THE
QUALITY OF LIFE
IN THE
GERMAN
DEMOCRATIC
REPUBLIC

The Quality of Life
in the
German Democratic Republic
Changes and Developments in
a State Socialist Society

Edited by
MARILYN RUESCHEMEYER
and CHRISTIANE LEMKE

M. E. SHARPE, Inc.
Armonk, New York   London, England

Available in the United Kingdom and Europe from M. E. Sharpe,
Publishers, 3 Henrietta Street, London WC2E 8LU.

Published simultaneously as Vol. 18, Nos. 3 and 4 of *International Journal of Sociology*.

Library of Congress Cataloging-in-Publication Data

The Quality of life in the German Democratic Republic / edited by
Marilyn Schattner Rueschemeyer and Christiane Lemke.
    p.   cm.
    Some articles translated from German.
    "Published simultaneously as Vol. 18, Nos. 3 and 4 of International
Journal of Sociology"—T.p. verso.
    Bibliography: p.
    Includes index.
    ISBN 0-87332-484-6
    1. Germany (East)—Social life and customs. 2. Germany (East)—
Social conditions. I. Rueschemeyer, Marilyn, 1938–
II. Lemke, Christiane, 1951–
DD287.3.Q35 1989
943.1087—dc19   88-4089
                                     CIP

Printed in the United States of America

Contents

Illustrations

LIST OF MAPS

LIST OF FIGURES

LIST OF TABLES

Preface

This book is about social life in a state socialist society—the German Democratic Republic or, in short, the GDR. It examines the social structures and institutions and the processes of change that shape the everyday life of people. We thus focus on the socialization of children in families and schools, on social life in neighborhoods and workplaces, on the involvement of GDR citizens in what is usually described as leisure time, and on the organizations and institutional structures that support and shape these various arenas of social life. Our emphasis on the experience of everyday life complements the analyses of the state that usually take center stage in the literature on Eastern Europe and the Soviet Union.

Although shaped and directed by government action and political leadership, institutional systems develop their own interests—even in state-dominated societies. These reflect collective and individual needs and experiences, which may well stand in some tension with those of the state and the leading party. At the same time, institutions and organizations typically compete with each other for power and scarce resources. Within the different organizational structures, those in leadership positions have to be at least minimally responsive to the concerns and interests of those ''below'' them. Failure to take their needs into account may result in a merely outward conformity coupled with passive inactivity, or in absenteeism and disruption. This is as true for workers and employees in factories and offices as it is for students in schools and universities. Such aspects of social life that give a limited autonomy to the ''grass roots'' are particularly important to investigate in the GDR precisely because of the dominant role played by the state and party.

Our focus on everyday life and the more immediately relevant social institutions also gives us an opportunity to examine the positions and problems of women in different arenas of GDR life. Women are rarely found in the highest positions of state and party. As women, they do not have sufficient clout to push for many of their social, economic, and political concerns. Although they have some representation in the Volkskammer (the GDR parliament) through the leading party and through subsidiary parties and mass organizations, their specific representation as women is through the Democratic Women's League (Demokratischer Frauenbund Deutschlands or DFD), an organization that has not formulated a coherent critique of the remaining contradictions that burden women under socialism. Women do, however, play an important role in GDR society—not only in "middle level" positions of political leadership but also in many other areas of institutional life, in neighborhoods, schools, and work organizations for example, where they are able to give some shape to the environment in which they live.

The contributions to this volume are written by authors from several countries—authors from both German states as well as from the United States, Canada, and Great Britain. We have tried to bring together research that deals with the most salient issues facing the GDR today. Social scientists working on the GDR in the West not only have different perspectives on that economically most advanced of the state socialist countries, they also experience differences in access to East Germany. Scholars from West Germany, for example, rarely receive permission to do field research in the GDR. In contrast, this opportunity does exist for other Western scholars if not in an unlimited fashion. At the same time, because of the particular connections—affinities as well as tensions—between the two German states, the Federal Republic has more researchers than other Western countries who study the GDR through its own publications and on the basis of excellent collections of GDR newspapers, journals, and literary works. These secondary sources are, of course, also used extensively by other Western scholars. GDR social scientists, on the other hand, not only have the advantage of their own primary experience and of access to research reports the circulation of which is variously restricted; they also have to be responsive to demands of practical relevance and ideological articulation of their work, demands that are fundamentally different from those faced by Western social scientists.

However one ultimately evaluates this form of social science, we think it important that the research of GDR scholars and their positions be known in the West. The very interesting contributions by the four GDR researchers in this volume illuminate aspects of scholarly orientations at the forefront of research in their country. They are at the same time examples of critical analysis from within GDR society.

In the first chapter, Bradley Scharf extensively discusses the role of sociology in the context of social policy in the GDR. He links his discussion of GDR social policy to research in the social sciences precisely because social science has a very particular role in the GDR: both empirical research and analytic reflection are guided by established state policy and serve in turn as advanced reflections on further policy development. In this sense, the analysis of social science must be an integral part of any examination of social policy.

The second section of the book, "Family, Sex Roles, and Socialization," deals with fundamental problems of social reproduction. The two contributions by

GDR scholars Irene Dölling and Hildegard Nickel highlight the role of women and, in their discussion of important changes and persistence of old patterns, focus in particular on gender socialization. The last chapter relates the issues of socialization to the political system.

The strong emphasis on advanced technology in the GDR and the corresponding hopes for development and an enhanced quality of life are reflected in the educational system and in the organization of work. Several problems related to these developments are discussed in the third section of the book—"Work, Technology, and Education"—as well as in the fourth and fifth sections—"Housing and the Environment" and "Culture and Leisure Time." We have decided to include, in addition, a chapter on the church in order to illustrate the role this institution plays in the GDR, which is quite different from its role in the West. It is also important to examine the sensitive balancing of goals and activities within this institution itself.

In the last section, we conclude the volume with several reflections on social complexity and structural differentiation and on the related partial autonomy of different groups and institutions. Both differentiation and autonomy are contained by a strong state and a nonpluralist party system under the leadership of the Socialist Unity Party (SED). This tension defines major issues and challenges for the GDR in the 1980s.

The editors of this volume met through the planning of a conference on "GDR Politics and Society" at Harvard University's Center for European Studies in the summer of 1984. At that time, Christiane Lemke held the German Kennedy Fellowship at Harvard University, which enabled her to spend a year's research leave at the center. Since then, the Center for European Studies and the Russian Research Center have sponsored a GDR Study Group, cochaired by Vojtek Mastny and Marilyn Rueschemeyer. We are very grateful for the support of both centers in their endeavors and especially for the encouragement and great help offered by Abby Collins of the Center for European Studies.

Acknowledgments

Marilyn Rueschemeyer is most grateful to Dietrich Mühlberg, director of the work group Kultur in the section Aesthetik und Kunstwissenschaften at the Humboldt University in Berlin, for his invitation to the conference on leisure time in socialism, Berlin 1986, and for the opportunity of selecting four conference papers for this volume. Rueschemeyer's participation in the Berlin conference was made possible by financial support of IREX. During the preparation of this volume, Marilyn Rueschemeyer was partially supported by a research grant from the Joint Committee on Eastern Europe of the American Council of Learned Societies and the Social Science Research Council, financed in part by the National Endowment for the Humanities and the Ford Foundation, which freed her from teaching obligations for one year.

Patricia Kolb of M.E. Sharpe Publishers not only supported this project but also encouraged us with her help and patience in the complex organizational work that led to the completion of this book. Volker Gransow of the University of California, Berkeley, gathered important materials for this project. The Zentralinstitut für sozialwissenschaftliche Forschung at the Free University of Berlin and its excellent library were important resources for the work of many contributors. The GDR program's director, Hartmut Zimmermann, and Dietrich Rueschemeyer of Brown University accompanied our efforts with ever renewed advice and criticism. To all of these colleagues we wish to express our deep appreciation. Finally, we want to thank the people in the GDR, colleagues and others, who maintained a dialogue with us over the years. The human intensity of these encounters has enriched our lives.

Part I

Social Policy and Social Conditions

Social Policy and Social Conditions in the GDR

C. BRADLEY SCHARF

In the German Democratic Republic, as in other modern societies, social issues are invariably also political issues. The essays about the GDR that follow are thus much more than descriptions of contemporary social conditions; political aspects emerge as appraisals of present governmental policies and as recommendations for future change.

My discussion, which addresses the impact of the political system on East German society, emphasizes three topics: (1) the interplay of ideology and politics in defining general social policy, (2) the featured components in the web of practical social programs, and (3) the institutions of social policy implementation. Occasional references to the comparative study of advanced capitalist nations provide a valuable interpretive frame of reference.[1]

The study of social policy shows that social conditions are the product of many variables, including aggregate personal choices, constraints of the physical environment, the intended and unintended consequences of government policy, and the public consequences of action by nongovernmental institutions. Furthermore, since social change is incremental, antecedent conditions are always the primary determinants of current conditions. The degree to which other variables are subject to influence by government policy, especially in the long run, is an important question that is not easily answered in any nation.

Marxism-Leninism and muddling through

For more than two decades following the birth of the German Democratic Republic, the very term ''social policy'' was an alien expression.[2] Since the days of Otto von Bismarck, when social security pensions and disability benefits were introduced to deflate the revolutionary pretensions of the labor movement, German Communists tended to regard "Sozialpolitik" as a cynical means to corrupt workers into accepting rule by a capitalist elite. Lenin echoed this view in his appraisal of prerevolutionary Russia. This understanding was unaltered in the extreme dogmatism of the Stalinist years and was carried forward to the GDR of the 1950s.

If the concept of social policy is understood to denote a comprehensive scheme for managed social change, it may be correct to say that the GDR had no such policy at that time. Instead, numerous ad hoc "social measures" were enacted to overcome the misery and economic instability induced by the war and to remedy the inequities inherited from capitalism. Marxist ideology provided merely a loose framework for these measures; apart from a general imperative to eliminate social injustices and the repeated assertion that everything would improve with the building of socialism, ideology provided no theoretical principles from which to deduce specific social programs.

After the closing of the Berlin border in 1961, an emergent elite consensus moved toward reconciliation with the general population and a strategy for enhancing the legitimacy of the regime. The decade began with a major economic reform and closed with an effort to infuse the labor unions with expectations of collaboration in the political process. The larger strategy was punctuated by attempts to tap public opinion and to respond with programs intended to satisfy popular wants—an approach that can be considered as either a cynical Bismarckian manipulation or the controlled beginnings of an authentic "socialist democracy." In either case, the results were the same: more political attention, increased funding for social measures, and tangible improvements in the standard of living. The unspoken justification was no longer the elimination of capitalist legacies, but the quest for popular legitimacy.

There remained, however, a striking lack of guidance from Marxist theory, and although the development of social measures acquired more positive connotations, it still was more or less case specific. In order to bridge the gap between the realities of practical social programs and the abstract realm of historical materialism, it was necessary to introduce empirically grounded sociology and social theory.

There were, however, major political obstacles to empirical social research in the GDR. The East German political leadership was painfully aware of the extent of popular discontent and was energetically trying to solicit citizen acceptance by means of economic and social achievements. Although the individual citizen was quite familiar with specific deficiencies in daily living, the political leadership suppressed information concerning the full scope of social problems, revelation of which would serve to undermine the image of progress and the desired mood of optimism. The vigorous workers' protests of 1953 had left a profound impression of the potential for political upheaval. Social research was, by its very nature, politically inflammatory, and even closely controlled research was dangerous, since it so often found its way to the West, where West German publicists were eager to disseminate negative findings back through the porous information screens into the GDR.

Ironically, it was the leaders' own commitment to more responsive public policy that led them to turn toward limited forms of social research which, beginning about 1963, was authorized into prevailing social conditions and corresponding public attitudes.[3] Numerous sociologists quickly came forward with the obvious justification: the previous prohibition of open empirical research was in fact profoundly un-Marxist, and social research should be seen as a superb expression of "scientific socialism."

If social *research* gradually won acceptance, the place of social *theory* was sharply disputed. Political leaders, generally far removed from academic life, were extremely wary. In the latter half of the decade there was most likely a rather intense contest between social philosophers and the upstart social scientists. I believe that the rapid advance of empirical sociology was symbolized in Walter Ulbricht's pronouncement at the 7th SED Congress (1967) that socialism was not merely a passageway into communism, but actually constituted a "relatively autonomous societal formation." Such an interpretation could be understood to imply the need for a "relatively autonomous" social theory, as well. Although Ulbricht's ideological deviation was subsequently repudiated, much of its implication remained.

Invoking the blessings of noted Soviet sociologists, GDR social researchers asserted the need for "middle range theory" in which content was derived from empirical studies and larger methodological perspectives were deduced from Marxist historical materialism.[4] However, apart from routine affirmations that "true" social progress is possible only in socialism, the impact of historical materialism remained very weak—its relevance might be better described as normative, rather than theoretical or methodological.

At the same time, program-oriented sociologists (notably the research group at the labor union college) rediscovered the ambivalent character of social policy which, in the sense of stepwise implementation of long-range social planning, might have been negative in the hands of Bismarck, but under the guidance of the SED would become decidedly positive. In utilizing the labor union structure for the assessment of real conditions among the working people, qualified sociologists forged a compelling argument for coordinated social change.

Although there were occasional open disputes in the continuing dialogue with political leaders and social philosophers, in 1974 a Scientific Council for Social Policy and Demography was formed, and was followed in 1978 by the creation of the Institute for Sociology and Social Policy as part of the GDR Academy of Sciences. (The Director of the Institute, Professor Dr. Gunnar Winkler, was also Chairman of the Scientific Council.)

In 1986 GDR social policy researchers undertook their second five-year plan. The task of constructing "middle range theory" as a means of accounting for change in developed socialist society seems to be still in its infancy—and linkage to a uniquely Marxist general theory of societal evolution appears as remote as ever. Empirical findings abound, some of which cast shadows over the ambitious promises of political leaders. The rapid growth of social policy research in the last decade has generated a plurality of approaches to social theory; pronounced divisions prevail among an expanding number of research centers. In what remains a markedly centralized system of power, prudent social researchers practice sensitivity to the rules of political disclosure. Yet the collective weight of GDR sociologists and social policy researchers has become a major moving force in the politics of social change.

The Politburo and the fire brigade

Both the stipulation of research tasks and the formation of social policy emerge through dynamic political processes, in which the participants are many and varied. All are members of the SED, and a great many of them can be regarded as "Party functionaries." It must be noted that such credentials do not imply monolithic agreement. On the contrary, a variety of personality and academic dispositions combine with diverse institutional affiliations and priorities to produce numerous points of controversy.[5]

The main participants involved in the authorization of research tasks represent four institutional sectors: the Council of Ministers, the Departments of the Central Committee (the SED staff departments, or the central apparatus), the labor union federation (FDGB), and a variety of academic and research institutions. Within the Council of Ministers, the Ministry of Health, the Ministry of Education, and the Bureau for Youth Issues are the principal contributors to matters of social inquiry, along with the Bureau for Labor and Wages. The Interior Ministry and the Ministry of State Security contribute data on social deviance and public opinion. Questions of funding, of course, directly involve the Ministry of Finance. Because the scope of social questions is very broad, several other ministries may be consulted from time to time. But my information suggests that Health and Education are clearly the lead units on the government side.

On the side of the Party executive, the SED Department for Science and Culture bears primary responsibility in the realm of social research. Additional major participants include the Departments for Labor and Social Policy, for Health Policy, and for Women's Issues. Again, the relevant network is potentially much more inclusive. These four departments are emphasized because their spokespersons have been especially visible in discussions of social issues.

The FDGB plays a special role as a sort of designated representative of "consumer" interests, including the interests of citizens as consumers of social benefits. National and regional units of the FDGB feature several pertinent commissions, notably Social Policy, Health and Safety, Women, and Youth. In addition, the FDGB College at Bernau retains a modest role in social research.

The participation of academic and research institutions is considerably more complex.[6] Leadership roles are exercised by two central institutions: the Party Academy for Social Sciences (Institute for Sociology), and the Institute for Sociology and Social Policy (Academy of Sciences). The Party Academy for Social Sciences has assumed the lead in efforts to develop "middle range" social theory. The task of evaluating applied social policy lies primarily with the Institute for Sociology and Social Policy. A review of continuing research reveals several areas of overlap between this institute and the Academy of Social Sciences.

Beyond these central institutions, secondary roles are played by sociology departments in the major universities and by specialized institutions, such as the Institute for Youth Research. Although distinctive research emphases are associated with each university and institute, most also carry teaching responsibilities; consequently, they endeavor to encompass several corollary areas of inquiry. Moreover, since there has been no effort to allocate any specific research focus to a single institution, there is competition among a number of research centers for funding and academic prestige. Despite elaborate structures for collaboration among academics from all of these institutions, a competitive mode predominates. The relative scarcity of empirical data (a situation that is commonly attributed to politically defined security requirements) may be partly due to "hoarding" by those institutions closer to the centers of political influence.

The process of authorizing and funding sociological research is carried on by two coordinating bodies: the Scientific Council for Sociological Research and the Scientific Council for Social Policy and Demography. The first group is chaired by Prof. Dr. Rudi Weidig, Director of the Party Academy for Social Sciences; the vice-chairman is Gunnar Winkler of the Institute for Sociology and Social Policy. It is the smaller of the two councils, with representation chiefly of an academic character, and it reviews research proposals with a theoretic emphasis. The Council for Social Policy and Demography is chaired by Gunnar Winkler, who thus provides a link between the two councils; its vice-chairman in 1986 was the Director of the Institute for Sociology at Humboldt University. This council includes more than forty participants, encompassing representatives of government ministries and SED departments, the FDGB, all major universities, and several social organizations such as Volkssolidarität (discussed below). The Council for Social Policy and Demography creates problem-oriented working groups, bringing together researchers and consultants from all participating institutions to share research results and evaluate on-going social programs.

In both councils, the initiative for proposing research projects rests with the academic professionals who will be directing the actual research. In the case of the larger Council for Social Policy, it may be necessary to solicit endorsements from affected administrative agencies. Every project must be presented within the context of priorities established by the five-year plan authorized by the SED Central Committee. This requirement is not terribly restrictive, because it encompasses a diversity of rather generally stated goals and also because the leading participants in the two councils have themselves been the major contributors to the stipulation of research priorities. The appropriate language of presentation is well known to all academics; working within their respective collectives it is not difficult to devise project proposals that fall within the approved guidelines. It is also possible to blend a personal research agenda into a large project with politically acceptable aims.

As proposals come before the respective scientific councils, there is an emphasis placed upon methodological soundness and the research record of the proponents. Patronage connections are perhaps most important. Academic communities in the GDR remain quite hierarchical, and each senior member of the scientific councils presides over a patronage network, which is based in his own institution but may occasionally cross into other institutions as well. The politics of social research funding consists in large part of allocating limited resources among the research groups linked to each of the research "elders." Because of the inclination to authorize multi-year projects and to alter funding incrementally, there is a certain degree of stability. In such a climate, innovative perspectives are not necessarily discouraged—and among the senior scholars there are sometimes individuals eager to support rising young social scientists. But success requires more than talent; it also requires sensitivity to East Germany's brand of "academic politics."

The role played by "Party functionaries" in this process is not that of aloof, disdainful ideologues.[7] Instead, they are minority participants who have had some relevant academic training and who help to shape—and are in turn shaped by—the evolving consensus about what constitutes legitimate research. Indeed, there is no sharp dividing line between "Party functionaries" and academic leaders. Just as the former are compelled to come to terms with new modes of inquiry, the latter must continually deal with the issue of what kinds of research results are politically "reasonable" at any particular time. In fact, much of the content of the politics of social policy lies in the efforts of each level of participants to convince the next higher level of the need to broaden the boundaries of open discussion.

Capping the whole mechanism of setting agendas for social theory and social policy evaluation are the nation's political leaders in the Politburo. The Politburo includes more than twenty SED and government officials. Although it sometimes functions as a body of collective responsibility, individuals or small clusters within the Politburo typically take the lead in articulating priorities for specific realms of public policy. The Politburo members most consistently identified with social policy are Prof. Kurt Hager, SED Secretary for Science and Culture, Harry Tisch, Chairman of the FDGB Executive Committee, and Ingeburg Lange, Director of the SED Department for Women's Issues. The central roles of these three individuals are occasionally supplemented by the contributions of Dr. Günter Mittag, SED Secretary for Economics, and Egon Krenz, SED Secretary and likely successor to Erich Honecker as General Secretary.

A more precise account of the politics of social policy requires a good deal of speculation. But the logic of the decision structure and the record of policy evolution permit some tentative inferences. First, the formation of social policy is essentially an inductive process. There exist multiple avenues for monitoring social problems and the pace of social change and for aggregating this information at successively higher levels. Administrative agencies of both the central and local governments readily identify social problems in their routine contact with citizens. Staff units of the SED at all levels solicit from basic party organizations periodic appraisals of the social policy performance of government agencies and public employers. Social policy commissions and other relevant divisions of the labor unions continually survey the needs and concerns of the working population. And academic and research institutions conduct long-term inquiries into social conditions.

Although there are a number of informal contacts among these four sectors and even an occasional formal local or regional assembly, I found no evidence of efforts to create intersectoral interest alliances or common policy positions as a means to alter social policy below the national level. As an illustration, it is not likely that government administrators, FDGB officials, and social scientists in Cottbus County will join together to recommend policy reform. Similarly, I found no evidence of efforts to build broad subnational alliances within the same institutional sector. For example, there seems to be no mechanism for aggregating the viewpoints of local health officials or local labor union officials as a means of advocating policy change. In short, there is a decided lack of horizontal politics—a feature that is not unique to the GDR or even to Marxist-Leninist systems. To some extent, it may be simply a consequence of bureaucratic competition within a centralized structure of government.

Instead, information on social concerns flows primarily upward through vertical hierarchies. Only at the national level—the Council of Ministers, the SED Departments, the FDGB, and the Scientific Councils—is there an opportunity to distill aggregated information into alternative policy proposals. Although this seems to be a rather narrow channeling of interests, a considerable diversity of viewpoints is represented within and among these four sectors. Just how these differences are resolved is not clear, but at some point the intervention of the three principal Politburo members becomes decisive. The nature of this intervention is probably much more consultative than dictatorial, and it would be a mistake to assume that "functionaries" in a single sector—such as the SED departments—act as "gatekeepers," screening the top decisionmakers from contending policy perspectives.

Second, decisions to amend social policy are a question of what is feasible and what is premature. There is no question of preserving or undermining SED power. Rather, the focus is on developing the most effective means for resolving social problems: the preservation of SED power should be a logical by-product.

This focus does not assure agreement on short-term priorities, nor does it mean that the aims and structure of SED power will remain constant.

Third, the SED style of political leadership, which might be characterized as a form of "democratic centralism" or perhaps "consultative paternalism," has specific consequences for the conduct of policy debates. On the one hand, the role of professional expertise is extraordinarily prominent. Professional social scientists are highly visible participants in shaping the social policy agenda. They occasionally have the satisfaction of seeing their research results directly translated into public policy. On the other hand, once the social scientists have made their case, final policy decisions are made behind closed doors and subsequent criticism must be severely muted.

Final policy decisions, of course, involve political trade-offs negotiated under conditions of budget stringency. In the last analysis, the Presidium of the Council of Ministers (the "economic cabinet") and the Politburo must allocate funding among competing demands. Social policy reforms are frequently very expensive and proposed changes are commonly delayed or only partially implemented, not because they are ideologically repugnant, but because they cost too much. Furthermore, the Politburo tends to avoid incremental policy change; highly visible, dramatic enactments are preferred, since they can be more readily featured in public information campaigns to attract public support. Consequently, social scientists may find an urgent recommendation apparently ignored for years, only to find it suddenly and enthusiastically featured in the next five-year plan. At this point, the Politburo expects a chorus of acclaim from all quarters, even if the adopted policy is a poorly conceived and compromised version of the original proposal. Social researchers cannot afford to offend the politicians whose support they must solicit for future proposals.

For the community of sociologists and social researchers, however, the mood is scarcely docile. Both politicians and social scientists realize that their relationship is one of mutual dependency. Social problems abound; the current pace of complex social change increasingly calls for a pragmatic, trial-and-error approach. And the experts retain ample means for alerting the highest authorities of the need for change. In the words of one prominent Party social scientist: "Social policy is the fire brigade—and the sociologists are the sirens."

The scope of GDR social policy

The most comprehensive statement of the purpose and scope of GDR social policy appears in *Sozialpolitik*, issued under the leadership of the Institute for Sociology and Social Policy. The 1985 edition characterizes social policy as "the expression of the politically, economically and juridically secured realization of fundamental human rights, which make possible lives of dignity and which serve the complete development of personality, the strengthening of families, and the just development of all citizens."[8] In typically Marxist-Leninist fashion, social policy is portrayed in extraordinarily broad compass, ranging "from job creation to the provision of social and cultural services in combines and firms, from the creation of socialist residential areas and the expansion of welfare and health services to the protection of the environment."[9] The implementation of social policy is a compound of multiple instruments and initiatives; it is "the sum of all measures and methods [employed by] the working class party, the socialist state, the labor unions and other political parties and organizations in shaping society."[10] This broad view subsumes at least seven more specific aims, which are presented here in approximate order of emphasis:

(1) to secure achieved material gains and gradually raise living standards for all;

(2) to guarantee employment and compensation according to performance;

(3) to gradually reduce differences among social groups;

(4) to promote a "social structurally differentiated" fulfillment of basic social rights;

(5) to provide support and care in all circumstances of life;

(6) to facilitate full participation in the social and recreational activities of society;

(7) to assure rational use of natural resources and preserve a healthy environment.[11]

A very strong emphasis is placed on the interdependence of economic and social progress—which is, of course, a fact of life that is valid in all societies. It is everywhere necessary to maintain a fruitful balance between investment and consumption and to recognize that improvements in productivity are the seeds of higher material standards of living. What is distinctive about the GDR is the degree to which public officials incorporate this universal principle in their messages to citizens.

GDR citizens are very sensitive to incremental change in their household consumption and have high expectations as a result of their television exposure to West German and American standards of living. At the same time, SED and government leaders have learned the costs of premature expansion of consumption. Like many of its socialist neighbors, the GDR participated in the wave of foreign borrowing in the late 1970s, on the assumption that imported technology would yield marked productivity benefits. Although the costs of excessive optimism were far less than in the disastrous Polish experience, GDR authorities determined to base future social programs on productivity achievements, rather than on projections. Thus, citizens are cautioned to moderate their expectations.

On the other side of the issue, the people are enjoined to consider the matter of productivity on a personal basis: productivity should be in large measure a question of employee responsibility—not only in terms of a manifest work ethic, but also in terms of actively seeking a more efficient work organization and rapid adaptation to technological innovation. In this sense, social policy benefits— including education, health care, consumer conveniences, improved housing, and cultural/recreational facilities—are expected to improve the physical, intellectual, and emotional resources of an increasingly productive workforce.

Although the thematic emphasis on the "unity of economic and social policy" appears eminently rational, there are potentially negative implications. GDR authorities seem to be consistently preoccupied with the economic side of this ostensibly reciprocal formula. The result is a markedly "economistic" approach to social policy in which the humanistic goals of Marxism may be systematically understated.

Although there is no uniformity of view, GDR social researchers explicitly recognize this tension and point to two specific consequences.[12] First, the overall profile of social spending suggests priorities among social groups, differentiated according to their productive potential. Thus, education and other spending for youth and young adults are strongly emphasized. The complex package of pronatalist programs, including maternity leaves and family allowances, is designed to assure a growing and more productive labor force. Middle-aged adults, without parenting duties but still in the workforce, receive correspondingly fewer social benefits, while lowest priority is assigned to pensions and amenities for the retired elderly and to the physically and mentally disabled, who make little or no contribution to economic production. This harsh characterization may be unfair. Progress toward meeting the needs of "unproductive" citizens is very real. Yet national priorities are open to challenge from specific groups of beneficiaries, as well as from concerned social scientists.

A second negative consequence of an "economistic" social policy involves the uneven quality of empirical data and its application to funding decisions. As a simple principle, the probability of enhanced spending for a given social program depends on its impact on measurable labor productivity. For example, it is relatively simple to show how improved public transit and enhanced retail services can lead to time-saving and reduced worker absenteeism and, thus, to better labor productivity. On the other hand, the link between the emotional benefits of after-hours and weekend recreation and worker productivity is far less clear. The absence of concrete data to support proposals for a wide variety of social programs does not mean that they are wholly neglected; rather, it means that the process of marshaling political support is considerably more laborious and that funding levels are likely to be modest.

Despite a tendency toward an economistic view of social priorities, the broader value orientation outlined earlier attracts considerable support. As a result, the GDR has gradually created a web of practical social programs that is among the most progressive and comprehensive in the world.

An inventory of social programs

A comprehensive review of GDR social programs would require far more space than this essay can encompass. In order to gauge the outcomes of the policy process summarized above—and to provide the state policy framework for discussions in the following essays—I will point out the major highlights of the social program network. There is no attempt here to systematically assess program outcomes, but I have inserted occasional interpretative comments where I believe they have special utility.

The classification of social programs in any society is itself something of a riddle. A classification scheme may be based on specification of beneficiaries (e.g., women, elderly), goals (equality, security), or means. GDR sources combine all three schemes. I prefer a means-based scheme, which is more conventional in the academic study of comparative social policy. The following review covers wages and tax policy, cash transfers, consumer policy and price modifications, and a diverse list of direct services.

Wages and taxes

GDR incomes policy features a commitment to eliminate "unjustified" wage inequalities and to substitute compensation based upon objective performance criteria. Wage differences derived from business competition, divergent labor union strength, and gender discrimination are considered "unjustified." On the other hand, it is both appropriate and necessary to link wage income to the employee's proportional contribution to productive output. In principle, income differences should reflect education and skill levels, work discipline, and direct contributions to enhanced productivity.

The implementation of performance-based income schemes is extraordinarily difficult and always incorporates arbitrary elements. Aggregate official data provide no clear measure of success, chiefly because employee categories are so broadly defined. But three kinds of problems loom rather large. First, in the service sector it is nearly impossible to apply productivity measures that are directly comparable to productivity measures in goods-producing industries. Even within a given industrial firm, it is difficult to measure the productive output of supervisory and staff personnel in relation to production workers. As a rule, the output of production workers is much more readily measured; consequently, cumulative adjustments to income schedules have favored skilled laborers over supervisors, and industry over services. Because the GDR operates within the framework of a modified labor market, these shifting compensation arrangements have led to an undersupply of qualified service-sector employees and a pronounced reluctance of production workers to acquire qualifications for supervisory positions.[13] Second, the economic prominence of certain "lead" industries (e.g., petrochemicals, electronics, scientific instruments) has enabled them to offer substantially higher wages than less privileged employers—even for jobs that are virtually identical. For example, secretary-trainees report that entry-level salaries for full-time positions vary as much as 60 percent among employers.[14] Third, the income structure reflects a number of anomalies under quasi-market conditions. For example, it is widely thought that refuse collectors in East Berlin are vastly overpaid. Apparently, in the 1960s there was a severe shortage of men to perform this ''back-breaking'' work. The problem was solved through large pay increases, which have been perpetuated up to the present day of hydraulic lifts and truck-mounted compactors. This wage anomaly is likely to remain for some time, because investment in new equipment has yielded higher productivity and because the authorities adhere to an ''unwritten'' rule that—since the 1953 workers' uprising—nominal wage reductions are politically unacceptable.[15]

The above problems notwithstanding, the GDR has made great progress toward realizing a pattern of incomes based on achievement. Unearned income (from property and stock ownership) has been virtually eliminated. The task of creating objective criteria continues in many fields of employment, most notably in education and science. As in the United States, ''equal pay for equal work'' is a watchword of East Germany's women's organizations. And it is a principle fully implemented, at least in a formal sense. But GDR women have also experienced a phenomenon familiar in the West: as some occupations come to be characterized by female employment, wage rates tend to lag behind increases for male-dominated occupations.

Finally, the increased visibility of independent small retailers and self-employed craftsmen (carpenters, plumbers) has meant a resurgence of incomes earned outside the socialist sector. Some of these incomes are rumored to be quite high, but official sources do not reveal their aggregate impact on the overall income structure. Despite data deficiencies, it is safe to say that the range of income inequality in the GDR is notably narrower than that found in North America, Western Europe, and even Scandinavia.[16]

The estimation of tax impact on different levels of nominal income is an arcane art that requires quite a number of assumptions involving household size and consumption patterns. Although the East German tax code relating to personal income is somewhat less complex than in market systems, it has numerous provisions that complicate our analysis.[17] Perhaps surprisingly, the nominal schedule for taxing personal income in the GDR is much less progressive than in most market economies; for example, Sweden's income tax schedule is far more progressive. Yet the GDR is exceptional in providing a relatively generous exclusion of all tax liability for incomes below a specified minimum. This threshold level varies according to source of income (i.e., there is a larger exclusion of income earned in the socialist sector) and according to type of household (i.e., the exclusion is smaller for single taxpayers, larger for families with two or more children). In addition, for certain ''intelligentsia'' occupations, special exclusions offset the progressive tax incidence for higher incomes. Further, certain types of bonuses, pensions, and state prizes are exempt from taxation. While it is evident that the personal income tax has some redistributive effects (most notably from self-employed single persons to multi-member households with double incomes derived from the socialist sector), there is no clear correlation between these effects and the distribution of nominal incomes. In aggregate, therefore, the East German system of personal income taxes appears to be very nearly proportional except for the very lowest income categories.

Like many market systems (but unlike all other CEMA states), the GDR assesses employees nearly half the cost of social security. In both the compulsory and optional supplemental programs, the employee contribution is 10 percent of gross income. Because most employees now participate in the supplemental scheme, the earlier upper limit on contributions becomes inoperative, and the effect of the social security tax on personal disposable income is proportional.

Taxes on the consumption of goods and services are a major element affecting disposable income. In the GDR such taxes are added to the final consumer price, ostensibly to discourage the consumption of scarce and imported raw materials and finished goods. Tax rates differ by type of commodity, and specific rates are not made public. If one assumes that such taxes are imposed primarily on "non-essential" consumer durables (e.g., automobiles, stereos, stylish clothing, and imported foods), their effect on disposable income should be progressive: these consumer items will claim a larger share of spending for higher income households. As household incomes have risen, increasing numbers of households presumably have adopted a narrower definition of "non-essential" consumption, with the result that some consumption taxes will be more proportional or even regressive.

The combined effect of wage and tax policies appears to be consistent with the goal of improving living standards without notably altering the basic pattern of income inequality. A steady increase in average household income has been achieved by shifting the entire income spectrum upward. For the most part improvements for lower- and middle-income households have resulted not from changes in wage rates, but from the movement of wage-earners into higher wage categories. This involves considerable upgrading in skills, chiefly among female spouses. In addition, the workforce participation rate of employable women has reached an impressive 88.5 percent.[18] This process has yielded a gradual reduction in inequality between "social groups" (i.e., between men and women), without an appreciable reduction in the range between high- and low-income households. Preserving visible income differentials is regarded as an essential incentive for workers to acquire higher skills and to become more productive.

The tax structure does not change this general picture. For lower-income households, nominal gains are partially offset by greater income tax burdens (as fewer families fall below the minimum taxable threshold); for upper-income households, nominal gains appear to exceed increased tax liabilities, but these households also carry a larger share of consumption taxes. The total tax effect is thus increasingly proportional, and the pattern of relative income distribution is maintained after taxes.

In 1975–1984, all income categories enjoyed real increases in both nominal earned income (36.1 percent) and disposable income (26.5 percent). The latter

Table 1

Social Fund Expenditures, 1975 and 1985 (%)

Total	1975 (Total Mill. Mark: 37,119)	1985* (Total Mill. Mark: 89,000)
Price subsidies	30.2	45.6
(Food)	(19.3)	(31.0)
Social security and other transfers	25.7	17.1
Housing subsidy	9.8	15.7
Education and training	20.7	13.0
Health and social care	8.2	4.7
Culture and sport	5.4	3.4
Credits for young married couples	0.3	0.2

*Preliminary data
Sources: *Statistisches Jahrbuch der DDR—1985*, 265;
        Statistisches Jahrbuch der DDR—1986, 107.

figure is lower because of higher taxes and slower growth in cash transfers. At the same time, average "effective" real income grew by 34.8 percent. The difference between disposable income and "effective" real income is explained by household consumption of goods and services paid by the social fund. For wage-earning households, social fund consumption represented an effective supplement of 46.1 percent of gross earnings, up from 21.8 percent in 1975.[19]

The GDR social fund resembles the "social wage" in developed capitalist states, but its impact on household consumption is much larger. The state covers roughly 84 percent of social fund expenditures, with the remainder coming from employers and voluntary organizations. The allocation and evolution of the social fund is depicted in Table 1. Overall, there has been a dramatic increase over the last decade, most of it accounted for by the large jump in price subsidies and the massive housing program currently underway. A summary of the dimensions of social fund expenditures is encompassed in the following discussion of transfers, price subsidies, and public services.

Cash transfers

Pensions for the retired elderly constitute the largest category of cash transfers (20.5 percent of social fund expenditures). With numerous modifications in the last two decades, the pension system has become increasingly complex. For new pensioners, those receiving both the basic and supplemental benefits, the monthly pensions can equal more than three-fourths of the last earned income. When the absence of income tax and social security contributions is taken into account, new pensioners can typically preserve their former standard of living. This outcome nearly matches the earnings replacement rate of the Swedish system, although with a significantly lower standard of living.[20]

But serious deficiencies remain in terms of assuring minimum security and equity. GDR pensions are closely tied to levels and years of wage earning. Consequently, a substantial proportion of older pensioners receive only the minimum monthly benefit of 300 marks (raised to 400 marks in 1986); this is only 75 percent of the minimum wage and 16 percent of average household income. Because many of these pensioners live alone, this income is plainly inadequate and must be supplemented by gifts from relatives or public assistance. And there remains a strong cultural resistance to accepting "welfare," especially among the older generation. At the other extreme, special pension schemes for selected occupations sometimes yield combined monthly pensions in excess of 2000 marks. As in developed capitalist societies, recipients of large pensions are far less "needy," since they have accumulated savings and personal property. Thus, the GDR pension system preserves inequalities created during people's working lives.

The second largest category of cash transfers is sick pay to cover wages lost during illness or short-term illness of a child. The highly publicized family allowances are the third major form of transfers; yet their impact has been quite small, generally accounting for only about 2.2 percent of median family income. (For comparison, note that the U.S. practice of tax exclusions for dependents generates an average of savings of about 2 percent of median family income.) In May 1986 this ratio changed substantially, with a threefold increase in allowances. Additional cash transfers include living stipends for university students, public assistance ("welfare"), income supplements to households with disabled residents, and the very popular one-year paid maternity leave. Cash grants are made for neonatal expenses (less than the cost of a new baby buggy), and substantial loans are available to newly married couples (repayment is partially canceled with the birth of each child).

Price subsidies

By far the most important social fund expenditure, price subsidies far exceed the total cost of all cash transfers.[21] The bulk of these price subsidies is applied to maintain low prices for basic food items; in nominal terms, food subsidies have nearly tripled in the last decade. Other major categories of subsidized consumption include housing and renovation, heating, transportation, essential clothing (especially, children's clothing), books, laundry services, institutional meals, and certain types of housewares. Retail specialists assume that there is an approximate trade-off between consumer taxes on "luxury" items and consumer price subsidies for "essentials." Overall, price subsidies are clearly redistributive across income levels, because low-income households spend a much higher percentage of their income on subsidized consumption. This holds true even though people at all income levels find that subsidies significantly enhance the utility of household spending. In time, of course, this redistributive effect will diminish, as there will be fewer people trying to get by at the low level of minimum pensions.

Direct services

Education easily ranks first in publicly provided direct services. In addition to universal elementary education, comprehensive secondary schools encompass a large share of the relevant age population (slightly higher than the European average, slightly lower than the U.S. average). Enrollment in universities and technical colleges (23 percent of the relevant age group) matches the West European average. Like most European systems, GDR higher education has a pronounced technical emphasis, although this has not produced a perfect labor-market fit: there remain significant numbers of university graduates and technical specialists whose current employment does not correspond to their training. High levels of funding and supplemental stipends have apparently eliminated educational biases derived from differences in family income. Nevertheless, the redistributive effect of education spending is mitigated by the fact that university admission is heavily based on academic record and there is yet no systematic effort to help working class youngsters to overcome learning disadvantages due to family environment. Children of educated parents are high achievers, and they compete vigorously for limited admission to the liberal disciplines, while some admissions quotas for technical fields go unfilled. Official reports claim that 80 percent of secondary school graduates enter the career of their "choice," but smaller studies indicate that only about 12 percent are able to fulfill their original career "wish." Apparently, school counselors successfully encourage youngsters to abandon their fantasies in favor of more realistic choices.

Compared to the world's most expensive health care systems (in the U.S. and Sweden), the GDR does not always provide the highest standard of medical technology. Yet it is a world leader in providing virtually universal access to sound care, in emphasizing prophylactic measures, and in achieving strong performance in such areas as life expectancy and infant mortality. Compared to the more market-oriented systems, the GDR's national health service provides especially well for the very young and the very old. Because these two categories include the majority of the economically disadvantaged, public health is an additional force for reducing the impact of financial inequality. While East German citizens occasionally register discontent with the quality of care, their expectations are also rather high, and they enjoy the benefits of a system that is, in general, very efficient.

Institutional day care for preschool children is extraordinarily important in an economy with such high rates of female employment. Long a source of dissatisfaction, day care is now provided to more than 90 percent of the population aged 3–6. Employers and/or labor unions typically provide day care for nominal fees; consequently, the quality of care is far from uniform and the staff–to–children ratio is rather low. Nevertheless, extensive child care represents a strong achievement in support of women's equality, as well as a moderately redistributive social program.

Broad access to cultural and recreational facilities is a much emphasized dimension of social policy. Capital costs for theaters, parks, sports facilities, and summer camps are financed through the state, employers, or labor unions. User fees are nominal. Such programs reflect a commitment to extend to all social segments the opportunity to participate fully in public life.

In addition to the four types of direct services mentioned above, social programs exist to respond to special needs of the population. Physical and mental rehabilitation programs are well established, but modestly funded. Personal counseling for divorce, child-rearing, and deviant juveniles appears underdeveloped (at least by American standards) and rather poorly funded.

Trends in social-policy administration

As is evident in the foregoing discussion, the GDR today has a very broad concept of social policy and an extensive commitment to social welfare. However, much of this current understanding has emerged only in the most recent decade; among major public officials, this inclusive approach is not yet universally accepted, and there is little common recognition that social policy is really anything more than the sum of its parts.

A generally fragmented view of social policy is not merely a result of deficient conceptual linkages; it is also the natural consequence of a piecemeal approach to creating social programs and their corresponding administrative institutions. Comparisons of advanced industrial societies reveal both many common social concerns and a bewildering diversity of administrative arrangements. Peculiarities in social policy administration result from the fact that different societies constructed their social welfare systems in different sequences and under unique historical conditions.

In the social disarray of the post-surrender period, the administration of East German social policy followed two tracks. The first involved taking over some long-standing administrative structures for macrosocial programs. Previous systems for social security pensions and workers' disability were adapted to new conditions and directed by the central authorities. Public education was similarly placed under central direction. The system of rationing consumer goods, later merged with a broader mechanism of central economic planning, became the basis for a centrally administered program of price subsidies. These three programs quickly become the main pillars of postwar social policy; today they still represent the largest categories of centrally funded social spending.

The second track consisted of locally improvised efforts to deal with suffering and deprivation. In the summer of 1945, the German Red Cross was revitalized in many distressed areas; additional voluntary organizations for mutual aid were established in most cities, with varying emphases and organizational forms. As winter approached, these latter groups were consolidated into a loose national federation, *Volkssolidarität gegen Wintersnot*, whose main aim was to assure food and heating fuel for those unable to care for themselves, chiefly the elderly. This emergency aid was strongly supplemented by the relief programs of regional churches and their international affiliates. At the time, local governments had only meager resources, most of which were devoted to establishing basic public services. To a very great extent, then, local social programs depended on donations of time and money from the private sector.

These two tracks—central public sector programs and local private sector programs—dominated the early postwar years. Health care was, of course, a pressing concern, and it soon became the major means for linking the two tracks. Central government allocations to local jurisdictions were essential to filling the gaping health care deficit; yet vital private health services, operated by the two main churches, continued to serve community needs.

Over time the social service role of local governments was gradually augmented, but restricted funding meant that city and district councils could not become the chief provider. At the urging of the SED, local boards of the National Front created committees to respond to cases of urgent need, calling upon state and/or private resources in an ad hoc fashion. As economic recovery progressed, public firms acquired resources which could be applied to answering local needs. Thus, the social problems committees of the National Front enlisted the participation of enterprise management and labor union officials. Although the national organs of the SED claimed to be the inspiration for this exemplary expression of "socialist solidarity," the basic pattern of citizen collaboration was clearly the result of improvised and spontaneous local initiative.

Economic reconstruction yielded more resources which could be tapped by the central government. Contributions to the churches and to such organizations as the Red Cross and *Volkssolidarität* also increased. But the major trend of the sixties and early seventies was a radically increased role for public enterprises. Economic reform brought a certain amount of managerial discretion into the socialist economy; it also meant the growth of large, profitable firms with both the will and the means to improve community public welfare. Many firms and their corresponding unions began offering a wide range of social benefits, including modern housing, preventive health care, child care services and recreational facilities. Thus, socialist enterprises gradually assumed the role of a vigorous third track for social policy administration. Efforts to harmonize this expansion of social programs were channeled through the regional and national bodies of the labor union federation [FDGB]. In 1972 the unions were symbolically elevated to a status of partnership with the state and ruling party in shaping public policy. Just as the National Front became the public-private linkage in the local communities, now the FDGB became a link between the social programs of the central state and the social programs of public enterprises. Each of these stages represented an important step toward a more responsive and more inclusive approach to social policy. Nevertheless, the diversity of funding and administrative institutions generated problems that could not be ignored. Duplication of efforts became increasingly obvious, as some social segments became the beneficiaries of similar programs from multiple sources. At the same time, other social segments were served badly or not at all. In addition, the prominent role of public enterprises meant that the quality of social programs varied greatly among communities, according to the disparate strength of local firms. Recognition of these problems grew against the backdrop of an expanding fund of empirical social research. Studies undertaken by the FDGB College, the Institute for Sociology of the SED Academy for Social Sciences, and the new Institute for Social Policy of the Academy of Sciences (along with excellent research at the major universities) all demonstrated the extent of problems resulting from the lack of a coherent social policy framework and from a lack of administrative coordination. Furthermore, the increasing transformation of the GDR into an advanced urban-industrial society had generated a sharp increase in problems of urban social ecology, e.g., domestic violence, juvenile delinquency, high divorce rates. Thus, a qualitative change in social programs seemed imperative.

In the administrative setting, two major reforms are now needed. First, there must be a substantial expansion of local government responsibility for the coordination and delivery of social programs. Much of the social budget of socialist enterprises can be put at the disposal of local governments either through local taxes or through multi-year contracts with city councils. Central authorities have urged the contract method, which reduces the potential arbitrariness of enterprise managers and permits better local planning; yet it does nothing to combat regional inequities. The 1985 reform of the law on local government is ostensibly designed to promote more integrated territorial planning for economic development, manpower allocations, and social programs.[22] One immediate effect is to transfer authority for housing allocations from the unions to city councils. But the larger consequences are not yet clear.

The second necessary reform involves the creation of a coherent administrative constituency for what might be termed a holistic view of social program development. There is, at the present time, no central government ministry for social policy. As noted earlier, the Ministry of Health and the Ministry of Education are customarily the lead state agencies in social policy formation, with assistance from the Ministry of Internal Affairs. Each of these ministries has its own bureaucratic perspective and its own educational institutions for training public employees. Local governments typically hire graduates of these ministry colleges to staff their social service offices. While these offices are quite small, they may include people of rather different training and different career aims.

The result is that each local social service office may reflect a different set of priorities, both in its internal operation and in its linkage to other local offices and to the central government. More importantly, there is no central agency—and consequently, no pool of career professionals—with an interest in asserting an integrated approach to social problems and a commitment to assessing particularly those problems that do not fall within the primary focus of the health care, pedagogical or public safety professions.

Conclusion

In a collection of scholarship devoted to vital dimensions of contemporary social life in the GDR, this chapter has highlighted deliberate efforts by state and Party authorities to consciously shape social change and to respond to social problems by means of official policy. By way of summary, six major points of this chapter deserve special emphasis:

First, the fund of Marxist-Leninist social philosophy has been proven wholly inadequate as a general theory from which principles of social policy can be deduced and applied to conditions of developed socialism in the GDR. Despite contrary claims by the leading scholars at Party and academic institutions, the Marxist paradigm of change—derived from insights into interacting forces in the industrial age—does not yield the kind of answers that can readily address the problems of intense systemic integration in what appears more and more to be a postindustrial society. It might be argued that Marxism-Leninism retains a certain vitality and utility for other purposes, such as depicting changes in global politics or differentiating capitalist from socialist societies. It is also useful as a heuristic approach to empirical inquiry. But it is very limited as a guide to policy. Consequently, macrotheoretical development of Marxism-Leninism has been tacitly abandoned in favor of modest "middle-range" theory, which is being constructed inductively from empirical foundations.

Second, the consequent ambiguity in social policy principles has generated enhanced flexibility in research approaches and a more overtly political process for setting the social policy agenda. Within the confines of a continuing power hierarchy, representatives from social research institutions advocate alternative policy priorities. Firm rules stipulate what is not permitted, but there is no consensus on a coherent new model of social evolution. Consequently, there is considerable evidence of controversy and experimentation in social program development. Third, one result of the need to accommodate diverse viewpoints has been a radical expansion of the basic definition of social policy which has become, in effect, a massive umbrella, under which a multitude of emergent perspectives can be subsumed. Thus, scholarly endeavors may focus on social subsystems (e.g., industrial sociology, urban sociology), social segments (women, youth, elderly), delivery systems (health care, education, social security), or middle-range theory ("unity of social and economic policy"). Overall social policy is not reduced to a simple catalog of social programs; there are continuing efforts to address systematic linkages. While the higher political authorities may not be fully supportive (or even fully aware) of this state of affairs, there nevertheless remains a potential for constructive innovation within academic circles.

Fourth, in addition to the latent tension among academic approaches, there is a pervasive and pronounced tension between what I choose to call the "economistic" and "humanistic" emphases in social policy priorities. This tension is manifest among social scientists and lower administrators; it is even more obvious at the level of top political decision-makers, where an economistic bias continues to dominate.

Fifth, despite the enormity of the problems of reconstruction and the retarded awakening of empirical research, the GDR has developed an extraordinarily broad range of active social programs. To be sure, there is nothing unprecedented about individual benefit programs; several highly industrialized liberal democracies have also constructed a wide variety of social benefits—often with substantially greater financial support. Yet, compared with nations at similar levels of economic development, GDR accomplishments are truly impressive. Sixth, the piecemeal development of complex social programs has left the GDR with a certain amount of administrative disorder. Social service delivery is sometimes erratic and inequitable, and there is far more bureaucratic inefficiency than might be expected from a marriage of "Prussian" culture and socialist central planning.

A final observation is in order for readers who are invariably drawn to evaluate the performance of GDR social policy. Western observers and East German citizens alike are inclined to hold the Party and state accountable for most persisting social problems. High citizen expectations appear prevalent in all modern societies. In the GDR case, such expectations are amplified by the occasionally extreme leadership claims to be constructing a new social order "on a scientific basis." But such claims should not be taken at face value: they must be understood as an element in an urgent quest for greater popular legitimacy, an overdrawn exercise in public relations. The GDR regime is neither omniscient nor omnipotent. It operates under considerable uncertainty over the kind of society it really wants to create. Despite significant advances in economic output and in the popular standard of living, the East German economy remains rather fragile; its capacity to generate the financial resources for addressing social ills is still very limited. Furthermore, neither politicians nor social scientists have yet mastered the knowledge required to thoroughly understand, predict, and control the forces of social change.

For readers tempted to either applaud or condemn the course of GDR social policy, it might be pertinent to note here that each of the points summarized above has its counterpart in the world's preeminent liberal democracies. In the United States and Great Britain, in France and the Federal Republic of Germany, contemporary social policy is marked by disarray. While social theorists squabble among themselves over sharply disjunctive answers to the problem of "paradigm shift," politicians energetically pursue mutually contradictory social programs in a frantic endeavor to "do something" about mounting crises over which they have diminishing control. Economistic perspectives are everywhere ascendant, and humanistic concerns are the exclusive preoccupation of peripheral political forces.

In the discussions that follow, the GDR will not emerge as a model that many citizens of Western liberal democracies will find worthy of emulation. The shortcomings of East German society are far too evident to provide much inspiration. Yet the story of GDR policy is the story of many people who still believe that progress is possible.

Notes

1. Much of this presentation is derived from three months of conversations with GDR sociologists, economists, and administrators in Berlin, Halle, and Leipzig during Spring 1986. I am most grateful to the IREX Board and to Seattle University for making this possible.

2. Peter C. Ludz, "Soziologie und empirische Sozialforschung in der DDR," in Peter C. Ludz, ed., *Soziologie in der DDR* (Köln: Westdeutscher Verlag, 1964), 327–418; Georg Assmann and Rudhard Stollberg, *Grundlagen der marxistische-leninistischen Soziologie* (Berlin: Dietz, 1977), 19–54.

3. Harmut Zimmermann, et al., *DDR Handbuch* (Köln: Wissenschaft und Politik, 1985), 1232–46.

4. Alice Kahl and Steffi Riedel, "Zu einigen methodologischen Problemen des Platzes der zweigsoziologien in der Struktur der marxistisch-leninistichen Soziologie," *Informationen zur soziologischen Forschung in der Deutschen Demokratischen Republik* 2 (1984): 37–46.

5. Based on interviews with a variety of participants.

6. Zimmermann, 1237–39 and multiple interviews.

7. Based on interviews with a variety of participants.

8. Günter Manz and Gunnar Winkler, eds., *Sozialpolitik* (Berlin: Die Wirtschaft, 1985), 22.

9. Ibid., 15.

10. Ibid., 14.

11. Ibid., 21–29.

12. This issue is frequently raised in discussion in a very wide range of settings.

13. Unpublished research conducted by the Institute for Sociology, Humboldt University.

14. Interviews with secretarial trainees in Karl-Marx-Stadt and Halle.

15. Heinz Siewert, "Sozialpolitik und soziale Unterschiede bei der weiteren Gestaltung der entwickelten sozialistischen Gesellschaft," *Thematische Information und Dokumentation, Series B* 9 (1977): 50.

16. Doris Cornelson, et al., *Handbuch der DDR-Wirtschaft* (Reinbeck bei Hamburg: Rowolt, 1984), 261–87.

17. Ministerium der Finanzen, *Besteuerung des Arbeitseinkommens* (Berlin: Staatsverlag, 1981).

18. *Statistisches Jahrbuch der Deutschen Demokratischen Republik 1985* (Berlin: Staatsverlag, 1985), 114.

19. Manz and Winkler, 139–42.

20. Staatssekretariat für Arbeit und Löhne, *Rentenrecht* (Berlin: Staatsverlag, 1985).

21. Manz and Winkler, 133–38.

22. *Gesetzblatt der Deutschen Demokratischen Republik, Teil I,* Nr. 18 (1985), 213–35.

Part II

Family, Sex Roles, and Socialization

Culture and Gender

Irene Dölling

I

The time structures of the human life process are sociohistorical structures translated into stable temporal segments, and processes of individual and communal life. The division of individual time into work time and leisure time, as well as the structure and internal relationships between the activities carried out in these two spheres, are the expression of specific social relations. Time structures also always display a gender-specific disparity. The transformation of social relations into the temporal dimension of individual activities or into gender relations consists of diverse and at the same time interrelated forms in which individuals produce and reproduce themselves in sociohistorically determinate ways. In the GDR, an average of 47.1 hours of housework per week per family has been a constant for about twenty years. About 70.7 percent of this work is done by women, and 13 percent by men.[1] Employed women with children have virtually no leisure time during the week and their free-time activities, hobbies, etc. often directly relate to the needs of other family members. Thus "leisure-time culture" is neutral with regard to neither age nor gender. Its analysis, therefore, requires a description of the essential social relations and conditions in which individuals manifest their lives. It also raises the question of whether, why, and how the fundamental social relations are manifested as gender relations, as fields of activities and temporal structures that are different for the two sexes.

II

Socialism is the first phase of the communist social formation. Economically it is marked by the absence of private ownership of the means of production, wage labor, and exploitation, or, in positive terms, by social ownership of the means of production, and the right and duty of all to work. The social objective of

27

production is the ever-greater satisfaction of the needs of all members of society and, over the long term, the establishment of social equality. The realization of this historical long-term goal is accomplished by socialism under material and technical conditions that objectively require the retention of the different forms of the Marxian "old social division of labor": the division of labor into predominantly physical or intellectual labor, into skilled and less skilled labor, and into decision-making, managerial, and practical activities. On the one hand socialism supersedes class society, although, on the other hand, it is not yet a society of real social equality: the existence of classes is a reflection of persisting social differences. The division of individual lifetime into work time and leisure time, into time for participation in social production and time for individual reproduction on one's own "private" responsibility is also a consequence of this, just as is the historical division of functions between the sexes—which at the moment is tending to disappear. Given these circumstances, how do the new socioeconomic relations of socialism assume significance for the behavior and everyday life of individuals? What concrete contradictory aspects of their way of life derive from the fundamental contradictions of socialist society—for example that between social ownership of the means of production and the participation of concrete individuals in social production within the forms of the "old division of labor," or in the exercise of a "particularized function"? To what extent are gender relations a concrete expression of these contradictions? In what (traditional or new) cultural forms are the relations between the sexes lived, practiced, and appraised? In what cultural forms do men and women live and "digest" what is new in their way of living and in what relation do the old or the new stand to one another?

Some aspects of these questions will be discussed in the following essay, which will deal more with women than with men, mainly because the changes that have taken place are more incisive and more conflict-ridden for women than they are for men.

First it is necessary to outline a few theoretical premises on which the discussion will be based.

1. The socioeconomic relations of society as such are not determinants of individual behavior but are mediated in the process of social and individual reproduction, in transformed structures, in cultural forms. One form of transformation of social relations is gender relations, which reflect social relations in a number of ways: in the gender-specific division of labor into social production and individual reproduction (in the family); in the social rating of activities exercised predominantly by men or predominantly by women; in the attribution of human properties to one or the other sex, as a devalorization, discrimination, or suppression of, say, the female sex. In the history of mankind, social (class) differences and conflicts have been made acceptable and livable for individuals by transforming them into social relations. This also applies to gender-specific norms, patterns, and strategies of male and female socialization.

2. Relations between the sexes are in practical terms reflected in the cultural forms, in particular in the norms, patterns, standards, and stereotypes that regulate and guide everyday life. These cultural forms are often historically older than the relations transformed by them at the level of relations between men and women. They have a relatively independent development and under certain circumstances can be functional for societies of diverse types.

3. Individuals become aware of changes taking place in social relations through cultural forms and react to these changes through cultural patterns of evaluation and interpretation familiar to them. In this way people give expression to their new experiences and in the process also modify the cultural forms themselves. Cultural forms can therefore convey totally different contents and different experiences, though their outward form is seemingly unchanged. The extent to which new changed (socioeconomic) relations assume their determining role in the everyday life of human beings is reflected in these modifications of handed-down cultural forms as well as in the production of historically new cultural forms.

4. Under socialism, gender relations are one form for the transformation of existing or newly generated social differences (not of social conflicts, as in class societies) at the level of personal relations. Gender relations are a form for the movement and development of social contradictions of the above type. In other words: they are a form of movement and development of relations that tend toward the abolition of the subordinate position of the female sex and toward the emancipation of both sexes as a concrete expression of the economic relations of social equality. This also means that the development of contradictions and conflicts at the level of gender relations takes a specific direction.

III

In his essay on the problems of the division of labor between men and women in social production and in the family, the author Hans-Jürgen Gericke observes: "Clearly, the shift that has so far been effected in the division of labor between society and family has contributed considerably to maintaining the old role patterns of the sexes and the old division of labor within the family. This situation is to the detriment of women and from it can be inferred the real social contradiction whose resolution will still require considerable effort, namely, the social contradiction between the almost complete integration of women into the social labor process on the one hand, and woman's dominant role in doing the work in the private household and in the family on the other."[2] Gericke describes *the* contradiction which at present is a fundamental determinant of the existence and the possibilities of development of working women in socialist society.

This contradiction, of course, also has consequences for men and children. At the least it calls into question the traditional division of functions between the sexes as well as the corresponding norms and stereotypes that are experienced at the practical level by most women. Often these also no longer function.

The contradiction observed by Gericke is premised on a separation in time and place of the processes of production and individual reproduction. This is relatively new historically: it began with industrial production, i.e., with the emergence of capitalist society. A functional transformation of the family and the gender division of labor is a consequence of industrial production, and of the division of the lives of the producers into paid labor time and leisure time. The family sees its function as a production unit, which hitherto had been crucial for its existence and for relations between family members (to which in the broad sense all the members of the "entire household" belonged), steadily waning. As it loses its function as a unit of production, the family, now reduced to two generations, derives its social and individual importance first and foremost from its functions of reproduction of the producers and their family. Under conditions of private ownership of the means of production the socialization of production makes the reproduction of labor power (including the socialization of future producers) the "private affair" of the producers. This means that the producers, personally free, are also in charge of their labor capacity and hence are responsible for their education (insofar as this takes place within the family), and for the maintenance and adaptation of their labor capacity to the market situation. This tends to create a new functional division between the sexes: "a gender-specific division between the male producer or provider and the female, who utilizes what is provided to maintain and conserve labor power,"[3] between socially productive paid activities and unpaid housework. This division assumes a specific form in the cultural patterns of evaluation and interpretation: housework and raising children become a "private service," a "service of love" performed by the housewife for her family members. This cultural pattern is reinforced by invoking the "natural function" of women as mothers and their purported proclivity for specific "housewife" activities. The functional division between the sexes into production and reproduction assumed a universal social character in the 19th century, after first being developed and imposed as a bourgeois ideal for women in the family, and as a norm for the bourgeoisie when it was in the process of acquiring economic and political power. In a society governed by the law of surplus value production, the effect of the law of exchange must be nullified in certain areas, e.g., raising and providing for children, in order to ensure reproduction, which now becomes an individual function and a private responsibility. This necessarily calls for special strategies, norms, and forms for this "socialization" of girls and women (working women as well), so that "private" reproductive work functions as a "service of love."

The contradiction between "public production" and "duties in the private service of the family"[4] was not abolished with the establishment of socialist production relations. The development of the forces of production and the socialization of production are not advanced enough to accomplish this, a fact which on the whole persists under socialism, if at different levels. The contradiction between social production and "private" reproduction acquires a new content on the basis of the new socioeconomic relations. It is no longer a manifestation of social *conflicts*, but of social *differences*, based in social ownership of the means of production. The cultural forms, patterns, etc., which were developed in capitalist society, i.e., the traditional divisions of functions between the sexes and the related rankings, are initially there to mediate this contradiction in the practical action of the individuals.

A peculiarity of this socioeconomic change in the content of the contradiction is that initially that which is new (socialist production relations) appears officially, in political programs, in propaganda, etc. as a radical break with the old. That is, radical changes in way of life, in relations between the sexes, and in claims for a meaningful life, etc. are derived directly from the new relations, and legal equality and the integration of women into gainful economic activity is crassly identified with women's emancipation. However, practical experience in building socialism showed quite soon that a comprehensive transformation in relations, down to the very shaping of daily life, is more contradictory and laborious. It became clear that the traditional cultural forms of, say, relations between the sexes, do not simply disappear or continue to exist in people's heads as an ideological "vestige." Rather what was found was that certain cultural forms are quite functional for the first stages of development of socialism, i.e., for undeveloped socialist relations, and are therefore reproduced on the new socioeconomic base. The view that the millenial problem of discrimination against women would be resolved with the integration of almost all able-bodied women into gainful employment, by corresponding measures in female and social policy, and with the proclamation and implementation of equal rights, proved to be one-sided. Equality of women, and even more broadly, the emancipation of both sexes from the onesidedness, limitations, and mentally debilitating effects of their hitherto contradictory existence presupposes a qualitative change in all social relations as well as in the subjective structures of women and men. For this to occur a long historical period is still necessary. At the same time, however, practical experience confirmed the postulate that the emancipation of women obtains a material foundation only when women are integrated into social production and "public affairs." From this perspective, major changes have without a doubt taken place in women's lives since the GDR came into being (1949), and these changes are often already taken as a matter of course.

How can these changes be described? What emancipatory effect does gainful employment have for women themselves and for men?

The first expression of the new socioeconomic relations was the juridical equality established between men and women: equal right to work, equal right to an equal wage for the same work, and equal right to education have been constitutional principles since the GDR was founded. They were introduced as early as August 1946 by the commander-in-chief of the Soviet military administration for the then Soviet occupation zone in his Order No. 253. In the same

Table 1

Educational Level of Employed Women in a Socialist Economy

Females employed with completed vocational training per 1,000 females
employed

Year	Total	With higher education diploma	With specialized higher education diploma	Diploma as master craftsman	Skilled worker diploma
1971	491.9	24.3	56.7		410.9
1975	607.2	34.7	75.0	6.7	490.7
1980	740.7	46.9	140.0[1]	7.9	545.6
1984	802.9	55.9	162.6	9.5	574.9

1. After 1976 when specialized vocational training schools were recognized, some employed women with a skilled worker diploma in public health were classified as having a higher specialized education diploma.

Source: Report of the GDR Government to the General Secretary of the United Nations, "Frauen in der DDR. Bilanz der Erfüllung des Weltaktionsplanes für die Dekade der Frau—Zeitraum 1976–1985."

Table 2

Share of Female Students among Total Number of Students (in %)

	1950	1960	1970	1981	(1984)
Higher education	19	25	35	49	52.5
Vocational schools	25	29	49	73	83.2

Source: "Gleiche Chancen für Frauen?" *Panorama DDR,* Berlin, 1982, 76. The figures for 1984 were supplemented with data from the statistical yearbook.

process the German administrative and health authorities, as well as the trade unions, were enjoined to revise the official lists of occupations, which prohibited women access to certain occupations for various reasons. As a result, only occupations that might be injurious to women's health were left in this list.[5] The practical consequence of this was that in industrial branches—which had been traditionally dominated by men and in which there was a shortage of labor because of the war—many jobs, machines, etc. were modified so that women could work on them.[6] The juridical equality of men and women meant then, and still does today, that any social policy was committed to creating the appropriate conditions for the practical realization of equal rights. This took place in different stages, with different aspects emphasized in each. In 1945, only very few women who were already employed or had just become employed because they had to feed themselves and their children had a vocational education. Since labor was needed everywhere, and skilled labor was often in short supply, the usual method for training these women was through trained specialized personnel or they were retrained to new tasks. In 1950, only about 5 percent of women in industry had a vocational certificate. A qualitative change occurred in the sixties and seventies, when the mechanization of agriculture and many hitherto manual jobs in industry, commerce, and the service sector eliminated the deficit in the vocational training of women. Today, the qualification gap between men and women in the age groups up to 40 has been closed (see Table 1). "At the end of 1984, 80.3 percent of employed women in the GDR had completed vocational training, with 57.5 percent as skilled workers and 21.9 percent with a higher or higher specialized education."[7]

"Over 99.9 percent of girls who do not choose continuing education were in a skilled worker occupation."[8] "Of 226 skilled worker occupations for 10th grade leavers, about 200 are accessible to girls."[9] Women are today very highly represented in occupations with higher or higher specialized educational diplomas. Women account for over 50 percent of university and technical school students, and over 80 percent of students in vocational schools (see Table 2). In some occupations, such as medicine or the educational system, they account for over 50 percent.

Considering also that women are increasingly more active in the political sphere as well (they account for between 36 and 42 percent of positions in communal, regional, and district representative assemblies, and almost 30 percent of all mayors and every second judge is a woman), and that they are represented at an average of 50 percent in trade union positions at all levels, we can say confidently that the social status of women has undergone a broad change. One effect of this, for instance, has been economic independence and a strong self-awareness. The realization of the right to work has tremendously broadened the horizons of women's experience and their social relations, and has brought them education and social recognition of skills and abilities which they could hardly have developed merely as housewives. Unlike "private" housework, occupational activity has given them the experience of seeing their work valued and recognized socially. "I was proud that my work was so respected, and so it also was fun for me. . . I had a responsibility and I knew why I was there,"[10] reflected a woman, now over 70, in her recently published memoirs. She had had to work very hard even as a child with farmers, began working after the war in a factory in Magdeburg processing vegetables, acquired a skill at the age of 40 and became a brigade leader. The material changes that took place in the life of women as a result of employment have had the consequence that traditional notions of male dominance, of the "woman's role" in marriage and the family, were at least called into question as were relations between the sexes. Another consequence is that women increasingly define themselves less in terms of their function as housewife and mother, and they regard their jobs—at most only interrupted briefly after the birth of their children—as being just as important for their own self-affirmation and for their personal development. For the young generation as well, gainful employment of women is to a high degree a permanent component of their value system and life plans—in any case much greater in percentage terms than for boys. [11] Correspondingly, boys (like their fathers) see themselves in traditional terms as responsible for women and as material providers for the family. [12] Nonetheless, even among men, the overriding tendency is to regard female employment as a self-evident matter, which was by no means the case 30–35 years ago.

At the same time women (and in another sense their husbands as well) regard gainful employment as a contradictory issue to which they have ambivalent psychological reactions. The traditional concept of housework as "a service of love," e.g., as almost a natural duty, conceals differences from male employment, and has corresponding emotional overtones. Perhaps much more blatantly than a comparison with housework, the division of labor between men and women that is evident in social production makes it obvious that social equality between the sexes is not automatically established when a woman takes a job. The level of development reached by the forces of production still requires—and will require for a long time to come yet—that the division of labor be maintained. The consequent differences in requirements with regard to individual knowledge and skills, differences in trade, etc., affect men and women equally. But within these differences in the content of their job functions, a gender-specific division of labor also takes place: women are still concentrated in comparatively less qualified jobs, carry out practical and accordingly less well-paid activities, and gravitate to occupations which in their content correspond to "typical female" functions in the household and family (see Tables 3 and 4).

At present 30 percent of females receiving a secondary education diploma go on to obtain vocational training in a technical skilled occupation. After their training, however, these women take on assembly jobs more frequently than men with the same qualifications (in comparison to the dominantly male preparatory or maintenance jobs). They take jobs involving the feeding and simple operating of machines, or do assembly-line work. As a study by the trade union technical college showed, "Such jobs are regarded as women's jobs in enterprises and are reserved exclusively for female employees." [13] Although there is no legal basis for this, the traditional cultural pattern assumes a spontaneous regulative function here. A gender-specific division of labor is also evident among persons with higher education or a higher level vocational training. Thus "every fourth male, but only every tenth female with a higher education works in industry and construction. The vast majority of women with a higher education are employed in the non-producing sectors of the economy. . . . Over half of all males with a higher education have jobs in construction and industry, while only one-fourth work in the non-productive sectors where, in contrast, almost three-fourths of all

Table 3

Proportion of Females Employed in Total Number of Employed and by Economic Branch (in %)

Economic branch	Year			
	1970	1975	1980	1984
Industry	42.5	43.7	43.3	41.9
Productive crafts	40.1	38.7	38.0	37.4
Construction	13.3	14.9	16.2	16.3
Forestry and agriculture	45.8	42.9	41.5	39.4
Transportation, post and telecommunications	35.5	37.3	36.9	36.0
Retail trade	69.2	71.4	72.8	72.8
Other producing branches	53.7	54.2	55.1	55.0
Non-producing branches	70.2	72.3	72.9	73.2

Source: See Table 1.

Table 4

Proportion of Female Teachers in Higher Education—Professors and Lecturers (in %)

1971	1981
3.4	7.4

Source: Informationen des wissenchaftlichen Rates "Die Frau in der sozialistischen Gesell-schaft," vol. 2, 1982, 24 and 42.

women with higher education work. A sixth of women with higher education work in industry and construction, so reflecting a gender-specific polarization into technical and non-technical occupations."[14] The general trend is for the proportion of women to decrease the higher one goes in the managerial hierarchy. In other words, the social division of labor, objectively not ready to be abolished, persists in gender-specific forms that have evolved historically. This is encouraged by the traditional patterns and norms of "gender-typical" behavior (e.g., in the minds of managerial personnel, but also in the minds of women themselves, with regard to "typical" women's jobs). It is also promoted—and I will come back to this in the next section—by the fact that "private" reproduction is still predominantly the responsibility of women. One of the contradictory consequences of the gender-specific division of labor in social production is that while on the one hand through gainful employment women expand their experiences, their abilities, and their knowledge as well as their self-awareness, on the other hand, the traditional notions of the subordinate, supportive, and auxiliary function of women are reproduced in their new area of activity in many spheres of work. So the corresponding cultural forms from the sphere of "private" reproduction remain functional and are passed on to the next generation. These considerations have occasioned a discussion as to whether this form of employment is truly able to broaden women's horizons, e.g., if one compares monotonous assembly-line work with the varied activities involved in housework, and especially in raising children. However, even when one enumerates the contradictory and often limited effects for the emancipation of women of many current occupations, the idea of returning to traditional female duties in the house and family is rarely mentioned. Being a housewife and nothing more is not a serious alternative for many women, even if a number of them, under the direct pressure of the stress of their jobs and their tasks in "private" reproduction, regard a brief interruption in their jobs as quick relief from their momentary situation. Over the long term, the contradictions of the gender division of labor can only be resolved by eliminating unskilled, one-sided monotonous jobs and creating jobs that are rich and varied in content. In addition to the economic and technical preconditions, the subjective attitudes of women will play a role in this: e.g., their positive experience in expanding their field of knowledge and activity, as well as the limited emancipatory impact of the gender-specific division of labor; their dissatisfaction with the progress made to date, as well as their interest in more meaningful jobs; their openness to technology and their willingness to continue their education. In the upcoming years, in the wake of the introduction of the new technology and new techniques (such as microelectronics and computer technology), it will be necessary in all productive and non-productive sectors of the economy to ensure that the level of vocational training achieved by women is fully utilized and that scientific and technical progress does not proceed at women's expense. Thus, the vocational availability of women must be increased by eliminating the still existing deficit in advanced vocational education. For example, at present "in industry the relative proportion of trained male skilled workers with an advanced qualification is two to three times as great as that of women."[15] Many firms—especially recently—provide special advanced training courses for women during working hours so that these courses create no additional burden. In addition, the state has made it incumbent on enterprises to ensure that when they introduce new technology, one-sided, stressful activities with low productivity, performed mainly by women, are abolished and that when new jobs with richer and more varied content are created, the "working conditions are a priori structured in such a way that women and mothers can also be employed in these jobs."[16]

To sum up, we can say that:

Today in the GDR over 90 percent of all women who can work do work. About 30 percent of these work in part-time jobs. Gainful employment for women has become a self-evident matter, a permanent component of the individual life plans of men and women. The traditional cultural pattern of the male as the producer and provider and the female as the "user" and housewife has been broken. Although this form of the gender-specific division of labor has largely lost its value for individuals, it does not mean that the gender-specific division of labor and the associated norms and evaluation and interpretation patterns have lost their function and are disappearing. In social production differences in the content of jobs make for the continuation of the gender-specific division of labor—thus there remain functional and effective cultural forms in which social differences appear as "natural" differences between the sexes, as the "biologically conditioned," better aptitude of men for certain jobs, and the dominance of men over women. Women's claim to gainful employment and economic independence has freed itself from the traditional restriction to housekeeping and raising children, but for the most part they still seek to cash in on that claim in "typical" women's occupations. Although most men regard it as self-evident that their wives should work, it is just as self-evident to them that they should tend to have more qualified, richer, and better-paid jobs. Although women have to a certain extent penetrated into the "typical" male occupations and now even dominate quantitatively in some formerly "male domains" (e.g., medicine), the converse is not the case: there are hardly any men in the "typical" female occupations (e.g., nursery school instructors, kindergarten instructors). In other words, women have by now reached the level of men in the process of their emancipation, and have developed the corresponding "male" attributes, abilities, etc. However, only the barest rudiments are discernible in the contrary direction.

IV

Many women do not take advantage of the officially equal access to most occupations. Despite manifold social efforts to recruit women and girls for technical occupations or for managerial jobs, these opportunities are often not seized. This has a deep-rooted cause which does not rest primarily with the content of these jobs: namely, the burden of housework and caring for children remains a heavy one for women, and the traditional concepts of "sex roles" are tenaciously adhered to in the division of labor within the family. The level of development of the forces of production has had a negative effect in this domain: individual reproduction has not attained the degree of socialization that has been achieved in social production, and therefore continues to take place in essentially "private" form. Under these conditions, the traditional cultural norm that makes women responsible for caring for and raising children, and for the functioning of the household, has a material basis for its continued existence. This is also reflected in the fact that discussion is always of the "double burden"[17] of women, but never of men.

One consequence of this situation is that dominant factors in the structure of everyday life and in self-conception are different for men and women. Men define themselves mainly in terms of their activities as producers and in "public

Table 5

Children in Children's Institutions per 1,000 Children in the Various Age Groups

Year	Nursery	Kindergartens (children between the age of 3 and the beginning of school)	School nurseries (school children between the first and fourth grades)
1970	291	645	466
1975	508	846	642
1980	612	922	748
1984	692	all children whose parents desire	all first through fourth grade children whose parents desire

Source: See Table 1.

Table 6

Duration of Pregnancy Leave or Weeks Off with Continued Payment of Full Salary

1950	11 weeks (5/6)
1963	14 weeks (6/8)
1972	18 weeks (6/12)
1976	26 weeks (6/20)

Source: Die Frau in der DDR, Berlin, 1978, 181.

Table 7

"Baby Year" Regulations

1st or 2nd child: 12 months, with payment of 70–90 percent of income and job guarantee
3 or more children: 18 months at the above conditions

Source: See Table 2.

life.'' Although the family is highly valued in their life plans, alongside their occupations, their function as spouse and father is of subordinate significance in their self-conception. For women, on the other hand, the ability to reconcile occupation with motherhood and household duties is the determining factor in their self-conception. Often the contradictory nature of the demands placed upon them in these different domains gives rise to serious individual conflicts and the need to find compromise solutions.

The specific feminist and social policy of a socialist state will reflect the existing, and as yet insurmountable contradiction between socialized production and "private" reproduction. The aim of this policy is to create facilities for working women with children under existing conditions and then to gradually improve these conditions so that they "can make full use of their equal rights."[18]

The GDR has built a comprehensive and essentially well-functioning system of caring for and raising children while their parents are working (see Table 5).

Comprehensive social policy measures have been undertaken, especially since the early seventies. These include—in addition to lengthening the leave of absence for pregnancy, and the weekly days off—the introduction of the "baby year," a reduction in the work day for women with two and more children under the age of 16, a monthly paid housework day, and paid leave for single mothers to care for a sick child (see Tables 6 and 7).

Thus ever better conditions are being created for compatibility of job and motherhood. The most serious problem, however, continues to be housework and the time spent doing it. The average is still several hours more than the weekly normal working time of 43 hours. (There are also considerable time differences among women depending on their social position. Whereas women with a higher education are below the average, spending 36.2 hours per week doing housework, the time spent by housewives in farm households is much higher than the average due to private crop raising and stockraising.) The more extensive use of household appliances and improvements in services and in the range of consumer goods have so far brought about no qualitative change in the situation. This also means that the responsibility traditionally borne by women for the household and for children continues largely undiminished. Women continue to do two-thirds to three-fourths of the housework, and they are responsible for the larger share of caring for and raising children. Changes are indeed discernible in the division of functions within the family; especially among young people and couples in which both partners do shift work or one has a higher occupational qualification, one can find more egalitarian views and practices in the division of housework and a greater male interest in caring for and raising the children. But these have not yet become dominant trends and the present forms of the sexual division of labor in social production serve to impede the elimination of the traditional family division of labor in the home. For most women the consequence is greater physical and mental stress. They must continually alternate between types of activity that have extremely different requirements, and they have little time for themselves. From this perspective, it is fair to say, as many do, that women are doubly burdened, even when from another perspective they regard their paid jobs as personally important and indispensable. Very many women with small children report that a reduction in their work day would considerably alleviate their situation—accordingly, a large number of women who are presently employed part time work 7–8 hours per day.[19]

For some time to come women will continue to experience a typical and crucial contradiction in their lives: they must acquire abilities and needs for two spheres, which in some cases have very different requirements, and must bring them into a relatively harmony with one another in their own self-conception. To feel responsible for the functioning of the household, for the emotional well-being of all members of the family, and for a harmonious, conflict-free family atmosphere, can thus stand in relatively stark contrast to the material requirements of their occupation, and to the interests of professional advancement and their own personal needs. The solutions that many women have chosen to meet these different requirements are marred by these contradictions, which include part-time work, temporary interruption in professional activity until the children are older, taking jobs beneath their acquired qualifications, near their homes, or without shiftwork, or foregoing their own professional development in favor of the development of their husbands. However, women at the top of the occupational ladder are less inclined to pursue such solutions; instead they look for ways to get as much out of their occupational opportunities as possible. Both the society in general and particular firms support them in this through such things as special promotional plans and individual work schedules. But for these women too the "double burden" is a problem with which they must cope individually.

If on the one hand women's focus on compatibility between occupation and motherhood, house, and home, may be seen as a demonstration that fundamental changes have taken place in their lives, on the other hand, it is also a very clear testimony to the contradiction in their ability to act which women and girls must develop differently from boys and men in the process of their "socialization." The socialization of girls continues to be highly, if not predominantly, oriented toward the family, and thereby reinforces the corresponding cultural forms and patterns especially in the informal and self-evident division (i.e., non-division) of chores within the family. From early childhood, the conditions of development within the family are still clearly different for girls and boys, and these differences lead to manifold different activities for young boy and girl adolescents. In many families, boys and girls are given contradictory orientations—on the one hand they learn about new egalitarian norms and value orientations of socialist society, yet they are still exposed to traditional influences,[20] and, we might add, this dissimilarity in orientations is experienced more deeply by girls. To be sure, the funds made available from the social consumer fund for social policy measures, for subsidizing children's institutions, and services, is tantamount to an indirect recognition of the work of "private" reproduction. But as unpaid "privately" performed work, it is still associated with the implicit assessment that it is not "real" work. And so the specific mechanisms for the "socialization" of girls and women are still broadly operative, making them individually willing and able to fulfill these "private" reproduction functions "voluntarily." Recent sociological studies have confirmed that there still exist clear gender-specific differences in the "socialization" process of the younger generation. Socialization in the family concentrates above all on cultivating the individual conditions for the exercise of "private" reproduction functions. Gender-specific divisions of functions and their traditional valuations are passed on and appropriated in the practical course of everyday family life. Unlike the activities carried out by parents at their jobs, which remain rather obscure to children for a relatively long period, the "private" work of reproduction and the valuations associated with it become visible very early, especially for girls, in direct family life, and, moreover, are practiced in play as well. Thus the traditional division of functions is passed on to children: today girls are still drawn much earlier and more regularly into household work than boys.[21] Furthermore, girls' activities soon acquire a predominantly personal orientation, one directed toward assuming the responsibility for the mental and physical well-being of all family members, correspondingly for seeing to it that the household work necessary for this is accomplished as harmoniously as possible, and for avoiding or diffusing conflicts in the family. A permanent concern for the well-being of others, seen as self-evident, as a proof of love and a partiality for one's intimate family, is considered to be a demonstration of feminine virtue. The highly personal orientation of the female socialization process—toward relations that have meaning and value in themselves because they are based in a seemingly unconditional love—has the consequence that a woman's own feeling of personal worth is dependent first and foremost on recognition by others in these direct "social" forms. The gender-specific peculiarities and consequences of women's socialization also have effects on their occupational activity, and on the methods they use to meet the standards of action required by their profession.

The occupational effects of the socialization of girls, especially in the family context, are manifested for instance in the fact that women concentrate in occupations that are highly person-oriented, i.e., they correspond with functions and demands within the family. Commonplace notions of what is a "nice occupation for women" or what is "really no occupation for women" probably even further reinforce the choice of person-oriented occupation, just as that choice evidently is also preprogrammed by a definite gender-specific definition of functions in the household. The fact that "in the division of household labor, women are assigned the uncreative household chores, while men take over the practical aspects of work in the home"[22] must certainly have something to do with "girls' lack of motivation for practical occupations."[23] In the process, the attitudes and values acquired in the assimilation of the "gentle" feminine socialization patterns (traditional norms and ideals of "femininity") evidently produce internal resistance within women themselves. This is seen in the prevailing notion that practical activities are for boys, so that it is "unfeminine" for girls to be interested in such things. However, probably more effective are more subtle behavioral regulations, based on the empirical perception that recognition, rewards, indulgence, and fulfillment of wishes can be had more rapidly and without great effort or conflict, if the traditional "feminine" tasks are performed as expected. The related tendency for demands and needs to be dismissed also necessarily engenders a defense reaction and anxiety vis-à-vis demands—and indeed possibilities of development as well—which go beyond the usual, the tried and proven, and the accepted.

The special training of girls for their future "duties in the private service of the family" has molded a basic posture which may be described as a "readiness for sacrifice," a readiness to forego one's own wishes and demands in favor of those of others. This traditional cultural pattern in women's socialization and its psychological consequences influence the concrete forms and solutions with which women today attempt to reconcile gainful employment with motherhood and household. Similarly, the job satisfaction of many women today is measured less in terms of job content, as is the case with their male colleagues, than in terms of factors such as work time, the transportation system, buying privileges within the firm, etc.—factors that are very closely related to the requirements of running a household and a family. Finally, women, especially those with a lower occupational qualification, have a pronounced interest in maintaining the traditional divisions of functions within the family to buttress their own sphere of influence and decisionmaking.

On the whole, it has been found that employment for women means another pace of life, another time schedule for all family members. Of course, it is not only women who experience their "double burden" as a point of conflict in family life; husbands and above all children do so as well. Children must adapt their schedules to that of their working parents, and their own way of using time is often in conflict with the way mothers or fathers use theirs. However, as I have attempted to show, these experiences have so far not resulted in a radical change in the division of labor between the sexes within the family. Rather, the predominant tendency at present is for women, often under the pressure of their husbands, to seek compromise solutions which not infrequently mean giving up their own development. Generous social policy measures thus have conservative effects as well, precisely because for historical reasons they have been aimed at relieving the situation of working women with children. For example, the shortening of the working day for women with two or more children under sixteen is sometimes taken by husbands as an argument for discarding new forms of the division of labor within the family. The first experiences with regard to the effects of the baby year on the division of labor within the family also betray a tendency toward a return to the traditional one-sided responsibility of women for the household. All these things make it clear that the indicated changes are undermining the traditional divisions of functions, cultural norms, and behavior patterns, so that they are perceived as out of line with the times. On the other hand, these changes are not so radical that they are breaking down these gender relations and the cultural forms in which they are practiced. The process of dissolving these relations and forms is by no means rectilinear. The contradiction in development can very easily result in an at least temporary revival of traditional forms.

V

But it would be very one-sided to see only the negative aspects of the above tendencies in present relations between the sexes. Experiences of their double burden, and improved conditions for caring for children, have given many women food for thought with regard to the importance of family security for a harmonious development of children, and the value of children for a happy and meaningful life of one's own. Because of their tasks and experiences on the job *and* in the family, women are more inclined than men to include the ability to raise children, the capacity for attentive, considerate, and loyal relations, and the demand for sufficient time to realize all this in their conceptions of emancipation. In a certain sense, their "double burden" has given women a lead over men in this respect. In contrast to their grandmothers and mothers, who saw gainful employment as a decisive step toward emancipation, and accordingly saw its reconcilability with motherhood as less problematic, many younger women today stress that they want both a job and motherhood. For them a harmonious partner relationship and children are at least as important, if not more important, as their professional development. The practical experience of the one-sided effects of a life direction predominantly oriented toward professional advancement is reflected in such valuations inasmuch as such an orientation has often entailed giving up important humanistic areas of life. Young women today have many experiences that their mothers and grandmothers had rather sparingly. Finally, such evaluations are also the expression of a negative experience of and with children who have received too little family care and attention.

If nowadays women emphasize their qualities of motherhood and caring, this must not be seen as a simple unbroken adherence to traditional functions and ideas of femininity. It also includes the idea of a unified harmonious development of individual needs and abilities. And this is an idea that embraces both men and women on an equal footing, one in which, over the long term, the one-sidedness of traditional male or female life contexts and the real or apparent privileges associated with them have been overcome. Women, and increasingly, men as well, find such a life worth striving for. Not a few men, especially among the younger generation, deem it a personal loss not to be able to spend as much time as their wives do with their children. Not infrequently social policy measures meant to alleviate the situation of working mothers have been popularly regarded as a partiality, a favoring of women, thereby overlooking to some extent their double burden. Gainful employment and reproduction work perhaps ultimately could become equally significant and important for a meaningful life for both men and women once a shortening of the work day for both sexes becomes economically defensible and the "old form of the division of labor" is abolished. The goals of social policy are not at variance with this. For example, as society develops further, the goal is to move from offering special supports for women to providing *parental* supports, provided that at the same time the "special burden of women compared with men"[24] can be eliminated. Further, since 1986, men have also had a right to a "baby year," or may share it with their wives (hitherto for men this was possible only without pay, and so was scarcely used). Such changes should help to break down customary "sex roles," or at least not revitalize them, an effect that many measures designed to deal with the special situation of women unfortunately still have.

VI

One of the questions we posed at the beginning of this essay was how that which is new in social relations becomes visible and subjectively operable in relations between the sexes, and in the changes or modifications in the cultural forms that regulate and set standards for relations between men and women in daily life. Our presentation should have made clear that a look into daily life, into the forms in which people in the GDR conduct their day-to-day lives, will show no spectacular and radical upheavals. The contradictory conditions—which moreover exist throughout the world—in which socialist society in the GDR is currently developing and which is experienced in daily life as differences between the sexes have had the effect that transformations in "sex roles" and in relations between the sexes occur more in the form of modifications in customary cultural forms than radically and abruptly. These modifications are often so gradual that individuals scarcely notice them as change. Thus the large majority of men and women of all age groups regard marriage and the family as a form of life together worth striving for. Even the relations between those who live together without being married are not so terribly different from those developed in marriage. The fact that in the last few years the relative number of unmarried women has increased considerably from 13 percent in 1970 to 34 percent in 1983[25] is not a direct indication that marriage is disappearing as an institution. The economic independence of women, generous state support to single mothers, and the eradication of moral discrimination against them are certainly factors that have had a modifying effect on the traditional cultural forms in which men and women live together. However, there are also other causes: single mothers receive apartments and nursery places more quickly, which influences the decision not to marry or at least not to marry immediately.[26] In many cases single mothers live in stable communion with a man whom they frequently later marry. Even the large number of divorces[27] is no proof of a rejection of marriage—in most cases the divorcée seeks and finds a new marriage partner.

Also, women do not carry out an unrelenting, voluble campaign against men's "patriarchal" behavior, instead they not infrequently adopt what appears to be an accommodating and approving stance with regard to the familiar patterns, e.g., they take on the bulk of housework. But often, within the traditional norms and behavioral patterns, they also evidence a change of conduct, a developed self-awareness and quite clear assessment of their abilities and of the compromises they continue to make. Thus it is often women who apply for divorce and who make attentive, considerate, and loyal relations, recognition of their claims and life goals, and equal status in the family, yardsticks for measuring their marriage.

On the whole, we find that the development of socioeconomic relations of socialism and the changes it has brought about in relations between the sexes, have not led to a radical shake-up in traditional divisions of functions, and in the norms and standards of "typical" male or female behavior. They have, however, made the traditional norms and practices in relations between the sexes more ambiguous with the result that they no longer function free of friction for either men or women. Rather, the changed life conditions are experienced by both sexes as conflicts of norms and in behavior. "A little" emancipation is generally rated positively today. However, a woman who pursues a professional career as ambitiously as her husband and demands of him a commensurate helping hand in the household and in raising children, or a woman who deliberately decides not to have children for the sake of her career, or a man who regards it as self-evident that he should take on the bulk of the housework while his wife is studying to acquire professional skills, or who stays at home when the children are sick and accepts that his wife earns more than he does—such persons must not infrequently expect the disapproval of the surrounding society.

Often new or modified modes of behavior exist side by side with traditional, unchanged behaviors, or the latter are employed and stressed more or less consciously to diminish friction and conflict with others, or to diminish uncertainty in identity, as when women who venture professionally into domains that were previously reserved for men stress "feminine" qualities in their external appearance and conduct, or when men stress "patriarchal" behavioral patterns among their colleagues in contrast to their own habitual behavior.

Measured in terms of the historical period of socialist development in the GDR, the changes that have taken place in relations between the sexes and in the cultural forms of regulating these relations have been great. Measured in terms of what must still be changed in the forms and norms of everyday behavior between men and women for the sexes to be able to experience their distinctiveness while still enjoying equal social rank and social status, these changes are only the very first steps and the very first fruits.

In an interview, Irmtraud Morgner drew up the balance sheet for the present situation: "In short: emancipation (and not only of women) is not a campaign theme, but an epochal problem, according to Marx. It is certainly not a secondary contradiction, or a fashion which is today in and tomorrow passé."[28]

Notes

1. Alice Kahl, Steffen H. Wilsdorf, and Herbert F. Wolf, *Kollektivbeziehungen und Lebensweise* (Berlin: Dietz Publishers, 1984), 99–101.

2. Hans-Jürgen Gericke, "Sozialökonomische Probleme der Arbeitsteilung zwischen Männern und Frauen," in *Informationen des wissenschaftlichen Rates "Die Frau in der sozialistischen Gesellschaft,"* no. 6 (1977): 15–16.

3. Kristine von Soden and Gabi Zipfel, *70 Jahre Frauenstudium*, Frauen in der Wissenschaft (Cologne: Pahl-Rugenstein Publishers, 1979), 69.

4. Friedrich Engels, "Der Ursprung der Familie, des Privateigentums und des Staats," in *Marx Engels Werke (MEW)*, vol. 21 (Berlin: Dietz Publishers, 1973), 75.

5. This order was preceded by practical changes. Thus for example a point in the program of action of the workers of the Leuna works of January 25, 1946, was "equal wages for equal work in all departments without regard for age and sex." Cf. *Zur Sozialpolitik in der antifaschistisch-demokratischen Umwälzung 1945–1949*, Dokumente und Materialien (Berlin: Dietz Publishers, 1984), 101.

6. On this point see: Rosemarie Eichfeld, "Zu Problemen der Teilnahme der Frauen am gesellschaftlichen Produktionsprozess im Land Sachsen in den Jahren 1945 bis 1949," in *Studien zur Rolle der Frau im Arbeitsprozess im Sozialismus*, Beiträge zur Geschichte der Produktivkräfte, vol. 14 (Leipzig: Deutscher Verlag für Grundstoffindustrie, 1979).

7. Report of the GDR government to the Secretary General of the United Nations, "Frauen in der DDR. Bilanz der Erfüllung des Weltaktionsplanes für die Dekade der Frau—Zeitraum 1976–1985—'Gleichberechtigung, Entwicklung, Frieden,'" in *Informationen des wissenschaftlichen Rates*, no. 2 (1985): 22.

8. Ibid., 20.

9. Burkhardt Gericke, "Zu Stand, Problemen und Konsequenzen der beruflichen Orientierung der Mädchen," in *Informationen des wissenschaftlichen Rates*, no. 6 (1984): 7.

10. Wolfgang Herzberg, *So war es, Lebensgeschichten zwischen 1900 und 1980. Nach Tonbandprotokollen* (Halle, Leipzig: Mitteldeutscher Publishers, 1985), 174, 176.

11. Rolf Borrmann and Hans-Joachim Schille, *Vorbereitung der Jugend auf Liebe, Ehe und Familie* (Berlin: VEB Deutscher Publishers der Wissenschaften, 1980), 91ff.

12. This is also reflected in the fact that for boys earnings rank higher as a motive for choosing an occupation than for girls. See Ute Bruhm-Schlegel and Otmar Kabat vel Job, *Junge Frauen heute. Wie sie sind—was sie wollen* (Leipzig, Verlag für die Frau, 1981).

13. Joachim Schindler, Erläuterung "Zur produktivitäts- und persönlichkeitsfördernden Gestaltung der Arbeitsbedingungen berufstätiger Frauen und Mütter," in *Informationen des wissenschaftlichen Rates*, no. 1 (1985): 10.

14. Hans-Jürgen Gericke, 10.

15. Information on the study "Die berufliche Qualifizierung der werktätigen Frauen als beitrag zur weiteren Förderung der gesellschaftlichen Stellung der Frau im Prozess der Gestaltung der entwickelten sozialistischen Gesellschaft," in *Informationen des wissenschaftlichen Rates*, no. 5 (1983): 10.

16. Schindler, 11.

17. I consider the term "double burden" an unfortunate choice and use it here only because it has become entrenched and hence is generally understood. It connects with everyday experience insofar as it is still typical for women that their occupation is in

addition to their duties in the home and family. However, in my opinion the term conceals the fundamental importance of an occupation for the emancipation of women insofar as the latter is seen as an additional burden. (For more details on this point see Irene Dölling, *Individuum und Kultur* [Berlin: Dietz Publishers, 1986], 131ff.)

18. Erich Honecker, *Bericht an den VIII. Parteitag der SED* (Berlin: Dietz Publishers, 1971), 62.

19. Schindler, 17.

20. Bruhm-Schlegel, 85.

21. "Not only do boys get assigned a smaller number of regular chores in the family than do girls, but in general boys are given household chores less frequently, for a shorter period, and with less responsibility than girls." Otmar Kabat vel Job and Arnold Pinther, *Jugend und Familie. Familiäre Faktoren der Persönlichkeitsentwicklung Jugendlicher* (Berlin: VEB Deutscher Publishers der Wissenschaften, 1981), 65.

22. Bernhard Schneemann, "Soziologische Aspekte der Persönlichkeitsentwicklung von Frauen im Hinblick auf die volle Verwirklichung ihrer gleichberechtigten Stellung und auf ihre Teilnahme an der Arbeit im Mehrschichtsystem," in *Informationen des wissenschaftlichen Rates*, no. 6 (1977): 45–46.

23. Kabat vel Job, 72.

24. Anita Grandke, *Familienförderung als gesellschaftliche Aufgabe* (Berlin: Staatsverlag der Deutschen Demokratischen Republik, 1986), 77.

25. See *Statistisches Jahrbuch der Deutschen Demokratischen Republik* (Berlin: Staatsverlag der Deutschen Demokratischen Republik, 1983).

26. See Jutta Gysi, "Lebensgemeinschaften in der DDR," in *Informationen des wissenschaftlichen Rates*, no. 6 (1984): 64–72.

27. The number of divorces increased from 27,400 in 1970 to 50,300 in 1984, cf. *Report of the GDR Government to the Secretary General of the United Nations*, 52.

28. Eva Kaufmann, "Interview mit Irmtraud Morgner," *Weimarer Beiträge* 30, no. 9 (1984): 1501.

Translated by Michel Vale

Sex-Role Socialization in Relationships as a Function of the Division of Labor

A Sociological Explanation for the Reproduction of Gender Differences

HILDEGARD M. NICKEL

In the GDR, boys and girls attend the same schools and study the same curricula. But in the past ten years educational sociology has conducted a number of studies that invariably show quite manifest differences of a social nature[1] (and this is the primary focus of sociologists' interest) despite distinct points in common in the conditions, activity structures, and value orientations of girls and boys. The studies show sex-specific action profiles. Is it primarily traditions and the tenacity of obsolete ways of life that are responsible for this? Or are there objective reasons, rooted in current social conditions, for the reproduction of gender stereotypes? In such a context, what should be the task of schooling?

Sex differences in empirical findings[2]

According to studies carried out in educational sociology, girls have more pleasant social experiences in school than their male peers[3] and hence are not only more willing to attend, they also are better achievers, at least as far as grades and the early school leaving rate are concerned. It may be concluded from the findings that girls are more disciplined, conform more to the norms, and are more adjusted in school than boys. Girls seem to develop in the home, at an early stage and to a greater degree than do boys, that potential for action and those structures of consciousness important in the school. The relevant qualities are discipline, industriousness, and the ability to adapt and subordinate oneself.

The mandatory and elective courses, as well as the political, social, and cultural life in the school are clearly perceived in different ways by the two sexes. Analyses in educational sociology have shown that participation in the social sciences and foreign language groups is relatively balanced within the general program, while boys seem to predominate in mathematics and the natural sciences. The ratio of girls to boys in the technical fields in the general program is flagrantly out of proportion: according to the findings of educational sociology, these disciplines are attended by 19 percent of boys but only by 2 percent of girls; the practical and productive disciplines in the general program are attended by 20 percent of boys but only 9 percent of girls, while the ratio shifts in favor of girls (30 percent to 11 percent respectively) in the cultural and artistic disciplines in the general program. This tendency extends into the voluntary school work groups, study circles, and interest groups. School athletics also show a gender differentiation, with more boys than girls attending such courses. On the other hand, girls are more active than boys in speaking out and in discussions in socially useful activities (solidarity bazaars, etc.) organized through or in the schools, and in social activities of a cultural, formative, or care nature.

Girls have electoral functions in the Federation of German Youth (FDJ) more often than boys, at least in the base organizations in the schools, and they also have comparatively better grades, although the pace-setting pupils in the class are mostly boys, in the judgment of both the other students and the teachers.

In leisure time relations and activities, the two sexes also show clear differences. Boys and girls show typical behavioral and relational patterns in the way they make use of their leisure time—girls read more often; more frequently meet their friends in discotheques, the cinema, and other cultural arrangements; pursue artistic activities more often; show a stronger preference for idly strolling about and doing nothing; and use more time for school work and FDJ work. Boys, on the other hand, spend twice as much of their free time as girls with sports, watch television more often, and are involved in acquiring specialized knowledge eight times more frequently than girls.

For girls, the preferred meeting place for contacts with boy friends and peers is their parents' home. For boys it is the street and parks near where they live. Girls spend their free time more often in the school, in youth clubs, and in ice cream shops. The social center, which is the preferred place to spend leisure time, also shows gender-specific patterns. In the case of older pupils, both the informal relations in leisure time with their peers, as well as the formal relations which they enter into in job communities and interest groups (the gender composition of which reflects the typical leisure-time patterns of the two sexes), are largely homogeneous with regard to gender, despite the greater interest shown by older pupils in the opposite sex. Girls meet girls and boys meet boys and both genders consider relations with their peers to be vitally necessary. The self-determined demarcation from the opposite sex is ultimately manifested even in the symbols of language and habit and observable in the spatial relations of sex groups, i.e., the subtle forms of distance and proximity, which seem to play a central role in self-identification of "masculinity" and "femininity." Groups of friends are focal points for exchanging the generational experiences typical of each sex. Girls seem to use their girl friends for a verbal exchange of experience and for intimate conversations. They exchange opinions on the "other sex," on questions having to do with their future occupations, on experiences in school, and on their life together with their parents and siblings more frequently than boys do among themselves. Boys are less interested in such intimate, highly person-oriented or social-oriented conversational themes, but are more interested in impersonal conversations, e.g., on sports. Interest in sports seems to be a key criterion of masculine self-definition, at least in the age group studied.

Secondary school pupils have extremely well-defined, stereotypical notions of their abilities (Wölfel, 1984)—a feeling that seems to get stronger in the later school years. Boys are more inclined than girls to have confidence in their technical skills, strength, and the ability to develop something new in their occupations (Wölfel, 1984). Girls, on the other hand, believe that they are able to handle smaller children, that they are skillful in handicrafts and in structuring their immediate surroundings (Wölfel, 1984). In their self-assessments, boys are better equipped for technical occupations, while girls are more convinced of their social abilities. Teachers also apparently have similar stereotyped pictures of the abilities of adolescents (Wölfel, 1984).

According to the findings in educational sociology, girls show just as great a readiness to take on productive work as boys. Almost as many girls as boys seek volunteer work during vacation, although the areas of activity sought by the students themselves, as well as those arranged through the school, show considerable gender differences: boys prefer the socialist industries, while girls work mainly in state institutions (nurseries, kindergartens) and in retail trade. So even at this level we see signs of those gender differentiations that were discernible earlier in occupational preferences and in the actual final choice of occupation: with respect to the level of occupational qualification, girls and boys are more or less equally intent on obtaining a solid education. However, the gender polarization that has been perceptible in the occupational structure of the GDR since the late sixties (Gericke, 1982) is clearly discernible in the distribution among the economic sectors and occupational groups. The findings of educational sociology show that adolescents largely take up those occupations that reproduce their own social stratum (Korn and Steiner, 1986) while there also exists a segmentation of occupations by gender (Nickel, 1986). Thus in the latest study, which analyzed actual choice of occupation of tenth graders (which, however, was done in a selected area in the GDR and was hence not representative for the country as a whole) almost two-thirds of the girls fell into the following occupational groups:[4]

Textile
Medical
Pedagogical
Retail trade
Service sector
Office jobs.

Two-thirds of the boys in the population studied fell into the following groups:

Maintenance mechanic
Electrician
Skilled construction work
Mason
Automobile mechanic
Engine fitter
Installations
Carpenter
Cabinetmaker
Skilled electronics fitter
Metallurgy
Skilled worker in supplementary instruments of production.

Although only four of these occupations were chosen exclusively by boys, there were on the whole fewer than 10 percent of the girls in the population who went into these professions.

Although informative, this is, of course, a very general level from which to regard gender distribution. It must be supplemented and defined more precisely in order for us really to be able to demonstrate differentiation and contradiction in present processes. With regard to determining the social activity, availability, and mobility[5] of adolescents, sociological methods that are able to pinpoint more effectively the content and material of the chosen occupations should then also perhaps be used. Although we do not yet have detailed empirical studies, it can be assumed that typical male and typical female occupations also differ with regard to autonomy, decision-making powers, and margin of freedom, as well as in the nature of the objects worked with (things, human beings, or symbols), and finally with regard to the complexity or intricacy of the demands of the job.

Gender differences as a function of the division of labor and socialization

Every new generation is born into a given context of social reproduction, and into concrete historical, economical, political, and general cultural relations. To the extent that these relations are assimilated through practical activity, specific generational experience is gained; but beyond that these relations themselves are reproduced in modified form. Socialization is at core the formation of the subjective characteristics that ensure social reproduction in its economic, political, and cultural dimensions (which is part of social change, which itself must start from concrete existing reproduction conditions).

Gender socialization[6] would then be that group-typical process which results in gender-typical action profiles and social identities (state of consciousness, subjective perceptions). It takes place as an educational process and on the basis of environmental and life conditions (which vary objectively by sex) and the accompanying requirements of action.

Gender socialization has its causal (but not its only) explanation in the concrete historical division of labor between men and women. From a sociological standpoint, gender socialization among other things prepares the new generation to reproduce masculine and feminine work capacities in modified form. Seen from this perspective gender socialization is not primarily an individual or even a contemplative act, but a practical social process in the course of which boys and girls, men and women, develop the necessary subjective capacities for social action, and especially for their role in the social organization of labor. In their own action (initially in the family, but later beyond it), in the transmission of experience by male and female adults (particularly the parents), and on the basis of concrete environmental influences boys and girls acquire those action potentials and subjective identities that enable them to reproduce the existing conditions as male or female working people or as fathers or mothers, and to be effective in a socially differentiated and gender-typical manner within social reproduction. Gender socialization is a relationship. It mediates the objective conditions of the gender-typical social division of labor and the associated gender-typical objective action requirements into subjective structures and action potentials, into concrete historical, and generation-specific female and male subjectivity.

Today, more than 91 percent of all females of working age are employed, going to school, or studying—which gives the GDR the highest level of employment of this population group of any country in the world. Differences in the level of occupational training between men and women have been further reduced; there are already no differences among young people (up to the age of 35). Presently, 81.5 percent of all women working in the socialist economy have a skilled worker diploma or even higher, while about a third of all its managerial personnel are women.

Thus both historically and in an international comparison the GDR has had tremendous success in the process of evening out the social differences between the sexes. Initially this involved the elimination of crass social inequalities that were biased to the detriment of women. But even under today's conditions, social labor is a manifoldly structured system that demands specific action, reflecting the division of labor, from men and women, fathers and mothers, and the male and female workforce in accordance with their objective position in it. Not only are the specific economic sectors and occupations more or less open to the two sexes (Tables 1 and 2), but as discussed by Dölling, the distribution of productive and reproductive labor, of socialized occupational labor, and individual or "pri-

Table 1

Share of Employed Females in the Economic Sectors (%)

Economic sector	Proportion of employed women in total number of employed				Proportion of economic sector occupied by women			
	1970	1980	1984	1985	1970	1980	1984	1985
Industry	42.5	43.3	41.9	41.7	32.3	33.0	32.1	32.1
Crafts	40.1	38.0	37.4	37.2	4.3	2.4	2.3	2.3
Construction	13.3	16.2	16.3	16.5	1.9	2.3	2.3	2.3
Agriculture and forestry	45.8	41.5	39.4	39.1	12.2	8.9	8.6	8.6
Transportation	25.5	27.4	27.0	26.9	3.0	3.2	3.2	3.2
Post and telephone	68.8	70.0	69.3	69.1	2.5	2.3	2.2	2.2
Retail trade	69.2	72.8	72.8	72.6	15.8	15.0	15.0	15.0
Other productive branches	53.7	55.1	55.0	56.1	2.6	3.5	3.4	3.3
Non-productive branches	70.2	72.9	73.2	73.1	25.4	29.3	30.9	31.1
Total	48.3	49.9	49.4	49.3	100	100	100	100

Source: Statistisches Taschenbuch 1986, 37. Data as of September 30.

Table 2

Apprentices by Economic Sector 1985

Economic sector	Total	Male	Female	% Female
	(in thousands)			
Industry	186.3	112.4	73.9	39.7
Crafts	15.0	11.9	3.1	20.8
Construction	46.7	42.4	4.3	9.2
Agriculture and forestry	41.1	24.5	16.6	40.3
Transportation, post and telephone	35.6	24.9	10.7	30.2
Retail trade	38.6	6.2	32.4	84.0
Other productive branches	10.0	2.7	7.2	72.7
Non-productive branches	24.7	6.3	18.3	74.3
Total	398.0	231.3	166.7	41.9

Source: *Statistisches Taschenbuch 1986*, 40. Data as of September 30, 1985.

vate'' labor within the family has gender-typical characteristics.[7] The system of the social division of labor and the place of the sexes in it leads to a specialization of activities and skills, and to different education for male and female capacities. This is evident in three empirical sociological dimensions:

1. In the different social positions of the sexes in the system of socialized labor, seen vertically (social positions, occupational positions) and horizontally (economic sectors and branches);

2. In the assignment of socialized labor and reproduction labor in the family, which differs by sex, "by nature," so to speak;

3. In the gender-typical division of labor in daily practical life in the family.

This system of the division of labor creates social differences between the sexes: first, it reproduces gender-typical differences at the level of occupational training, in social positions, and in incomes, to the detriment of women. It contains "unjustified differences in level" (Lötsch, 1985), and differences respecting social inequality. In the GDR we have been effectively and steadily eliminating this type of social differences, but they have by no means all been overcome. Second, it contains "functional" differences. Gender-typical specialization in specific occupations and economic branches is today still predominantly functional for the economic progress of our society. However, functional differences can become dysfunctional at any moment. This seems to already be the case where women are inadequately prepared for the demands of science and technology as a result of their one-sided channeling of abilities in the socialization process, and especially in the growth of "social" or "welfare" occupations. Third, the system of social division of labor brings to light the "social disparity" between the sexes. In the historical process of the division of labor, the sexes have evolved specific subjective abilities, social disparities, which have congealed into the "nature" of the two sexes. As socialism evolves, we must ultimately consider to what extent these historically evolved cultural forms of subjectivity may still be regarded as a boon to society, assuming that the deleterious effects still associated with them are systematically abolished.

The social division of labor is an extremely dynamic relation. Under socialist relations of production, and as the scientific and technical revolution proceeds, the "old" forms of the social division of labor have changed considerably. A work-related concept of gender socialization gives a historical perspective on gender relations, roles, and stereotypes themselves, as something that can change objectively over the course of time. What are the present discernible trends? On the one hand, the use of new technologies in the GDR makes possible, indeed even makes necessary, the continued dismantling of one-sided action profiles of the sexes. On the other hand, a number of counter-tendencies are discernible. In the process, social planning must be put to active use if it is really to contribute to social progress for both sexes. The changes in work brought about by the introduction of new technologies in the GDR have meant a reduction in monotonous and physically heavy labor, have entailed restructurings of occupational groups and redefinition of occupations, have tangentially affected proportionalities in entire economic branches and sectors, have impinged upon the organization of labor time and of "work" in the family, and have affected the demands made on education and training, and on availability and mobility. They affect both women and men. Over the long term, living labor is being supplemented, and indeed in some cases even replaced, by computer labor. Initially, however, sizable labor redundancies in industrial production are to be expected. Unskilled and semi-skilled work is affected, and in industry 60 percent of this work is done by women. Similar tendencies are discernible in the nonproductive sectors. In the occupational groups "administration," "testing and control," and "production implementation," there will still be monotonous and simple work carried out primarily by women. Finally, the need for labor will increase in areas in which the qualification requirements also rise: research and development, designing and drafting, maintenance and repair. Although 40 percent of all persons participating in continuing education in an attempt to meet the new scientific and technical standards are women (as indicated in the annual report to the 11th Party Congress), these occupations are still entered by only a minority of girls. Girls' interest in the technical occupations has been declining since 1976, and they presently make up less than one-third of those in technical skilled labor occupations in industry. Furthermore, these are usually occupations which allow only a small chance of developing challenging technical abilities. New technologies thus do not automatically lead to a reduction in the gender polarization in work. However, social labor and its gender-typical distribution remains the central point. To take gender socialization as a point of departure and to expect decisive changes to come from it is essentially to turn things upside down. Gender socialization is a function of the social division of labor, not vice versa. Ultimately the concrete conditions for and the requirements placed on gender socialization and education depend on the level of development of work. Socialized labor has reached a level of development that forces us to reconsider this process and the schools' responsibility in it. The important point is not the formal male-female proportions of the respective sectors, but whether and how both men and women master scientific and technical progress. The society's educational institutions, that is, all schools prior to the ten-year general educational polytechnical schools, have manifold opportunities to lend a systematic and guiding hand to the process of gender socialization.

Gender education as a special case of gender socialization may be seen as that process with which and during which the two sexes acquire or should acquire the subjective capacity necessary for social action, and in particular for their role in the social organization of labor, by assimilating essential social powers specifically chosen to that end. This capacity is acquired in a conscious, guided, and controlled manner, i.e., in a fundamentally planned and regulated way, as well as in forms showing varying degrees of social institutionalization and organization. As a socially differentiated process which takes place in institutions created especially for it, gender education under socialist conditions is governed by the equality principle: boys and girls are educated and developed for ten years of their life in schools in the same way and with the same contents regardless of their sex. At least this is formally so. Actually, as we have seen, the same school material is apprehended differently by the two sexes. Creative awareness of this process is necessary if scientific and technical progress is to be undertaken equally by the two sexes. Because of their experiences in their surroundings, and in particular in their own families, by the time they enter school boys and girls are in many respects already socially different. Formally identical school conditions encounter social disparities; they thus reinforce differences instead of breaking them down. Much is left to automatic processes, and the educational efficacy of schools in this specific important respect remains far below its potential. Pedagogical strategies for action concerning this question seem largely to be lacking. A systematic intervention into this process requires that teachers become conscious of what they are doing, often in spite of themselves. Instead, research shows that teachers, and indeed even many textbooks (Vogt, 1984) systematically and manifestly reproduce sexual stereotypes. In particular, some thinking must be done about the practical aspects of instruction in the natural sciences and about forming technical and natural science communities. Girls must be consciously recruited again for the technical occupations. But this requires a long and meticulous development of appropriate interests in girls. Many new ideas are required in this area, as well as in the facilities and opportunities offered for leisure time for girls both in school and regionally. Truly life-relevant instruction cannot evade the question of reproduction of sexual roles and stereotypes. The school has certainly more potential for cultivating boys' ''social'' abilities than is currently realized.

Education can be regarded as only one part of socialization overall. Yet in the course of historical development, and above all in socialist society (whose construction and further development is a conscious and planned process) education has become an increasingly crucial component and an ever more extensive sector of socialization. Nevertheless both partial processes of socialization carry their own particular weight and differ in the extent of their relevance. Just as the overall influence of societal relations on the young generation must not be reduced to the effects of education, however powerful the latter may be, education can likewise not be reduced to the more diffuse forms of socialization. On the one hand, there is the overall social environment, which has its own potential with regard to influencing the formation of the new generations of men and women in the classes and layers in socialist society. It is this potential that is operative as the younger generation acquires its experience, i.e., through practical action in the context of their own immediate lives. On the other hand, upbringing in general, as well as gender upbringing in particular, is a necessary, controlled, and purposeful complement and in part (of course only within limits) a corrective on spontaneous socialization. Upbringing will be more effective the more it understands how to take into consideration in its strategies the material effects of the social environment on young people.

There is an objective, although of course not mechanical, interaction (and it is just this that must be shown) between the level of development of social labor and gender socialization. Both the conditions for and the demands placed on gender socialization ultimately depend on the level of development of labor. Conversely, gender socialization and upbringing are active aspects of this process, although there are limits to the scope of its effective influence. Analytically, they may be regarded on three levels, differing with regard to the aggregational level of the subject:

Gender socialization is a process that

(a) takes place at the level of social classes and strata, where it is the gender-typical assimilation of work and life conditions which vary depending on the social structure, and which thus have their class-specific and stratum-specific characteristics;

(b) takes on generation-specific characteristics as a consequence of historically changing conditions and is accompanied by concrete and varying generational experiences;

(c) takes place under the influence of the exercise of, or of training for, gender-typical social functions, e.g., in concrete gender-typical occupations or in the social functions associated with motherhood or fatherhood;

(d) is effected in direct interaction in everyday activities and in the direct routine reproduction of life in micro-groups.

Socialization and upbringing take place primarily in everyday action in a specific configuration of life spheres, in which adolescents are integrated in socially typical ways, e.g., by social origin, social age, and gender, as a spontaneously and systematically pursued cultivation of those abilities that enable them to act independently in this concrete social environment, to control it, and to master it. Gender socialization and upbringing, considered from this perspective, constitute a spontaneous and guided development, respectively, of male and female competencies.

Notes

1. We shall not address the question of biological differences here, as they are basically irrelevant to the issue concerning us, however interesting they may be in detail.
2. The empirical findings stem from educational sociology studies at the APW, namely studies on life-style (1976–1980) and studies of the social experience of senior students (1981–1983) done at the Department of Sociology of Education, APW, Berlin.
3. The studies in the main concerned 9th graders, i.e., 15-year-olds.
4. Since the choice of occupation is always dependent on territorial conditions, it is not possible to draw conclusions that would be representative for the GDR, although the results show a generally valid trend.
5. The current research project at the Sociology of Education Department at the APW concerns this question. It will be completed in 1990.
6. This approach derives from a discussion begun by A. Meier (1984) on the concept of socialization.
7. About 75 percent of women do housework for an estimated 40 hours per week.

References

Gericke, H.-J. "Sozialökonomische Probleme der Arbeitsteilung zwischen Männern und Frauen," in *Informationen des Wissenschaftlichen Rates "Die Frau in der sozialistischen Gesellschaft,"* no. 5 (1982): 6.
Korn, K. and Steiner, I. "Arbeitsgruppe: Bildung und Qualifikation als Triebkräfte ökonomischen Wachstums," in *Soziale Triebkräfte ökonomischen Wachstums, Materialien des 4. Kongresses der marxistisch-leninistischen Soziologie* (Berlin: Dietz Publishers, 1986), 303–12.
Lötsch, I. and Lötsch, M. *Soziale Strukturen und Triebkräfte . . . Jahrbuch für Soziologie und Sozialpolitik* (Berlin: Akadamie, 1985), 159–78.
Meier, A. "Sozialisation und Erziehung als gesellschaftliche Prozesse" (Thesis), *Pädagogische Forschung*, no. 1 (1984): 27–32.
Nickel, H. M. "Geschlechtersozialisation in der Familie und als Funktion gesellschaftlicher Arbeitsteilung—Ein erziehungs soziologischer Erklärungsansatz für die Herausbildung weiblicher und männlicher sozialer Identität," Dissertation (B) (Berlin: Humboldt University, 1986).
Statistisches Taschenbuch der Deutschen Demokratischen Republik, 1986 (Berlin: State Publishers of the German Democratic Republic, 1986).
Vogt, E. "Inhalt und Struktur von Geschlechtsrollenbildern in Schulbüchern der unteren Klassen," Dissertation (A) (Erfurt, 1984).
Wölfel, I. "Unterschiede in Lehrerurteil bei der Einschätzung der beruflichen Voraussetzungen von Jungen und Mädchen," in *Informationen des Wissenschaftlichen Rates "Die Frau in der sozialistischen Gesellschaft,"* no. 6 (1984): 38–43.

Translated by Michel Vale

Political Socialization and the "Micromilieu"

Toward a Political Sociology of GDR Society

CHRISTIANE LEMKE

Political socialization usually describes the process through which members of a society receive their political knowledge, adopt beliefs and values, and learn behavior concerning political life. As part of the political system it constitutes the major link between the individual, society in general, and the state. A socialist system, like a Western society, cannot operate effectively unless there is considerable congruence between its institutions and objectives, and the prevailing ideological and political orientations of the people. It is in this respect that political socialization is of major interest. As Archie Brown, Walter Rosenbaum, and other scholars of Communist studies have argued, political socialization plays a major role for the political culture of Communist systems. In Brown's words the relationship between the process of political socialization and political culture "involves consideration of what are the major components of the *official* political culture. . . . The *efficacy* of socialization into the official political culture is a major concern here. . . . The large and important question which follows on from this is: how successful have the holders of institutional power been in *changing* the political culture—in replacing traditional values and creating a 'new man'?"[1]

The GDR today is a highly complex industrial society, and the traditional Marxist-Leninist concepts of creating a "new man" and mobilizing the population into the Communist "goal culture" had to be adapted to the needs and social conditions of advanced industrialism. SED party secretary Erich Honecker's emphasis on new technologies and forced economic growth, and its effect on society and nature, necessitate a recasting of political education in the GDR. The involvement by some of the younger generation, the intelligentsia, and artists in peace and ecology activities, the rise of feminist thinking, the development of a distinct youth culture apart from the official youth organization, the upgrading of the church, and the significance of informal groups and networks are clear indicators for a differentiation within society.

Against this background political socialization can be viewed from two different analytical perspectives. From a political perspective it is mainly an ideological concept held by political elites to use their power to legitimize and stabilize the existing political system. From this perspective the ideology itself, derived from Marxist-Leninist thought, is of major interest. This line of inquiry suggests such themes as how political socialization is executed in the educational system from crèche to adult education, the role of political organizations, the degree of social and political pressure, and the results of such efforts. Notably, political socialization of political elites, the cadres, is a basic concern. Studies by Thomas Baylis, Peter C. Ludz, Gert-Joachim Glaessner, and Gerd Meyer have provided insightful information on this aspect of political socialization. From another perspective, one can also view political socialization as a sociological phenomenon. As part of everyday life, political attitudes, values, and behaviors are formed by social and political conditions of life, the experience of individuals and different social groups and their relationship to political institutions. Differences between the public and the private sphere, between elite and mass consciousness, and between ideology and reality come into focus.

For the political sociologist it is precisely this linkage between political and sociological aspects of political socialization that is of major interest. In the pages that follow I will assess the significance of the socialization process from this perspective. Based on social science research conducted in the GDR and on Western perceptions of current GDR politics and society, special attention will be given to this linkage on the level of the "micromilieu" of social and political settings within small segments of society. It is precisely in the realm of school experience, family life, peer group culture, and informal networks where the "quality of life" is experienced and where it becomes part of political learning.

Communist goal culture: the socialist personality

The basic goal of political socialization in the GDR is the socialist personality. By definition this personality follows the precepts of socialist morality, such as community spirit, feelings of duty and responsibility toward the state and society, and an optimistic outlook on life and the aims of socialism. Moreover, the socialist personality is willing to put his or her knowledge, capability, and talents to full use in the cause of the socialist society, and is willing to learn and acquire skills needed to master the scientific-technical revolution and to help increase productivity.

Philosophically the concept of personality is based on Marxist-Leninist theory.

As Marx and Engels argued, the key for the understanding of personal life is to be found through analyzing the basic conditions of the society, the character of labor and social relations deriving from the way production and consumption are organized. But how to proceed from these to individuals, their way of life, aspirations, values, and behaviors? Unresolved by Marx and Engels, this question remained to their successors, and throughout the history of Marxism the dispute over what function a theory of personality could have and how its subject can be defined has been carried out with some bitterness.

It was Lenin who, pursuing the cause of the revolution in Russia, introduced the leading role of the Communist party for political consciousness-raising. Rejecting Rosa Luxemburg's notion of a "spontaneous mass consciousness," Lenin claimed that Communist politics relies on political education through the party.

The heritage of these two lines of argumentation is essential for the concept of socialist personality in the GDR.[2] During the 1950s, when the role of Marxist-Leninist thought as state ideology grew and attempts to de-Stalinize science were made by giving more attention to psychology, sociology, and other previously neglected fields in theory and research, first efforts to develop a Marxist theory of personality were made by the social psychologist Hans Hiebsch in Jena, whose work was influenced by the Soviet psychologist S. L. Rubinstein. Other social scientists followed suit as increased significance was attached to the individual in socialist society. The "scientific-technical revolution," as the fostered industrialization and modernization of science, technology, and economic management was labeled in the late sixties, needed politically conforming but highly qualified workers and intellectuals. The concept of socialist personality was no longer simply a moral and political vision of the Communist goal culture but a category for managing socialist society; it was introduced as a major aspect in academic research as well as in the politics of the state. A comprehensive educational reform in the 1960s, encompassing the ten-year general polytechnical school, vocational training, and university, was designed to socialize flexible, highly qualified "socialist personalities." Similarly, the Youth Act, passed in 1974, pursued a policy of early and continuous political socialization according to the "developed socialist society," a term that was used since the early 1970s.

On the level of social science research and theory, the "socialist personality" became the most popular term during the Honecker era. Closely linked to the "socialist way of life" (*sozialistische Lebensweise*), personality development is a highly sensitive term to measure the quality of life under state-socialist conditions. Jürgen Kuczynski's study *Geschichte des Alltags des deutschen Volkes* (1980) with its focus on everyday life and everyday culture was trailblazing for the diverse and data-rich literature on *Alltagskultur* (everyday culture) of GDR society, whose flowering we are presently witnessing. Several research projects as well as individual publications shed light on social conditions of the development of socialist personalities.

An excellent example of the current trend in research and probably the most advanced study concerning the theory of socialist personality is Irene Dölling's publication *Individuum und Kultur* (1986). The author insists on the validity of the Marxist assumption that personality development is determined by the socio-economic conditions of society, but points more explicitly than traditional arguments from this school of thinking to individual experiences, needs, and expectations as well as to culturally determined symbols.[3] Here, she lines up with the French Marxist Lucien Sève and the Western school of "critical psychology" of Klaus Holzkamp and Ute Holzkamp-Osterkamp. Dölling promotes a concept of "historical forms of individuality" (*historische Individualitätsformen*), valid for socialist society, in which the individual is emphasized in its own right. Her excursus on the contradictions within the personality development of professional women gives a lively account of how social and political conditions shape the personality when seen from the angle of the individual rather than from the prevailing political ideology and the Communist goal culture.

Likewise arguing in favor of reflecting individual, cultural, and social conditions and differences of the socialist personality is Albrecht Kretzschmar, a leading sociologist from the Academy of Social Sciences of the SED. In his book on "social distinctions and distinct personalities" Kretzschmar points to significant differences in value orientations, patterns of behavior, and life-styles of members of different social classes and groups in GDR society.[4] Based on empirical data, the study reveals a tendency to rank the influence of the "social milieu" much higher than previous studies on social structure and personality development. His conclusion that attitudes and behavior are apparently shaped more by the social conditions and the cultural environment of the micromilieu than by class membership goes well beyond traditional Marxist-Leninist argumentations.

These two examples of current social science research in the GDR may illustrate the direction in which works on the socialist personality have moved. Within the framework of Marxist-Leninist ideology and language more room is given to the individual, the cultural and social environment, and the micromilieu of living.

Formal political socialization: the educational system

The major policy instrument to implement the Communist goal culture and cultivate socialist personalities is the educational system. The current debate in the GDR about the scope of general education (*Allgemeinbildung*) underlines the importance of political education and points to the way in which future political education will be shaped. Emphasis is put on two major aspects, the modernization of the curriculum and the improvement of political and ideological training. As Gerhart Neuner, the president of the Academy of Pedagogical Science, explains, general education in the ten-year polytechnical school has to recognize the fact that new technologies such as microelectronics, robotization, and genetic engineering, which will be introduced in the GDR on a large scale in the near future, call for new skills and knowledge.[5] Thus the curriculum for the polytechnical education has been reformed, giving more room to topics such as "automatization of production" and "electrotechnics." Electronic calculators are being used in mathematics beginning in grade 7, and computers are provided for the polytechnical training centers. Extracurricular study groups (*fakultative Kurse*) are established for grades 9, 10, and grades 11 and 12, which lead to the *Abitur*, focusing on electronics, data processing, and microbiology. To recruit a scientific elite capable of meeting the challenges of the "scientific-technical revolution," talented students are promoted in their career.

Parallel to these efforts more emphasis is put on ideological, political, and moral education. For example, starting in 1983 new curricula were introduced in civics. According to Neuner, ideology is the basic condition for general education. The scientific-technical revolution requires a clear and optimistic view of technology and science according to socialist values. Teachers of civics, history, science, and mathematics are requested to work together to improve ideological education. By strengthening this aspect of school education GDR political elites hope to meet the challenges set forth by the dynamic in value structures and behavior patterns produced by introducing new technologies. Also, it should be kept in mind that the opening toward the West as part of détente policy under the Honecker administration has fostered the official policy of ideology demarcation and strengthening of the Communist view of the world (*kommunistische Weltanschauung*) vis-à-vis the capitalistic world. Education, including political education as a major component, clearly is organized systematically, beginning with the preschool, continuing in the ten-year general polytechnical school, in vocational training, university education, and in adult education, such as the *Volkshochschulen* and *Akademien* (academies). The underlying political theory in the GDR holds that the socialization process is a continuous one with a gradual adaptation of political values and attitudes, and that it is successful because of the developed network of socialization agents. As in most other socialist systems, growing up in GDR society includes a high amount of political education at all stages of the socialization process. The educational system is intertwined with political organizations, in particular with the youth organization, the Free German Youth (FDJ), and the Young Pioneers. Further, the school and other institutions are requested to work closely with the parents to fulfill educational goals.

Basically we can distinguish three major aspects of political education within the educational system: first, the subjects taught and the scope of the class curriculum; second, the environment of learning; and third, the function of the educational system for guiding later careers.

The kindergarten curriculum already contains several features for political education, both in respect to values as well as to behavior. Among the latter are the training of community spirit and social responsibility taught through collective education (*Kollektiverziehung*). The values include "love" for the socialist GDR, support of the official peace policy, which includes appreciation of the army, and an optimistic outlook on managing life. The combination of intellectual skills with moral and emotional training is characteristic for political education and will continue throughout the socialization process. In school, political learning is part of the regular curriculum as well as of extracurricular activities in the study groups. Generally speaking, 41.7 percent of formal instruction time is devoted to German language and social science, 29.8 percent to mathematics and science, 10.6 percent to foreign languages (in particular Russian), 10.6 percent to polytechnical education, and 7.9 percent to sports.[6] Subjects designed specifically for political education are civics, history, polytechnical education, and—since 1978—premilitary and civil defense training. The reforms of the curricula mentioned above led to an upgrading of political education; the curricula were adapted to the current politics of the state and restructured according to new psychological and pedagogical findings. In most subjects general and political education were merged to educate socialist personalities.

Political socialization is further determined by the general environment of learning—above all the concept of collective education. The enormous significance of this concept for political, economic, and social life has been pointed out by several social scientists in the West. For example, Otto Stammer finds for the early phase of the GDR that the ideology held by the collective, or as he calls it the "moral of the group" (*Gruppenmoral*), is one of the major instruments of political education, designed to train behavior and attitudes stabilizing the power system.[7] Other authors have stressed the social and psychological function of the collective, pointing to certain supportive elements for individuals by the group.[8] Generally speaking, the collective generates socialist value, and idealistically the more "advanced," active members hold locomotive functions for the rest of the group. Collectives of this sort are, for example, the class at school, youth brigades at the workplace, and most notably the youth group of the Free German Youth (FDJ), which are closely linked to the everyday life at schools and other educational institutions.

Another important aspect of the learning environment needs to be mentioned. As Christel Lane and others have argued, socialist systems need political symbols and rites to foster identity and stabilize political power. In her book *The Rites of Rulers*, Lane gives a lively account analyzing the political role of rites in the Soviet Union. For the GDR, Ralf Rytlewski has lately drawn the attention of Western observers to the role of rites and political symbols in the political and social life.[9] As part of the political culture, rites mainly serve to foster socialist identity, integrate individuals and groups, and thus stabilize the political system. Rytlewski particularly points to the *Jugendweihe*, a ceremony introduced in 1955 for pupils at the end of eighth grade. In this ceremony themes of patriotism and solidarity with the Soviet Union are interwoven with those of civic virtue. Several special lectures at school precede the ceremony. In a formalized and ritualized manner the pupils publicly commit themselves to the socialist ideology and the GDR as their state. The ceremony symbolizes the admission to the world of young adults; it also marks the entry of the youth into the youth organization FDJ. While because of the highly symbolized procedure, the real significance of this formula for the values and attitudes of young people should not be overestimated, it is without doubt that these rites—"initiation rites" as Rytlewski calls them—signify the political culture of everyday life for school children and, taken together with the collective education, form political socialization.

The educational system further gears political socialization inasmuch as the ten-year school (but even more advanced institutions, in particular the universities), destine political careers and political biographies in general. From the founding of the GDR the educational system has been a tool for policy implementation. General political goals, such as social equality and economic planning, played a large role in educational policy. In fact institutions of education have been used to restructure society and reform the social structure. In the centrally planned system, admission to the twelve-year school (*erweiterte Oberschule*) is given on the basis of ability, encompassing grades achieved as well as political activity, society's needs, and the social structure of the population. In applying these criteria, the GDR has acquired considerable leeway in regulating the numbers and kinds of entrants. In the early period students of worker and peasant backgrounds have been given admission on a priority basis, a policy that considerably increased the proportion of these students. Yet, in recent years more emphasis was put on the ability of applicants, promoting talented students. This shift in admission policy is based on the guideline that economic progress needs highly qualified, creative, and gifted students. Thus we observe a "reproduction of the intelligentsia," meaning that children of academics, whom sociologists have found usually to have better preconditions and basic skills for learning than others, are given more attention.

The impact on political aspirations and expectations should not be underestimated; frustration for those whose upward mobility is blocked, permanent renewal of intellectuals as a social group, and alienation between workers and intellectuals are possible.

What is the result of the enormous effort put into formal political socialization within the educational system, or in other words how successful have the holders of political power been in raising socialist personalities? According to empirical studies conducted in the GDR, socialist values have increased and are now dominant among the youth.[10] Western observers, however, have noted that the gap between verbal acceptance of the system and actual behavior is quite significant. Karl Schmitt, for example, concludes his survey of political socialization in GDR schools with the statement that attitudes and behavior are congruent for only a small group of students.[11] His study confirms the argument presented by Archie Brown that it is important to distinguish between attitudes and behavior since in socialist systems the gulf between those two may be especially wide.[12]

GDR scholars themselves acknowledge that political education often remains rather formalistic. They critically address the problem that the curriculum in school insufficiently reflects and refracts social experiences of children themselves.

Particular mention is given to two groups who seem to trouble political elites. One is the group of pupils already leaving school after eighth grade. These pupils, roughly 7 percent of the students, some of whom have difficulties learning while others are dropouts for various social reasons, often refrain from political activities, mobilization campaigns, and collective life. Their identification with socialist goals remains highly questionable.

The other group is to be found among university students. Trained to become future leaders of politics, economy, and society, these students are confronted with high expectations concerning their political values and activities. Several surveys, however, indicate that only a small group actively supports socialist ideas and activities while others are either not interested or do not participate in social political life.[13] One is also reminded that critical or even dissident views were in several cases nurtured at universities. For example, active supporters of the unofficial peace movement were found among academics. Prominent dissidents such as Robert Havemann, Rudolf Bahro, or Hermann von Berg came from university backgrounds and, in particular in the case of Havemann, had appeal among students.

Considering the selection among applicants, the finding of official GDR surveys about low or absent political activity is rather astonishing, but it confirms the assumption that the gap between values and attitudes verbally acknowledged and existing behavior is notable even in the "developed socialist society." Going beyond this one might question whether it is at all possible to implement socialist ideology as an overall guideline for behavior. More likely in highly industrialized, complex modern societies only a small group of intellectuals follow the precept of an ideological system while others hold rather inconsistent belief systems. Thus Arthur Hanhardt's conclusion that the gap between "is" and "ought," between goals and realities characterizing GDR in the 1970s holds true until today.[14]

Family socialization and informal networks

Sociological changes as well as the politics of child raising have resulted in a shift from socialization within the family toward socialization within public facilities. About two-thirds of all children from the ages of 6 months to 3 years spend part of their day in the crèches and more than 90 percent of the 3- to 6-year-olds are in kindergarten. Official policy supported these collective, public means of education, partly because of ideological reasons and partly because of the mobilization of women for the labor force, since shortage of labor has been troubling the GDR since the early period. Usually both partners in the family work; with more than

90 percent of its women working (or studying), the GDR rates in the top range of female labor force participation.

Several studies conducted in the GDR have found, however, that despite these trends the family still plays a large role for young people in the process of socialization. Surveys conducted by the Central Institute for Youth Research in Leipzig have found that 90 percent of the 12- to 23-year-olds have a positive emotional relationship to their parents. More than two-thirds of the sixth to eighth graders and over one-half of the tenth graders prefer their parents as advisors in all personal matters.[15] Even for older students the attachment to the family remains strong. As Kurt Starke reports, the studies of the Central Institute have found significant correlations between students' attitudes and those of their parents.[16] These findings suggest that despite the strong support for collective, public education, the family remains an influential socialization agent, a fact that in the GDR led to a careful reevaluation of the family. A newly founded project on "Family and Society" at the Institute for Sociology and Social Policy at the Academy of Sciences, directed by Jutta Gysi, aims to follow up with some of the sociological changes as well as with the new role of the family in society.[17]

The major point here is that families constitute the most important informal network for children and grown-ups. In everyday life, the family represents a private niche, a realm of individual freedom and social relatedness that is characteristic for GDR society. Günter Gaus, the former first representative of the Federal Republic in the GDR, who has summed up his experiences and impressions in his book *Wo Deutschland liegt* (1983), rightly characterized this high appreciation of the privacy in such niches with the term "Nischengesellschaft." In addition to providing for this popular desire for privacy, the family also serves as a network for social and emotional security. Especially since the GDR is mobilizing all resources of society to achieve an "intensified reproduction of society," meaning an intensive use of all resources including the human one, the family embodies a resting point in the dynamics of modern industrial society. In her book *Ganz in Familie*, the sociologist Irene Runge describes the various aspects of everyday life, the *Alltag*, of the family and enlightens its role as "social network" (*soziales Netzwerk*). She sees a strong correlation between the functioning of the family as social network and the appreciation of family life. Generally speaking she asserts, "The GDR is a highly family oriented country."[18]

In everyday life, the family represents a microcosm in which values, attitudes, and life-styles are transmitted informally from one generation to another. As various studies suggest, there is a significant continuity of such patterns. Starke, for example, finds that 83 percent of the students claim to have the same political opinions as their parents.[19] It is much more likely that politically active students come from socialist-oriented families than from other backgrounds; political activity of parents themselves, particularly their previous membership in the youth organization FDJ, provides role models for children, as Starke argues.

Role models of parents definitely do not follow the socialist ideology in all respects. Negative examples can especially be found for sex-specific attitudes and behavior patterns, a fact that not only hinders equal opportunities for women in their job but also in their advancement into leading positions and political careers.[20] This is not to say that only the family is responsible for the continuity of traditional male-female patterns; other aspects, such as the culture of institutions, official family policy, and social policy also play a role. Considering the significance of the family for those growing up, though, the importance of role models and expectations of parents can not be questioned. The influence of parents on leisure time and job choices of boys and girls and their sex-specific differences has been documented in surveys by the Central Institute of Youth Research in Leipzig as well as by the Academy of Pedagogical Sciences. Clearly these differences contradict the aims of social equality promoted by the socialist state. Here the more conservative function for socialization becomes obvious. In the realm of privacy within the family, attitudes and behavior seem to be quite resistant to change; the everyday culture of the family constantly recreates gender specific role models.

Besides the family, other informal connections have proved to be significant for political socialization. In a discussion about her famous novel *Kassandra* (1984), Christa Wolf, one of the most prominent writers in the GDR, shares an important observation she made about society. Asked about the question of preserving peace, the very sensitive issue she raises in her novel and the related Frankfurter lectures, she argues that she does not stand alone with her critical approach to current peace policy but that she finds a new infrastructure emerging, encompassing groups of those interested in these issues.[21]

This informal network of groups was confirmed by the young writer Sascha Anderson who very recently left the GDR to live in West Berlin. As one of the critical writers, Anderson reports that others who thought like him or were interested in his writings met regularly in private homes, discussing problems of literature, culture, aesthetics, and politics. These two examples may represent a number of others in which political learning is part of the informal groups and networks. At present, most of these informal groups are formed by intellectuals and writers. Sheltered by the privacy of individual homes, or, in other cases, by the church—the only autonomous large organization—new centers for political thinking emerged.

The peer group culture

The peer group culture is an important aspect of social and cultural life, especially for young people in the GDR. This culture did not emerge in the FDJ but rather in friendship circles and informal groups. These groups generate a distinct youth culture, expressed in leisure time habits, preference for certain music (in particular rock music), dress fashion, and hair styles. In big cities such as Berlin there is a wide variety of cultural expressions of youth; "punks" and youth culture at the "*Prenzlauer Berg*," a quaint old district of Berlin, are the most spectacular forms of this culture.[22] Despite the fact that these informal groups share mainly leisure time activities and interests, their impact on popular values, aspirations of youth, and behavior patterns should not be underestimated. As Sabine Hoffmann writes, studies conducted at the Academy of Pedagogical Science found that 80 percent of the 14- and 15-year-old students discussed "lively" political topics in their friendship circles.[23] Good students, FDJ members, and those who come from middle- and upper-class backgrounds are more likely than others to be interested in politics during their leisure time. The documented importance of the friendship circles and informal groups for young people suggests that there is a significant influence of the peer group culture on political attitudes and behavior.

It was Walter Friedrich, the director of the Central Institute for Youth Research, who very early pointed to the significance of "micro-groups" for the personal development of children and youth. In his book *Jugend heute* (1966) Friedrich writes that small groups constitute the basic network for those growing up and thus are more important than so-called macro-groups, such as class membership. Norms, values, and behavior patterns are shaped by a "group moral" of micro-groups. Similar arguments were presented by the social psychologists Hans Hiebsch and Manfred Vorwerg in the their book *Einführung in die marxistische Sozialpsychologie* (Introduction to Marxist Social Psychology, first published in 1966). Social groups, in particular the family, are from their point of view major social institutions forming individual personalities. Considering the prevailing Marxist-Leninist theory, which at that time insisted on the primary role of class membership and social conditions determined by the class structure of society, this was quite remarkable. Despite their acclamation of Marxist-Leninist theory, their study reveals a tendency to rank the role of small groups and social networks important in everyday life higher than others. Interestingly enough they use the term "socialization" for the active relationship between the individual and society, a term that was labeled "bourgeois" and rejected by leading social scientists until the 1970s.

Empirical knowledge of the great impact of the peer group culture on youth dates back to the early 1970s. At that time, though, this connection was basically seen negatively, as a means to generate anti-socialist values and behavior. Ideally, the official youth groups of the FDJ, the collectives, should determine the way of life of pupils, students, and young workers and should result in political attitudes and behavior according to the ideal of the socialist personality. For example, the sociologist Arthur Meier, a leading expert on educational policy and the educational system from the Academy of Pedagogical Sciences, writes that the friendship circles which exist as part of leisure time have great impact on job choices and leisure time activities as well as on ideological belief systems, values, and expectations of youth.[24] While in some cases these groups do conform with socialist values and overlap with the collectives of the FDJ, in other cases they may act dysfunctionally, inasmuch as the latter may often nurture delinquency of youth. Meier is expressing a view that was dominant at that time. He concludes that the influence of organized groups, the youth organization, and the schools on leisure time activities should be extended, encompassing all activities of youth.

Youth policy designed to follow this advice could not do away, however, with the growing importance of informal friendship circles and the emergence of a distinct youth culture which is characteristic for most complex industrial societies. To follow up with this trend, recent publications indicate a shift in the perception of the peer group culture and the evaluation of the role of these groups.

Summing up the results of studies conducted at the Central Institute for Youth Research concerning leisure time activities of youth, the authors of a recent publication fully acknowledge the role of informal, non-organized leisure time groups. From their point of view these groups function as agents of "secondary socialization."[25] They clearly reject the assumption that the non-organized groups nurture criminal habits, even though they assert that in some cases this can be true. However, for the majority of the youth groups their culture and activities are normal aspects of the way of life with no negative impact on personality development.

Their findings show that 22 percent of the pupils, 19 percent of apprentices, and 12 percent of the young workers belong to several non-organized leisure time groups.[26] Further, they find that:

—boys are more often members of non-organized groups than are girls
—group membership is significantly higher between the ages of 16 and 18 years
—members of the learning youth (pupils, students, apprentices) join these groups more often than young workers
—there are no regional differences
—the group members are usually of the same age
—group activities include informal gatherings, discussions, listening to music, dancing, going to see movies, sports
—approximately 15 percent of all youngsters are members of several leisure time groups at the same time, including organized groups.[27]

As Table 1 shows, relaxing activities obviously rank above political activities.

Starke reports that about 50 percent of the students belong to informal friendship circles. Similar to Voss and others he finds no correlation between the membership in a non-organized group and anti-socialist or criminal behavior. Rather he asserts that, except for some very few groups, friendship circles today can not be seen as a "competition" to the organized activities of the FDJ.[28]

Research projects focusing on the culture of everyday life of youth have likewise underlined the significance of the peer groups. Hoffman finds that these groups express the need of those growing up to share specific experiences and needs, apart from organization and guidance by grown-ups. Habits and symbols, values and attitudes embody the specific youth culture and generate the search for

Table 1

Group Activities of Non-organized Groups

Percentage of youth indicating that they often perform these activities

Activity	Pupils	Apprentices	Young workers
listening to records and tapes, collecting and exchanging them	70	62	53
sports	49	49	42
visiting discotheques	47	51	41
visiting movie theatres	44	40	25
visiting other dancing activities (except disco)	32	51	56
talking, joking	25	14	14
having parties	24	37	42
discussion about political problems	18	18	24

Source: *Die Freizeit der Jugend*, authors collective directed by Peter Voss (Berlin: Dietz Verlag, 1981), 246.

identity among GDR youth.[29] As we know from other sources this includes the import of Western culture, which is very popular among GDR youth.

It is precisely at this point that peer group culture becomes important for political socialization. The values, aspirations, and behavior patterns transmitted by peer groups clearly stand for the diversification of cultural expressions in the GDR. Official policy has to face the fact that the education of socialist personalities has to recognize the growing importance of leisure time in general, a desire for more individual freedom, and the search for identity found among youth. It is against this background that the emergence of new values concerning, for example, the protection of the environment, or the upgrading of the church must be seen. For the majority of friendship circles, however, the fact that political discussions rank at the bottom of group activities indicates that individual lifestyles prevail over politically determined interests. The peer group culture stands for individuality rather than for conformity.

Conclusion

Political socialization in the GDR today is shaped both by the ideological concept held by state authorities as well as by sociological changes within society. Influenced by the fostered modernization of the economy, traditional Marxist-Leninist ideology merged with the aims of the "developed," highly industrialized society. Changes in the ideological concept of the socialist personality signal the need to adjust the concept to this development. Notably it has led to the upgrading of the role of individual personalities, capable of mastering new technologies and of promoting modern management of society and economics. Political education at schools was reformed so as to ensure socialist values and belief systems along with "optimistic" views on technology development and achievement-oriented values. In this respect the politics of the state set new guidelines for political socialization.

As a sociological phenomenon, political socialization proves to be influenced by sociological changes partly promoted by state policy—most notably the emergence of the new scientific technical intelligentsia and the new role of women— but partly uncontrolled or even unwanted. The high appreciation of the family as a private niche, the emergence of informal networks and subcultural groups have become part of everyday life and popular culture in the GDR. By focusing on the micromilieu of these social groups rather than on elite political socialization I have attempted to show that beyond organized, ritualized political learning there is a broad variety of parameters influencing political values, attitudes, and aspirations. In the future it is most likely that these parameters will increase their influence and produce a divergence of values. Studies on the changing political culture have likewise confirmed this tendency. This development may harbor conflicts inasmuch as the need of state authorities to legitimize and stabilize the existing political system will contradict the expectations and aspirations emerging in the realm of new social networks, the privacy of the family, or the peer group culture. The quality of life in the GDR will then be measured in terms of room to maneuver.

Notes

1. Archie Brown and Jack Gray, eds., *Culture and Political Change in Communist States* (London: Macmillan & Co., 1979), 16.

2. For a detailed account on the intellectual history of the theory of socialist personality see Christiane Lemke, *Persönlichkeit und Gesellschaft. Zur Theorie der Persönlichkeit in der DDR* (Opladen: Westdeutscher Verlag, 1980).

3. Irene Dölling, *Individuum und Kultur. Ein Beitrag zur Diskussion* (Berlin: Dietz Verlag, 1986).

4. Albrecht Kretzschmar, *Soziale Unterschiede—unterschiedliche Persönlichkeiten? Zum Einfluss der Sozialstruktur auf die Persönlichkeitsentwicklung* (Berlin: Dietz Verlag, 1985).

5. Gerhart Neuner, "Entwicklungsprobleme sozialistischer Allgemeinbildung," *Pädagogik* 40, no. 9 (1985): 657–83.

6. Neuner, 660.

7. Otto Stammer, "Sozialstruktur und System der Werthaltungen der Sowjetischen Besatzungszone Deutschlands," *Schmollers Jahrbuch* 76, no. 1 (1956): 99.

8. Marilyn Rueschemeyer, "Social and Work Relations of Professional Women. An Academic Collective in the German Democratic Republic," *East Central Europe* 8, no. 1-2 (1981): 23-37.

9. Ralf Rytlewski, "Politik der DDR als Ritual—das Beispiel der Jugendweihe," *DDR-Report*, no. 12 (1984): 714-17.

10. Walter Friedrich and Werner Gerth, eds., *Jugend konkret* (Berlin: Verlag Neues Leben, 1984).

11. Karl Schmitt, *Politische Erziehung in der DDR* (Paderborn: Schöningh, 1980).

12. Archie Brown, ed., "Introduction," in *Political Culture and Communist Studies* (London: Macmillan & Co., 1984), 4.

13. Kurt Starke, *Jugend im Studium* (Berlin: Deutscher Verlag der Wissenschaften, 1979), 117.

14. Arthur Hanhardt, "East Germany: From Goals to Realities," in *Political Socialization in Eastern Europe. A Comparative Framework*, ed. Ivan Volgyes (New York: Praeger, 1975), 66–91.

15. Otmar Kabat vel Job and Arnold Pinther, *Jugend und Familie. Familiäre Faktoren der Persönlichkeitsentwicklung Jugendlicher* (Berlin: Deutscher Verlag der Wissenschaften, 1981), 33.

16. Starke, 124–27.

17. Jutta Gysi, "Frauen- und Familienentwicklung als Gegenstand sozialistischer Politik," in *Jahrbuch für Soziologie und Sozialpolitik 1984* (Berlin: Akademie-Verlag, 1984), 95–109.

18. Irene Runge, *Ganz in Familie* (Berlin: Dietz Verlag, 1985), 9.

19. Starke, 125.

20. A most enlightening essay on female identity in the GDR is published by Irene Dölling, "Social and Cultural Changes in the Lives of GDR Women—Changes in their Self-Conception," in *Studies in GDR Culture and Society* 6, ed. Margy Gerber (Lanham: University Press of America, 1986), 81–92. See also Christiane Lemke, "Women and Politics in East Germany," *Socialist Review* 15, no. 3 (1985): 121–34.

21. Christa Wolf, "Documentation Christa Wolf. Ein Gespräch über *Kassandra*," *The German Quarterly* 57 (Jan./March 1984): 109.

22. See, for example, Norbert Haase, Lothar Reese, and Peter Wensierski, eds., *VEB Nachwuchs. Jugend in der DDR* (Hamburg: Rowohlt Verlag, 1983).

23. Sabine Hoffmann, "Soziale Erfahrungen der Schuljugend—Ergebnisse bildungssoziologischer Untersuchungen," in *Informationen zur soziologischen Forschung in DDR*, ed. by the Academy of Social Sciences at the ZK of the SED, no. 5 (1984), 66.

24. Arthur Meier, *Soziologie des Bildungswesens. Eine Einführung* (Köln: Pahl-Rugenstein, 1974), 320–25.

25. *Die Freizeit der Jugend*, authors collective directed by Peter Voss (Berlin: Dietz Verlag, 1981), 245.

26. Ibid., 248.

27. Ibid., 244.

28. Starke, 141.

29. Hoffmann, 65–66.

Part III

Work, Technology, and Education

Technological Transformation and Educational Policy

GERT-JOACHIM GLAESSNER

For four decades the educational policy of the SED has been molded by the notion that socialist society must give every citizen the opportunity to obtain a higher education and skill, and that this is a prerequisite for an individual gaining access to cultural and educational goods. This is an essential element in the emancipation of the working class and is formulated by the 1976 Program of the SED as follows:

> The educational system has the task of educating and training young people who, equipped with solid knowledge and abilities, are able to think creatively and act independently; whose view of the world, based in Marxism-Leninism, pervades their personal convictions and behavior; and who feel, think, and act as patriots of their socialist fatherland and as proletarian internationalists.
>
> The educational system serves education and training of fully developed personalities who unfold their abilities and talents to the good of socialist society, and are distinguished by their love of work and readiness for defense, by a sense of community, and by a striving toward high communist ideals.[1]

If the SED has outlined the ideal picture of an all-round educated socialist man, it does not merely mean by this that all citizens should, if possible, achieve an educational diploma. As the quotation from the SED program shows, it also linked other substantive notions to the concept of education or general education. Thus the educational policy of the SED was aimed not only at breaking the monopoly of the bourgeoisie on education in order to strip the old ruling classes not only of their economic base, but their social privileges as well but to create a new content for education: general education was and is understood to mean the appropriation of all the goods of cultural education and at the same time a preparation for later occupational and social praxis. In this regard, at the 9th Party Congress of the SED Margot Honecker said that in the three decades of SED educational policy a "pseudo-education for the masses," which for the vast majority of people meant training to function as a machine (Marx), was replaced by "the all-round education of the personality" and an upbringing that led to a "crippling of the spirit was replaced by education to be free-thinking individuals."[2]

Recent discussion in the GDR calls into question some key axioms of the previous education and science policy: the issue is how the educational system will be able to respond to the qualititatively new challenges of scientific and technical progress, in particular microelectronics and information technology. In an article in the central organ of the SED, *Neues Deutschland*, Rudi Weidig, director of the Institute for Marxist-Leninist Sociology of the Academy for Social Sciences, attached to the Central Committee of the SED, popularizes views that have been setting the tone for some time in the debate in the social sciences, but which still have a way to go before they become part of general consciousness. These may be summarized as follows:

1. The guiding idea of upbringing and education in the GDR, namely, the all-round educated socialist personality, requires a correction. An elementary understanding of informatics and information-processing technology must become a permanent component of general education. In the modern world, general education has a clear natural science and technical component which is growing in importance.

2. Modern society requires flexible, highly skilled workers prepared to take risks and to understand education and training as a "continual, unceasing, and dynamic process."[3]

3. The capacity of the educational sector for innovation must be reinforced. "Peak performances" and "top talents" must be promoted even further.

4. But this does not mean that the present general level of qualification will rise. A quantitative expansion of the relative proportion of the labor force with a technical certificate or specialized higher education cannot be expected. The number of skilled workers and foremen will stabilize at around 67 percent, that of persons with diplomas from technical schools or institutions of higher education will reach 23 percent, and a certain portion of the work force will continue to have no completed education with diploma.

These predictions show that educational policy in the GDR is at a crossroads: the aims and concrete structuring of education and upbringing must be reviewed. The answers found in the fifties and sixties in the wake of socialist restructuring of the educational system have lost their validity.

Today the question is how the education system must respond to the challenges engendered by the change and partial disintegration of the old pattern of large-scale industrial production, growth of the service sector, and the change in the world of work brought about by the microelectronic and computer revolution. It is the traditional aims of education which have shaped educational and cultural policy in the GDR for forty years that are primarily being challenged. These trends raise the question of the role of education and science and the status of the education and science sector in the GDR society. The education system provides a graphic example of the tension between the demand for an all-round education, which pervades everything that is written in the GDR on educational policy, and an orientation of the educational sector to the concrete qualification requirements derived from the existing and the projected organization of labor processes in industry and elsewhere.

The status of the education sector in the social system of the GDR

Educational requirements are determined not only in industry, but also in other areas and sectors of society. Thus it is not exclusively the requirements of the socialist economy that determine what the "occupation sector" expects of the educational system. The qualification requirements, both quantitatively and qualitatively, are quite different in the different domains of society. It is a key task of the educational system to respond to these differentiated requirement profiles. In order to meet the expectations of the employment sector, the education system must have at its disposal the necessary material resources, and projected needs must be formulated which define the expected skill and occupational structure and the requirement characteristics for specific occupational profiles.

The education system, however, does not only have the tasks of training people for their occupations. All educational policy documents refer to the political ideology and social function of education. The education system is expected to achieve two aims: the cultivation of thoroughly educated socialist people, and the preparation of youth and adults for the requirements of the scientific and technical revolution. The expectations of society and of the political and administrative system with regard to the education system is that it should bring about the desired social and political socialization of children and youth and educate them to be loyal citizens, and that it consciously shape occupational and social advancement through the way it distributes educational opportunities and thereby contribute to the planning of the development of the social structure. In descriptions of the educational system in the GDR, the specific conditions engendered by the system of domination under "real socialism" often remain unmentioned. But they have a considerable influence on the interdependence among the educational system, the political and administrative system, and the occupation sector. The claim of the SED to political and ideological leadership has led to the formation of a peculiar sector in society, the "nomenklatura," which comprises all positions and functions that are regarded by the Party as strategic. Since a considerable portion of professional leadership positions in all areas of society is subject to the functional conditions of the cadre domain, i.e., the criteria of cadre policy, the general educational system also is involved to a considerable extent. The establishment of formalized courses of study, the setting of specific qualifications for the assumption of managerial positions, and the differentiation of methods for planning the needs for cadres and for cadre administration have crucial feedback effects on the educational sector. The social function of educational processes and the special status of the educational system within the social whole of "real socialism" thus requires that the educational system not be seen in isolation, but as a part of a functionally differentiated political and social system. For the GDR, despite all the changes that have occurred since the fifties, the political adminis-trative system still dominates all areas of society, including the educational system. Decision-making powers in regulating institutional and legal frameworks of the activity of social subsystems lie unequivocally in the political domain. However, the growing complexity of society makes it increasingly necessary to concede more powers to specific areas of society for formulating their social political goals and concrete strategies. The educational system has a special importance in this context in that it provides the indispensable preliminary func-tions for shaping all other areas of society. It is therefore understandable that educational policy has always been a crucial element in the SED's overall policy.

Stages of the educational reform

As in all systems of the Soviet type, the educational sector in the GDR has been regarded from the very outset as an important sub-area of the new social order under construction. Educational policy was and is a special aspect of overall policy in the socialist countries.[4]

Changes in the educational sector are and have always been a part of and a reaction to trends in other social areas in the GDR, and are supposed to support or correct planned, but also unplanned de facto political, economic, social, and cultural processes. In this respect the development of the educational system in the GDR is seen as an "inseparable part of the socialist revolution" [Handbuch DDR, 1984, 469]. Thus educational policy is integrally linked to the pre-estab-lished long-term projective political and social goals set forth by the ruling party. Since it is an important element of the social policy of the SED, it is understanda-ble that the educational system was included in the far-ranging program of economic reforms adopted at the 6th Party Congress of the SED in 1963. The "new economic system of planning and managing the economy" was accompa-nied by a comprehensive reform of the educational and science sector which was deemed by the Party leadership to be a prerequisite for realizing, and securing over the long term, the economic goals of the reform. The reform itself affected several sectors:

—The school system was restructured by the "law on the unified socialist education system" of 1965;

—A restructuring of the technical and higher education system took place after 1967 as part of the third reform of higher education;

—A decision from the Council of State from 1970, initiated a restructuring of vocational training;

—A decision of the *Volkskammer* in 1970 gave the go-ahead to the expansion of a unified system of adult training to skill;

—In the same year, the organization of science and research began to be restructured in the GDR, and the function of the Academy of Sciences as the coordinating center for research for the whole of the natural sciences and technical sciences, as well as select areas of the social sciences, was strengthened.

The reform of the educational system within the framework of the new economic system had a dual aim: first the training of all occupationally employed was to be improved with an eye to the expected developments in scientific and technical progress and the greater requirements this would place on the training of the labor force. Second, the level of education of cadres, technical workers, and specialists was to be raised to meet the new requirements of "scientific management." These tasks could not be achieved within the former education and science system, which had been formed bit by bit over time and was heterogeneous in its overall structure.

These comprehensive reform projects were molded by the notion that all areas of society, and not merely the economy, were plannable and needed planning by the socialist state. The idea that the educational and research system must be oriented toward the social whole and had a direct social function was not new; what was new was that the political emphasis, which persisted to the end of the fifties, now receded into the background in favor of an orientation to modern sciences and the exigencies of the scientific and technical revolution.

The structure of the educational system

The educational system comprises the formal institutions and establishments that are components of the "unified socialist educational system." These are:

—Nurseries, kindergartens, play-and-learn afternoons, which, while not obligatory, are nonetheless preschool establishments based on the state educational and upbringing plans with their precise pedagogical goals;

—The ten-grade general education polytechnical upper school [Allgemeinbildende Polytechnische Oberschule (AOS)];

—Establishments of vocational training;

—Establishments preparing for entrance into higher education, especially the "expanded general polytechnical upper school" [Erweiterte Allgemeinbildende Polytechnische Oberschule (EOS)];

—Engineering and technical schools;

—Universities and colleges;

—Establishments for adult education and training.

Unrestricted movement among the individual stages of education is an essential structural element of the educational system, i.e., as a rule there are several possibilities, adapted to the various periods of life and occupational careers, for achieving a specific skill or qualification. The basic decision to permit such unrestricted movement is especially evident in educational establishments leading to a secondary school diploma, i.e., the general qualification for entry into higher education:

1. Most secondary-school graduates study in the expanded upper school (EOS), which at present receives about 13 percent of students from the tenth grades of the general polytechnical upper school (AOS). Preparatory classes, which comprise the ninth and tenth school years, and are intended to prepare for entry into an EOS, existed from 1967 to 1981; however, it was not absolutely necessary to attend them in order to transfer to an EOS.

2. Exceptional talents were to be cultivated in special schools or classes, which owe their existence to the attempts undertaken after 1963 to improve over the short and middle term the qualification profiles of, above all, managerial personnel, through specific educational measures. These establishments have now become an integral part of the educational system and are set up primarily for intensified courses in language, mathematics, natural sciences, arts and music, and athletics. Exceptionally talented eleventh- and twelfth-graders are prepared for advanced study in these schools. Some of them later begin their advanced studies in the second rather than the first years; thus the first stage of study is completed within the special classes.

3. Vocational training is regarded in the GDR as an integral part of the unified socialist educational system. After the ten-year education in the general educational upper schools, the students who do not go on the EOS enter vocational training, which on the average lasts two years. The roughly 5 percent of pupils who leave school between the eighth and tenth grades without obtaining a diploma receive a three-year occupational training.

> The purpose of vocational training is to train well-rounded, highly skilled workers who are distinguished by a high socialist consciousness and socialist mode of behavior, have a high level of general education and comprehensive occupational knowledge, abilities and skills that can be put to use on a broad basis in the labor process, apply their efforts creatively for the further development of socialist production and, as key shapers of socialist society, collaborate in planning, management, and functioning not only directly in the production process, but also in the overall development of the society.[5]

The current regulations on skilled labor occupations specify the contents and the general contours of the different forms of vocational training. A skilled labor occupation is marked by the combination of "general, polytechnical professional education, communist upbringing, and vocational training." In contrast to the notion that the graduates of each of the stages of education already specialize to a high degree during their training period, the regulations stress the necessity of a broad basic education and "occupational flexibility" of those who complete vocational training. With a broad general and vocational basic education as a foundation, a youth can then go on to acquire the specialized knowledge regarded as necessary for the graduate of vocational training to achieve "a stable level of performance as a skilled worker" when he enters working life and be sure of a successful exercise of his occupation.

4. After the ten-year school, *Abitur* classes in vocational training schools lead directly to the *Abitur* (secondary school diploma) in a three-year course of study in preparation for the trade school final examination. Whereas training in an EOS is distinctly science-oriented, and is mainly a preparation for the university, in vocational training with a secondary school diploma, general education is more closely interlocked with the vocational disciplines. Although courses in the general education disciplines follow essentially the same curricula as the EOS, so that the secondary diploma thereby received is of equal status, this course of study in fact leads to a *Spezialabitur*—a special secondary school diploma—for technical sciences. The engineering colleges, established in 1969 as part of the third reform of higher education as a consequence of a transformation of the already existing engineering schools, recruit their students mainly from among the graduates of this course of study, since these colleges usually have trade school training in addition to the *Abitur* as a prerequisite for admission.

5. The *Volkshochschulen* (but also the factory academies of large factories), afford employed people the opportunity to make up their eighth, tenth, or twelfth school year at a later date. The *Volkshochschulen* offer "comprehensive courses of study" for the completion of the eighth, tenth, or twelfth school years. In the courses for the twelfth school year (*Abitur* course) employed people with a completed ten-year education and vocational training may receive their *Abitur* diploma in a two-year course. This diploma corresponds to the EOS diploma. The comprehensive courses of study for the tenth school year, like special preparatory courses, are for employed persons to obtain the required qualification for acceptance into a course of study for foreman or master craftsman or for a study in a technical or engineering school, in addition to their vocational training.

6. The engineering and technical schools (*Ingenieurschule and Fachschule*) are also regarded as potential preparatory stages for admission into higher education. Study in these establishments requires completion of the tenth grade, training as a skilled worker, and practical occupational experience. These admission prerequisites, like the specialized areas of emphasis (mainly in the technical and economic sciences), demonstrate that it is primarily persons who were formerly gainfully employed who study in technical schools. The graduates are then hired principally as middle-level technical personnel in industry, but also in agriculture, public education, the health system, trade, the arts and other areas of social life. Considering these ends, they cannot be regarded directly as an intermediate stage

between secondary school and higher education. Nonetheless, they give employed people the chance to enter higher education by way of vocational training followed by study in a trade school.

7. One institution that was extremely important in the early sixties as preparation for higher education has largely lost its function: namely, the workers' and peasants' faculty (ABF). Between 1951 and 1963, 33,729 graduates of the workers' and peasants' faculty went on into higher education. The ABF Wilhelm Pieck at the Mining Academy of Freiberg is the last of these institutions; it accepts candidates for the disciplines of mining, foundry work, and natural sciences, and offers them a higher education. The participants are assigned by their factories to the ABF for the purposes of a specific course of study, set down in an agreement to train to skill. The ABF Walter Ulbricht at the University of Halle was established in this form in 1966 and serves to prepare people for study abroad. However, because of the declining importance of the ABFs, this possibility of achieving a diploma qualifying a person for entry into higher education outside of the "normal" paths no longer plays any role.

This brief depiction of the educational paths provided for in the unified educational system has made clear that the structure of the educational system is attuned to allow for a large measure of openness and to that extent has conformed to the intentions of the educational reform in the sixties. However, the development of the educational system since the early seventies shows very clearly that an analysis that is limited to its structural characteristics tells us nothing about the performance or potential of the educational system. Despite the great openness among the different educational stages, which the structure of the unified socialist educational system allows, the facts of social policy and economics resulted in the system's selection function assuming a steadily increasing importance. The structural reforms undertaken by the education law of 1965 indeed continue to offer the possibility of entering technical studies or higher education by various routes, but the real chances of the individual have deteriorated considerably since the early seventies in light of the attenuated projections of educational policy.

Qualification versus "socialist personality"?

The educational system is society's institution for socialization; in the GDR it is shaped by the requirements of a hierarchically organized and centralist system. The aim, shaped by the model of the all-round socialist personality, of forming responsible and autonomous personalities and citizens, encounters insurmountable obstacles not only in the general conditions of social policy, but also in the concrete requirements of the world of work. The value of an all-round education, i.e., education seen as the ensemble of the skills of thinking, discovering, and acting, stands in a tense relationship to the development of skills, learning the aptitudes of work. It cannot be overlooked that in the GDR, especially in recent years, education has been much too often reduced to this narrow aspect of training skills. The requirements of the world of work contrast to the ideal picture of an all-round educated person who is thereby also able to participate equally in the political decision-making processes. Moreover, such an education is of only limited use, if any, in the area of a person's essential life activities, i.e., work. These political and social conditions make the narrowing of education to skill training more comprehensible.

As long as the notion of the sixties seemed to ring true, namely, that the scientific and technical revolution would alter the former structures of the world of work within a relatively short time, and so sweep away the restrictions it currently places on the individual, the emphasis on training skills might have seemed justified. It was argued that a comprehensive education would be, as it were, the natural effect of further scientific and technical development. It was expected that the proportion of intellectual and creative work would increase very rapidly at the expense of heavy physical work and that therefore not only the higher practical skills, but also new creative abilities and a greater flexibility and mobility of the labor force would become possible or even necessary. This development was to be supported by the educational system, which was supposed to prepare its graduates for these expected conditions. Education and upbringing has always been understood as a process that prepares for the future. But the educational system encountered limits for which not it, but the political system, was responsible.

In the GDR the determination of future developments is not seen as an open process of search in which the various institutions and social groups participate, but as something that is formulated authoritatively by the political system. The political ideological reservations of the Party and state leadership are somewhat dysfunctional when faced with a broad independence of thought as one possible result of formal educational processes or of scientific research—and not only for the lower levels of the educational system. The most acclaimed social scientist of the GDR, Jürgen Kuczinsky, called attention to this with regard to technical and vocational education. In his opinion an education that produces uneducated non-independent, although technically highly qualified specialists (Kuczinsky speaks explicitly of specialized idiots) who are therefore unsuited for coping with the manifold problems that they must confront in their occupational practice, will be also unable to deal with present developments and even less with future developments in the society at large.[6]

The observation of Kuczinsky also reflects a likely reaction of university students (and probably also of many advanced high school students) to the continuing comprehensive demands of party and state: studying means fulfilling a social mandate, developing a "socialist personality" and proving oneself as such. The students are expected to perform at a high level and to develop "socialist collective relations" with their fellow students. In return, they are promised social and economic security. These socialist collective relations are supposed to be shaped "by the shared striving for high achievement at work, in professional studies, in sports, and in the learning of the treasures of culture. These relations are marked by mutual respect, by trust and help, by deep responsibility for one's own work and behavior as well as for the development of the collective."[7]

All of this is to be learned in the collective of the Free German Youth (FDJ) group, of which all students of the same level are members. Since the vast majority of students live in dormitories, the activities of the FDJ group can be extended to the private life of students without considerable organizational effort. In reality, it is true, many students elude these demands. Leisure time activities undertaken with fellow students are made to appear as activities of the FDJ group.

The advantages of such an organization of studies are as obvious as its disadvantages. About 85 to 90 percent of those who begin a course of studies successfully complete it. They are not left alone with the various difficulties and problems they encounter during their studies. On the other hand, there are clear limitations to individual development, and it takes great effort to insist on the individual character of one's life as a student. The state expects the students to shape their whole life collectively—studies, leisure time, and vacations (for instance, in university-owned vacation homes and camps or during the obligatory labor periods). It is difficult to withdraw from these comprehensive demands since this can easily be interpreted as an indication of deficient personal and political maturity.

In spite of these restrictions, sociological studies have found indications that in universities and other institutions of higher education much has been conserved that always characterized these institutions: "That special atmosphere of lectures and seminars, that peculiar 'world' between lecture hall, rented room or dormitory, reading room and pub . . . (these) are experiences . . . which in this form cannot be made by apprentices in an industrial enterprise or on a farm."[8]

To be a student in the GDR means on the one hand to be confronted with the demand of orienting one's work and life to the model of the "socialist intelligentsia." At the same time, it offers free spaces that workers amd employees of the same age cannot enjoy. The students in the GDR seem to be quite conscious of this social privilege. At the universities and other institutions of higher education a social milieu has developed that in many respects continues old academic traditions and that often contains traces of academic pride and snobbery. This milieu has a tendency to close itself off from the rest of society and thus to support a process that one may call the social self-recruitment of the intelligentsia.

Equal education, equal chances?

The educational practice in the GDR calls into question not only the general idea of an all-round educated socialist man, but equally the promise of achieving social equality for as many citizens as possible, if not all, through a broad education. This was the undisputed goal of educational policy, at least until recently. There was too little reflection on the fact that all existing educational systems are more or less selective. Educational policy, which is committed to emancipatory goals, is therefore always confronted with the problem of how to bring this selective function of the educational system—which decides on the social and occupational chances of the individual—into line with the postulate of equal opportunity. This conflict, which has characterized the discussion on educational reform in Western countries, is formulated differently in the GDR: equality of opportunity is not exclusively or even preponderantly considered with reference to the individual. Rather, it is essentially oriented to creating equal opportunities for social groups, strata, and classes. It thus has one eminently important component. In the early years of the Soviet occupation zone and the GDR, the SED wanted to open the doors to higher education for the very first time by a "redistribution of opportunities," which meant a conscious decision to impose a handicap on individual talents from those social strata that had hitherto kept the majority of the population, i.e., members of the working class and peasantry, away from institutions of higher learning. After a new "socialistic" intelligentsia had thus been created, elements of individual inequality of opportunity remained. The selective principles still contain the aspect of "social origin" in addition to the criteria of professional performance and active sociopolitical work as defined by the SED.

The task, originally seen as only temporary, of ensuring appropriate educational opportunities, a solidly based education, and training in skills, as well as equal access to cultural goods to all social groups, strata, and classes commensurate with their numerical representation in the total population, has become a lasting commitment. However, since almost 80 percent of the population are ranked in the working class or the class of cooperative farmers, the retention of such broadly defined concepts of "working class" has also proven to be problematic in the educational sector. The living and working conditions within these large social groups are very different. However, from the perspective of equality of social opportunity the aim should in fact have been to include these differences in the basis on which selectivity decisions are made.

In light of this problem it is not surprising that the different social classes and strata and hitherto disadvantaged groups such as women are represented in courses of study in higher education in numbers commensurate with their relative proportion in the total population. However, it is impossible to say whether and how diverse socialization conditions are at work in selection decisions—such as children of unskilled workers compared with children from skilled worker or white-collar families, or regional differences deriving from the city-countryside gap, which is still considerable. More recent sociological studies from the GDR show that there are considerable social differences between and within classes and strata, and between city and countryside in the different domains of society, and that the conditions of socialization of the upcoming generation thus are extremely differentiated despite the great influence of state educational institutions. The influence of the social environment, regional differences, and the city-countryside gap influence social conditions more strongly than traditional Marxist-Leninist social structure research would have liked to assume.

Not only social differences between and within classes and strata, and between physical and intellectual work, but also social differences between the city and countryside and between social domains influence the conditions of the development of the personality. . . . The role of classes as a socially differentiating factor with regard to individuals and their assimilation of the essence of society tends to diminish as class antagonisms are eliminated and the socioeconomical, political, and ideological points in common among classes and strata assume clearer contours. In other words, the differentiating influences exerted on the development of the personality that are caused and nourished by the existence of classes are gradually suppressed. A specific type of social differentiation of individuals, namely, that linked to the existence of classes, is thus gradually reduced. The contradictions of this process, however, consist in the fact that other socially differentiating conditions and factors in the development of the personality, specifically those whose effect under capitalism is in a sense overloaded by class antagonism, move more into the forefront. Thus another type of social differentiation of individuals becomes more prominent in the theoretical and practical interests of socialist society as well.[9]

Sociological findings support the thesis that the influence of different life environments on the formation of the consciousness of social groups in the GDR is increasing and is repressing the common basic orientations of social classes and strata which had long been dominant. How the educational system will be able to create equality of social opportunities against the background of such a development is a still unanswered question.

But even a conceivable "fair" selection procedure in the educational system would not automatically ensure equality of opportunity in the employment system. The politically motivated selective mechanisms operative in filling strategically important positions in administration, mass organizations, etc., speak a clear language, just as does the small number of women in these positions. Political selection criteria have shaped educational policy and educational planning in the GDR just as much as the target of gearing all educational processes to the requirements of the employment system. The decision of what material resources must be made available to the educational sector was and is an optimization problem for educational planners. Such a shortsighted view reduces to a dependent variable of economic rationality and optimal economic growth what has been the primary goal, ever reiterated, of educational policy of the SED, namely, that of shaping and cultivating an all-round educated socialist personality. The upshot is that this educational goal is included in calculations only insofar as it does not contradict economic goals.

This contradiction was resolvable, it seemed, only in periods of quantitative growth. Since the agenda of the next decade includes only a consolidation of the qualification level already achieved, with no notable expansion of the sphere of higher qualifications, the educational system can no longer pursue both goals. In all likelihood, the target will be to alter the proportions between particular areas and disciplines of education which only imperfectly meet the requirements of industry, administration, and other social domains, and ensure a uniform development. The achievements of the educational system would then become calculable over the long term for those who employ its graduates who enter working life. This consolidation has a feedback effect on the educational system itself: its transforming function with regard to the development of social structure, e.g., toward a greater political and social equality, should diminish further. The task of adjusting and correcting for divergent sectoral and regional trends remains essentially a fact of educational policy.

Social differentiation

In contrast to former notions that a high education and qualification for all or for as many as possible will promote a process of social homogenization, lately the necessity of social differentiation has been stressed. This is reflected in educational and science policy in terms such as talent, top talents, promoting intellectuals, elite, top performances, etc. The (self-imposed) need to adapt to necessities of a highly technologized society has raised the question of a suitable development of social structure and of the consequences for education and science. This has become a key question in the political and social system of the GDR.

Since the early sixties the GDR has been passing through a second phase of sociostructural change. The significance of this change for social policy was at least as great as the transformation of the old class structures after 1945. As was also the case in the first years of the Soviet occupation zone and the GDR, the educational system became the most important instrument of planned sociostructural change. The forecast expectations with regard to the development of the qualification structure were reflected in an expansion of the educational system and of higher education such that the boundaries between the working class (unskilled workers, semiskilled workers, skilled workers, and foremen) and the intelligentsia began to blur.[10]

The educational reform was based at the very outset on the idea that the social requirements placed on the labor force in a developed socialist society would make the old limits on education and qualification obsolete. It appeared that the scientific and technical revolution would make the dream of a society of equals and all-round developed socialist personalities possible. Twenty years had a broad sobering effect. At the 8th Party Congress of the SED in 1971, the SED acknowledged that the goal of educational policy which had been pursued hitherto, namely, the quantitative expansion of higher qualifications, and especially technical school and college and university education, could not be continued on the scale envisioned. The growth figures were reduced, but the long-term goal was retained—it still seemed to be reasonable to make a technical or higher education available to as many persons as possible. The future communist society of equals was to be a society in which all citizens would acquire a higher general education and an occupational skill. These notions are today regarded by leading GDR sociologists as false oversimplifications and exaggerations which must be discarded. There had been "truncated and unrealistic notions with regard the possibilities of a transition to the second phase of the communist social formation."[11] In 1981 Manfred Lötsch, a leading GDR sociologist, had cast doubt on the thesis that the general qualification level would develop in such a way that differences between the working class and the intelligentsia would diminish steadily because in the course of the scientific and technical revolution workers would have to acquire more and more of the knowledge and skills specific to intellectuals.[12] The high proportion of graduates of technical schools and universities at work in the GDR economy, in administration, and in other areas of the society cannot itself tell us whether these people are employed in accordance with their formal qualifications. Actually, sociological studies from the GDR demonstrate that many graduates of technical schools and universities are employed at levels below their qualifications, or that the proportion of administrative and routine jobs that require a lower level of qualification is often extremely high. Consequently, routine reigns, especially in areas in which new innovative types of work are necessary. Despite the high proportion of university and college graduates, it has not yet been possible to organize research and development in large factories in the GDR in such a way as to enable them to keep pace with international developments.[13]

Sociologists now admit that the educational reforms of the sixties were based on a false premise: it was believed that the goal of social equality could be achieved by increasing the proportion of graduates from technical schools and universities. The second assumption was that the scientific and technical revolution would require such a large number of highly skilled workers that there would be no difficulty in employing everyone in conformity with their qualifications. The developments of the last twenty years have roundly refuted these hopes. But the implications are just being acknowledged today. For years practical policy has been to reinforce the status quo in educational policy, and it has only been recently that the necessity of a change in educational policy has been theoretically grounded.

As regards the sociostructural conditions and consequences of educational policy, the following aspects of the present discussion may be mentioned:

—A more realistic view of social development in the GDR society seems to be gaining ground. The view that the qualification level (and thus also social opportunities) will increase steadily has been discarded. In a recent publication, the same author says that the qualification structure will settle in over the long term and that the qualification of skilled workers will change, but will not rise further to any perceptible degree. What is new is the acknowledgment that the category of semiskilled workers, which was tending to disappear (or so it was thought for a long time), has shown a "distinct capacity to persist" and "not mainly because a certain proportion of youth leave the education system prematurely as 'conditionally inclined' or 'conditionally capable' of an education, but because a specific proportion of corresponding jobs had to be filled."[14]

—As regards intellectuals, it became clear that the "structural explosion" of the past decade was past. An important thesis—which does no more than acknowledge the implications of the real situation—for the social status of intellectuals is that in the future more members of the intelligentsia will be working in material production. Lötsch calls for a redefinition of the intelligentsia since the definition of this group as the totality of cadres with a higher and technical education is "gradually drifting away from the heart of the matter." A higher education diploma is becoming increasingly a kind of basic qualification after which skills specific to the intelligentsia must be acquired: in the same way as the working class developed, the internal educational and qualificational spectrum of the intelligentsia is becoming broader and more differentiated. More and more members of the intelligentsia, says Lötsch, will be working directly in material production, and a distinctly smaller proportion of the intelligentsia involved in creative work will have to be relieved of routine tasks which cadres having a middle-level technical education will be able to fulfill.

—This discussion is so important for the GDR's ideological self-conception because the discussants are not content merely to concede that social equality had not been achieved to the degree that had long been thought possible, but because the arguments imply that social inequality on a new level is a permanent component of socialist society. Social differences manifested no longer along the axis "property vs. class," but on the axis of the division of labor and qualification, are no longer seen as relics of the old capitalist society or flaws of socialism, but rather are ascribed a productive function (the function of a driving force). The different interests growing out of this social inequality are then not antagonistic, but productive and innovative elements of social and societal development. Implicit in this view is the notion that different interests can in socialist society give rise to something on the order of "artificial competition" among individuals or social groups, and in this way produce innovations that will bring economic and scientific and technical developments up to par with those in the Western industrial countries.

Power and knowledge: the political function of the education sector

The political function of the education sector can be described with three concepts: unity, differentiation, and hierarchization. GDR educational policymakers apply the concept of unity de facto to only those parts of the educational sector that may be ascribed to the "unified socialist educational system." Even accepting this description, the evolution of educational policy over the last decade forces a rethinking of the problem of unity and differentiation in the educational system. The unified school, which for decades has been regarded as a guarantee of a socially just and politically desired allocation of educational opportunities, is undergoing an increasing structural differentiation. In opting for a differentiation of the educational system in the secondary domain, the GDR found itself faced with the problem of how to achieve a balanced and ideologically defensible relationship between the special promotion of the individual, on the one hand, and equality of opportunity for all, on the other. These tendencies toward differentiation are especially conspicuous in "special classes" in general education schools, or the "special schools" which are designed to accept a "limited number of pupils with high achievements, in order to meet the special demands of the economy, science, sports, and culture, and promote talents in specific ways."[15]

The securing of equal educational opportunities and an ever higher general education for all makes such a differentiation of the educational system or of its individual stages problematic. The purpose of differentiation is to discover special talents early and to promote them—which may satisfy the postulate that the educational system must ensure unobstructed access to the advantages of education on a graduated basis, in accordance with a standard oriented to "achievement." But since it neglects the social factors that determine talent, it can only too easily lead to a de facto privileging of certain social groups at the expense of others (e.g., working class and peasant children).

The decision as to what degree uniformity in the educational system can be maintained in light of the increasing social differentiation and diversification remains a question of political power. The structural decision for a uniform (above all an open) educational system has not formally been revised. However the tendencies in educational policy since the early seventies have cast doubt on this structural principle. An intensified selection process for access to the institutions of higher learning is matched by a distinct cutback on "compensatory" educational measures. The chances of acquiring a qualified educational diploma in any other than the "normal" way have continued to deteriorate.

The real chances of the individual to acquire a higher educational diploma by various paths have deteriorated considerably. For the socioculturally disadvantaged strata of the population, as well as for women, this development means a serious restriction on their occupational, and hence social, chances which hitherto had been considerably greater in comparison with the capitalist system. To that extent it is only partially true that the educational system of the GDR is marked by a high degree of flexibility and openness that makes it possible to achieve any desired goal of education via several paths, and especially by combining employment and education.

The unity and openness of the educational system is however challenged to a far greater degree by the fact that parts of this system have been given the task of training cadres for the different managerial apparatuses. This is evident first in the maintenance and expansion of the internal educational institutions of the SED, the state and economic apparatus, agriculture, and the mass organizations, and second by the increased use of the institutions of the unified educational system, and especially the technical schools and universities, for the training and advanced training of managerial workers of this apparatus.

The central institutions for educating managerial cadres are separated in both structure and content from the unified educational system. They are accessible only to those who have been especially selected by the cadre divisions of the various organizational units, with participation of the relevant department of the SED, on the basis of their political and technical achievements and in consideration of cadre need. This enables the individual apparatuses to apply their own criteria of evaluation and selection in the educational process itself. The increasing technologization of managerial functions has also meant that cadre policy has acquired a greater importance in the unified educational system. Success or failure in higher education (admission to which is actually decided on entrance to the EOS in light of the lower failure rates in the upper school) are important criteria for a future career as managerial cadres, and since all higher education graduates are regarded as potential cadres, such criteria are probably also operative in the selection process for general educational institutions.

Educational institutions designed especially for the training of managerial personnel are wholly excepted from the general admissions regulations. However, since the essential selection criteria of the general educational system cannot be applied in the case of cadres, it is no coincidence that no legal norms have been established as part of an admissions policy binding on all institutions of higher education and similar institutions.

Apart from further education in colleges and universities, the fact is that cadres are trained only in the educational institutions of the apparatuses, structured in stages in correspondence with the hierarchy of those apparatuses' managerial structures. This isolation from the general educational system, motivated by cadre policy, means that specific qualifications and organizational knowledge, managerial techniques, and knowledge of the apparatus (insofar as this cannot be acquired by experience through work in the organizational system) is accessible to only a limited, carefully chosen group of persons.

Thus is formed a hierarchy in the transmission of knowledge which closely follows the functional principles of the system of authority. The entrenchment of the educational system and the shift of its target function is a part of the attempt to maintain the social and political structures of the GDR as intact as possible. Changes take place within the narrowly prescribed, legally codified, and ideologically legitimated limits of the system. As with social policy in general, in educational policy as well this has led to a pragmatization which has departed from the long-term utopian idealistic goal of ''equality'' and adjusts ''opportunistically'' to social circumstances and problem situations.

The educational sector, which has always been taken as proof that equality could be realized in it almost prematurely, earlier than in the world of work or in politics, is losing its legitimating function for the system as a whole. In view of the close intermeshing of the educational system with the functional conditions of a bureaucratic authority it can hardly be expected that it will be possible even partially to meet the crude requirements of the need of the economy and the direct ruling interests of the Party, or that the various social interests and needs will be given a chance to formulate and put through their demands on the educational system. However, this would be a precondition if education is to become more than qualification for the labor process and a prop for the existing political and social structures, instead of encouraging the assimilation of human civilization and culture.

Notes

1. *Programm der Sozialistischen Einheitspartei Deutschlands* (Berlin [GDR]: Dietz, 1976). *Das Bildungswesen der Deutschen Demokratischen Republik* (Berlin [GDR]: Volk und Wissen, 1979).
2. *Protokoll des Verhandlungen des IX. Parteitages der Sozialistischen Einheitspartei Deutschlands* (Berlin [GDR]: Dietz, 1976).
3. Rudi Weidig, ''Persönlichkeit—Qualifikation—Bildung,'' in *Neues Deutschland* (March 5, 1987): 3.
4. Helmut Klein, *Bildung in der DDR. Grundlagen Entwicklungen, Probleme* (Reinbek: Rowohlt, 1974).
5. *Handbuch Deutsche Demokratische Republik* (Leipzig: VEB Bibliographisches Institut, 1984), 490.
6. Jürgen Kuczynsky, ''Fachstudium kontra Allgemeinbildung? Spezialisierung und intersisziplinäres Verhalten,'' in *Forum* 34, no. 4 (1980): 8.
7. *Das Hochschulwesen der DDR. Ein Überblick* (Berlin [DDR]: Deutscher Verlag der Wissenschaften, 1980), 177.
8. Albrecht Kretzschmar, *Soziale Unterschiede—unterschiedliche Persönlichkeiten? Zum Einfluss der Sozialstruktur auf die Persönlichkeitsentwicklung* (Berlin (GDR): Dietz, 1985), 97.
9. Ibid., 123f.
10. See Eva-Maria Langen, *Technisierungsgrad der Arbeit und Qualifikation der Produktionsarbeiter. Ein Beitrag zu Fragen der Vervollkommnung des sozialistischen Charakters der Arbeit* (Berlin [GDR]: Akademie Publishers, 1979), 48f.
11. Manfred Lötsch, ''Arbeiterklasse und Intelligenz in der Dialektik von wissenschaftlich-technischem, ökonomischem und sozialem Fortschritt,'' in *Deutsche Zeitschrift für Philosophie* 33, no. 1 (1985): 31.
12. Manfred Lötsch, ''Sozialstruktur und Wirtschaftswachstum. Überlegungen zum Problem sozialer Triebkräftlich des wissenschaftlich-technischen Fortschritts,'' in *Wirtschaftswissenschaft* 29, no. 1 (1981): 67.
13. Fred Klinger, ''Die Krise des Fortschritts in der DDR. Innovationsprobleme und Mikroelektronik,'' in *Aus Politik und Zeitgeschichte*, Beilage zur Wochenzeitung Das Parlament, B 3/87, 3.
14. Lötsch, ''Arbeiterklasse,'' 36.
15. *Das Bildungswesen der DDR*, 63.

Translated by Michel Vale

Individual Burden—
Societal Requirement?

Human and Social Aspects of Shiftwork in the German Democratic Republic

MICHAEL DENNIS

Introduction

GDR politicians and economists frequently refer to the vital contribution of shiftwork[1] to the country's prosperity and the future of the socialist system. By helping to raise productivity and to reduce costs, shiftwork is represented as a key factor in the struggle between socialism and capitalism. After the relative slowdown in the expansion of shiftwork from the mid–1970s to the early 1980s (see Table 1) the merits of shiftwork have returned to the forefront of the GDR's economic strategy, and mass publications such as the trade union daily *Tribüne*, the women's magazine *Für Dich*, and the FDJ newspaper *Junge Welt*, are now urging workers to participate in this type of work. The Free German Youth movement organizes campaigns to persuade young workers to fulfill this "societal requirement." A target of 35,000 has been set for 1986.[2] A relatively high proportion of women are on shiftwork: in 1979 40 percent of all two-shift and 25 percent of all three-shift workers in industry were women and, according to a 1985 report, about 50 percent of women production workers under 25 were on shifts.[3]

The SED's goal to increase the three-shift utilization of its machinery and investment-intensive plant may, however, entail considerable social strains and

An earlier version of this paper appeared in *GDR Monitor*, no. 9, Summer 1983.

Table 1

Proportion of Production Workers on Shiftwork (%)

Year	Daywork	Two-shift	Three-shift
1962	62.0	18.8	19.1
1966	61.4	17.0	21.6
1970	61.3	14.6	24.0
1976	57.6	14.8	27.5
1977	57.5	14.3	28.2
1978	57.5	14.2	28.4
1979	57.8	13.6	28.6
1980	58.1	13.5	28.4
1981	58.0	13.0	29.0
1982	58.1	12.8	29.1
1983	57.8	12.9	28.3

Sources: Martina Jugel, Barbara Spangenberg and Rudhard Stollberg, *Schichtarbeit und Lebensweise* (Berlin: Dietz Verlag, 1978), 142 and *Statistisches Jahrbuch der DDR* (Berlin: Staatsverlag), vols. 1977 to 1984.

burdens upon the individual. Shiftwork, particularly if it includes nights, has been found by most American and West European researchers to evoke little enthusiasm among workers and to be disruptive of their family and social life. It tends to be associated more frequently than so-called normal daywork with gastric ulceration, especially among ex-shiftworkers, fatigue, the disruption of normal sleep patterns, and the disturbance of circadian rhythms.

Observers of shiftwork in the GDR have often adopted a highly critical attitude toward the social and human costs of this method of working. The American international relations expert Lawrence Whetten identified shiftwork as one of the four major adverse social complications arising from the economic reforms of the 1960s. Shiftwork, according to Whetten, "met strong resistance, despite special incentives, because it interfered with family life and reduced opportunities for 'moonlighting.'"[4] The West German sociologist Axel Bust Bartels interpreted the rising proportion of shiftwork in the 1970s as one of the indicators of a general intensification of workloads and as typifying the priority accorded productivity increases over improvements in working conditions.[5] From within the GDR, reservations are expressed by labor scientists and trades union officials. A research team headed by Rainer Sinz stated ". . . it's of little use to the worker if he obtains a wage adjustment in return for socio-cultural deprivation or instead of good health."[6] It recommended the application of new job designs in order to minimize the negative effects of nightwork. A wide audience, the readers of *Tribüne*, must have been interested in the open disagreement between two trades union officials. Karl-Heinz Schiller, the chairman of the Leipzig district executive of *IG Metall* was reprimanded by Gerhard Muth for expressing the opinion that "Shiftwork is naturally not the goal worth striving for in socialism."[7] Muth, the head of the labor and wages division of the national executive of the FGDB, countered that shiftwork should not be dismissed as an expedient; it is a requirement of contemporary society. Shiftwork benefits socialism as well as the individual.[8]

Central to the question of shiftwork is the need to devise solutions to enable workers to cope with three major problem areas, that is, sleep, social and family life, and circadian rhythms. As all three are interrelated, a failure in one area may undermine the success achieved in the other two. The nightworker's need for sleep in the day may clash with the household routine. Certain leisure activities such as organized sport and having a drink at a pub may be precluded by evening work. The disturbance of circadian rhythms which follow the 24 hour day and night cycle may affect the workers' quality of sleep, bodily function, and work performance.

The term circadian rhythm is applied to those regular fluctuations in bodily activities such as heart rate, blood pressure, and body temperature that exhibit a rhythmicity of about 24 hours. These internal rhythms are subjected to external influences known as *Zeitgeber* or synchronizers. The synchronizers include social habits (for example, meal times), the cycle of light and darkness, and awareness of clock time. The bodily rhythms become locked or entrained in the periodicity of the synchronizers. Nightwork and shift rotation disturb the stability of the circadian rhythms. Some individuals are able to invert the circadian rhythm of body temperature after two or three days on the night shift; others require almost a week. For some, inversion is impossible or only partial. So-called morning types have been found to react to late shiftwork with sleep deficiency and the accompanying pathological symptoms. Whereas "evening types" are constitutionally less vulnerable because of their delayed circadian rhythm phase position. The complexities of the underlying physiological features and the potential harmfulness of shiftwork, especially if it includes nights, raise fundamental questions about its desirability. In an International Labour Organization publication Marc Maurice expressed the kind of doubts that should also trouble GDR planners: ". . . since it [shiftwork] has been created by industrial society, it may also be asked to what extent man should adapt himself to a state of affairs that disturbs, in particular, his fundamental rhythms, and whether it would not be better to change certain aspects of the situation, at the risk of reducing the productivity of the undertaking."[9]

On the other hand, the considerable corpus of research has failed to demonstrate that shiftwork is linked with above average cardiovascular and nervous symptoms, absence from work due to sickness, or higher mortality. Given optimal schedules of shiftwork, frequent medical checks, accommodation conducive to undisturbed sleep, and some restriction on nightwork, an appropriate balance might be struck between the needs of the individual and those of society for the shiftworkers' services. This essay will examine how GDR workers have responded to the "societal requirement" of shiftwork and how the GDR authorities seek to mitigate the ill effects of shiftwork on health and its disruption of social and family activities.

The case for shiftwork

The basic arguments in favor of shiftworking, although not, of course, specific to the GDR, are to secure the best returns on expensive machinery and plant before obsolescence and depreciation occur, the technological imperative of a continuous process in the chemical and other industries, the provision of vital public services, and seasonal requirements in agriculture.

Various calculations have been made to demonstrate the economic advantages. Professor Otto Reinhold, SED Central Committee member and rector of that body's Academy of Social Sciences, estimates that the change from one or two shifts to three shifts represents a saving of 20 to 30 percent on costs.[10] In 1982 Harry Tisch, FDGB chairman and *Politbüro* member, put the benefit of an extra ten minutes of operation each day of highly productive machinery at an additional 4.5 billion Marks per annum in industrial goods.[11] One simply cannot, argued Claus Thiele, the deputy director of a combine in Leipzig, allow highly productive machinery and machining centers worth up to one million Marks stand idle for forty-eight hours per week.[12] This explains why the operation of such machinery has increased in recent years from 11.2 hours per calendar day in 1965 to 14.9 in 1979. By 1984 it had reached 16.2 hours.[13] The 1986 National Economic Plan has set a target of 17 hours for major capital equipment and 19 hours for investment-intensive plant in the basic industries.[14]

The more intensive utilization of fixed assets in conjunction with an expansion of shiftwork occupies a central position in the economic planning of the SED leadership. In his speech at a major conference in 1983 Günter Mittag[15] described the increase in the operation time of fixed assets as the GDR's most important reserve for improving economic performance; a considerable expansion of the three-shift system would therefore be required. Three years later, in his report to the Eleventh Party Congress, general secretary Erich Honecker[16] specifically referred to shiftwork in point six of the SED's economic strategy until the year 2000. An increase in shiftwork, not only in industry but also in the LPGs and scientific establishments, was expected to play a major role in improving work efficiency.

The inadequate utilization of fixed assets was only one of the main obstacles to greater economic efficiency frequently referred to by politicians and economists in the 1970s. Other constraints included the increase in the costs for raw materials due to unfavorable natural conditions, lack of manpower, unsatisfactory utilization of materials, downtime, high repair costs, and obsolescence of fixed assets. The rapid deterioration of the GDR's terms of trade in the late 1970s and the early

1980s rendered the situation critical. Her growing indebtedness to the West rose from \$3.5 billion in 1975 to \$12.6 billion in 1981. The increase in the price of Soviet oil since 1975 also hit the GDR hard. After the sharp increase in 1982 a record deficit of 3.0 billion Valuta Marks was recorded in the GDR's trade with the Soviet Union.[17] The SED leadership responded to the crisis not only by reducing imports from the West and by expanding the domestic production of lignite, but also by unveiling a ten-point economic strategy at the Tenth Party Congress. Although the individual items were far from novel, the package did confirm intensification as the central feature of the party's economic policy. Intensification emphasizes qualitative factors such as reducing inputs and production costs, increasing capital productivity, and reducing manpower needs by increasing actual working time. The instruments of economic management were refined and the application of key technologies—microelectronics, robotics—was accelerated. Honecker announced that 40,000 to 45,000 industrial robots were to come into operation during the 1981–1985 plan. The present Five Year Plan envisages the production and application of an additional 75,000 to 80,000 robots. (One explanation for this apparently extraordinary achievement is the GDR's extremely generous definition of the term robot.) The number of CAD/CAM work stations will expand rapidly from 11,200 in 1986 to between 85,000 and 90,000 by 1990.[18]

The robots are to be operated on a multishift basis and each robot, it is hoped, will release on average 2.5 workers for other activities. Workers are to be released in particular from jobs in which levels of mechanization and efficiency are low, mainly ancillary jobs such as repairs, transport, and maintenance. This labor rationalization program, whose model is the "Schwedt Initiative" of the Schwedt petrochemical combine, is often unable to achieve this modest goal, by international standards, of 2.5 workers. This relative failure has been attributed to the shortage of comprehensive and integrated automated systems, the application of robotics to out-of-date plant and equipment, the lack of experience of enterprises and combines, the limited potential of the widely deployed first-generation robots which perform only a set program, and management and worker resistance. Nevertheless, rationalization schemes do release appreciable numbers of workers for shift systems. For example, of the 7,600 workers released by the end of 1981 in Frankfurt-am-Oder district 30 percent were engaged in shiftwork.

Workers' attitudes

It is popularly believed that the physiological stress and the awkward working hours make shiftwork unpopular among workers or, at best, tolerated. Alastair McAuley has unearthed Soviet findings on widespread dissatisfaction with shiftwork among women.[19] However, national studies do not always present a uniformly pessimistic interpretation. In a general survey of the literature, Sergean, whilst conceding that many workers dislike shiftwork and fiercely oppose plans to introduce it, concludes that "... for many it is a perfectly acceptable way of life...."[20] In fact, considerable evidence exists to show that job satisfaction increases with the length of time spent on shiftwork. For many Western firms, the real problem period, when resistance and job turnover are most likely to be high, appears to be immediately before, during, and immediately after the introduction of a shift system. Attitudes toward specific shifts vary widely. For example, women have been found by some investigators to respond favorably to the two-shift system as they are able to cope more easily with the double burden of housework and job.

The attitudes of GDR workers do not appear to deviate markedly from this general picture. Several major investigations in the 1960s and 1970s provide evidence of widespread antipathy and coolness toward shiftwork. "Shiftwork" was a major reason for job turnover in Dieter Voigt's 1965/1966 study of 911 relatively young assembly fitters. About 25 percent had left their previous job in order to avoid shiftwork and the assembly line.[21] House interviews revealed that shiftwork was one of the main reasons why workers had left a Berlin enterprise in 1964, although the official reasons had been recorded as "financial and health."[22] On the other hand, this type of work most certainly does not encounter universal and outright rejection. In fact, the 1971–1975 national survey of workers in industry revealed that 38 percent of 577 women on shifts liked their work, 44 percent derived some enjoyment, and 18 percent none at all. On the three-shift system 92 percent of women enjoyed or partly enjoyed working on shifts.[23] Such questions and responses are pitched at perhaps too high a level of generalization and in order to capture the nuances of workers' attitudes a finer differentiation according to a range of variables—type of shift, community values, age, gender, marital status, number of children, level of qualifications and earnings—is required.

Several GDR investigations have revealed that the higher the qualification, the greater the reluctance to accept shiftwork. At a *Filmfabrik* in Wolfen the qualified women were more eager than the semiskilled or unskilled women to avoid shiftwork, especially the three-shift system with Sundays. Shiftwork tended to be associated with monotonous and unqualified activities and a lack of identification with one's job.[24] Age, too, is an important determinant of attitudes. Members of Leipzig's Central Institute for Youth Research admit that one reason for younger workers' unenthusiastic response is shiftwork's disruption of leisure pursuits such as dancing, cinema visits, and motor sports.[25] An evaluation of job turnover in Berlin by the *Hochschule für Ökonomie* established that a high proportion of shiftworkers under age 25 left their job because of the demands of shiftwork.[26] There is also evidence that suggests that adolescents and young people experience greater difficulty in adopting physiologically to the frequent changes in circadian rhythms resulting from nightwork.

Marital status and children influence attitudes too. In the late 1960s Führich

Table 2

Women's Attitudes to Shiftwork according to Marital Status (%)

	Married	Not Married
Willing to work on shifts	26	56
Unwilling to work on shifts	74	44

Source: Wulfram Speigner, "Soziologische Untersuchungen zur weiteren Entwicklung der gesellschaftlichen Stellung der Frau in der DDR," Dissertation, Humboldt Universität, Berlin, 1972, 111.

and Johne found that married women were significantly less willing than unmarried women to work on shifts (see Table 2). The Wolfen study and the 1971–1975 national survey both support the Führich/Johne finding. One possible determinant of a woman's negative attitude was identified in the national survey as a husband's dislike (19 percent of the husbands) of his wife's involvement in shiftwork. The same investigation revealed that women with two or more children were less satisfied with shiftwork than those with one or no child.[27] On the other hand, Johne discovered that married women dayworkers with children, especially mothers with three or more, were more willing than those without children to work on shifts. No difference in willingness was established among the men.[28] Obviously we are dealing here with an interplay of variables, of which the number and age of children, partner's attitudes, and the need or desire for higher earnings shape the level of satisfaction with or the willingness to undertake work on a specific shift system.

Shift bonuses are frequently cited as one of the main reasons workers prove willing to participate in shiftwork. Good earnings was one of the four main reasons why women three-shift workers at a Berlin textile enterprise were prepared to work on this type of system. The higher income was particularly significant for women without a partner but with children to look after.[29] In the important survey conducted in 1972 by a team of sociologists at the university of Halle-Wittenberg, the day- and shiftworkers rated additional income as the second most import advantage of shiftwork (see Table 3). The men and women on the three-shift system in the 1970s national survey[30] ranked the shift bonus as the second most important material reward behind the end-of-year bonus but ahead of additional holidays and a shorter working week.

However, the complex and delicate nature of the interrelationship between the variables is well illustrated by the attitudes of women in the lower income groups at Wolfen who preferred the less intensive shift systems because of age and family factors. The researchers[31] found a high proportion of women in the lower income groups who merely desired to supplement their parents' or husband's income, who had young children and consequently sought part-time em-

Table 3

Advantages of Shiftwork (%)

	Dayworkers		Shiftworkers	
	Men (No. = 232)	Women (No. = 229)	Men (No. = 217)	Women (No. = 154)
No reply	73.3	70.3	41.9	22.1
More money	9.9	9.6	22.1	20.2
More time for housework	4.3	6.1	11.1	18.2
Family's care of children always guaranteed	3.5	3.9	8.4	9.8
More work-free time	11.6	11.4	28.1	37.7

Source: Rudhard Stollberg, *Arbeitssoziologie* (Berlin: Die Wirtschaft, 1978), 222. The survey included 832 married production workers, day as well as shift.

ployment, or whose husband enjoyed a higher income by virtue of his skilled worker qualification or his higher education attainment.

Social and family life

In his review of the Western literature James Walker has pinpointed some of the general problems facing shiftworkers in the fulfillment of family and social roles. These observations have a bearing on the situation in the GDR where the problems are compounded by the relatively high proportion of women on shift and by the expansion of the three-shift system with weekend work. Walker[32] argues that shiftworkers need to supply companionship and emotional support and satisfy the sexual needs of partners. They have to provide companionship to their children and to act as a model for them. Irregular hours, night and weekend work may disrupt the family routine while the cumulative effect of numerous disturbances may reduce marital happiness. Western investigators such as Mott, Ruthenfranz, Nachreiner, and Banks[33] have identified in their research a number of major family and marital problems: women's greater responsibility for the children, the lack of time spent together by family members, less opportunities for sexual relations and, possibly, a higher divorce rate. However, as Walker has observed, if domestic life can be adjusted to the demands of irregular hours, the advantages of shiftwork can be exploited.

One area of great concern in the GDR is the negative effect of shiftwork on childrearing. At Wolfen the women's evaluation was highly pessimistic and the Halle-Wittenberg sociologists discovered that shiftworkers were less likely than their daytime colleagues to believe that they had sufficient time to spend with their children. Serious difficulties arise when both parents are employed on shifts, if there are several children in the family, or if the mother is on nights.[34] Many couples in the Halle-Wittenberg study (about one half) opted for different schedules in order to look after their children. Those married couples with children aged three to seven preferred different schedules rather than a weekly institution for their children. Weekly care is inferior in terms of children's development to that provided in day institutions. Eighty percent of children aged nought to three had parents on different systems. Conditions for childrearing varied according to which system was being worked. The early shift was the most advantageous: school and work hours as well as the free time of parents and children fell within the same time period. The night shift, though desynchronizing the life of parents and children, provided family members with a greater pool of common free time; unfortunately, the free time was often spent at the expense of the parents' sleep. The loss of sleep, in Stollberg's view, was especially serious for women who, after returning from the nightshift, performed various household chores and slept on average four to five hours per day. The most disadvantageous shift was the late or afternoon one: children were left to themselves during the afternoon and evening. If a grandparent or other person was unable to help out, the children were left to determine for themselves how to spend the day and their free time.

A disproportionate share of childrearing is borne by the mothers, even if they too are shiftworkers. In fact, Dr. Walter Richter[35] recommended in the pages of *Für Dich* that women who are employed in farming should not be expected to work on extended shifts as these are often incompatible with their tasks as mothers. We are obviously dealing here with the stereotyping of gender roles, as in the case reported by Manfred Hainich, the director of the Friedrich-Engels school in Altenberg. One husband objected to his wife changing her shift system and thereby leaving him with the responsibility for looking after their three children, a task which, in Hainich's opinion, the father regarded as unworthy of the head of the household.[36]

In a 1974 publication, one of the GDR's leading authorities on shiftwork reported that schoolteachers were increasingly requesting enterprises to withdraw mothers from shiftwork because of their children's educational problems.[37] Among the problems identified by GDR researchers are the greater difficulties experienced by shiftworkers' children in becoming integrated into the class collective and their relatively poor academic performance. An analysis of the school grades of 818 third-form boys and girls at 12 schools in Magdeburg indicates that shiftwork is associated with below-average attainment.[38] The Halle-Wittenberg team, too, discovered a similar pattern. The most interesting details of their research do not appear in published form but in an article for the house journal of the scientific council ''Die Frau in der sozialistischen Gesellschaft'' of the Academy of Sciences. An examination of the school grades of 918 children in the fourth and sixth forms of six schools in the Bitterfeld district related average grades to parental occupation. The children of shiftworkers were clearly disadvantaged. As childrearing obviously posed considerable problems if both parents were on shifts, the researchers, Martina Jugel and Barbara Spangenberg, recommended that only one parent be employed in this type of work.[39]

In view of their children's problems it is desirable for shiftworkers to have frequent contacts with school. However, the Halle-Wittenberg study shows that shiftworkers attended parents' evenings less frequently than other workers and were also less likely to hold an office in parent-teachers' associations.[40] Furthermore, there was less discussion in shiftworking families between parents and children about school problems. Parents often gave lack of time as the reason for being unable or virtually unable to help their children with homework.

GDR workers do show great concern about the impact of shiftwork on marital relations. One possible solution to the lack of free time together is for both partners to work the same shift, but this is disadvantageous for the upbringing of children. The most problematic variant, for married life, is when both partners are on the three-shift system but on a different rotation. Indeed Rudhard Stollberg has recommended the introduction of the continuous three-shift system only if it is economically and technologically necessary.[41] Stollberg's Halle-Wittenberg research team drew special attention to the irritability and strife between shiftworking couples, above all between nightworkers who tended to suffer from inadequate sleep. Another contributory factor to marital stress was the greater housework burden on women.

The numerous family and marital problems arising from, or compounded by, shiftwork—irritability, insufficient shared time, gender stereotyping—have been interpreted by the West German Friedrich-Ebert-Foundation[42] as major factors in estrangement between couples and subsequent divorce in the GDR. Although this argument is persuasive, and highly significant at a time when one in three new marriages ends in divorce, it is not known whether the incidence of divorce is higher among shiftworkers than among dayworkers. Much more sophisticated research is required to elucidate the role played by shiftwork in marital breakdown.

In objective terms shiftworkers enjoy more work-free time than colleagues on "normal" time. In 1977 all workers on three-shift systems, including those working weekends, were granted a 40-hour week and those on two shifts one of 42 hours; dayworkers continued on 43.75 hours. In January 1981 the supplementary leave of shiftworkers was increased by four days. Workers on three shifts enjoy ten days extra leave and those on two shifts eight days.

The additional work-free time is perceived as one of the main advantages of this type of work. Women regard the extra time for sleeping and housework as a considerable gain (see Table 3). In practice, the amount of disposable free time is eroded by housework tasks, childrearing, journeys to and from work, and sleep requirements. As among other groups of workers, the men enjoy more free time than women (see Table 4). Many women at Wolfen were of the opinion

Table 4

Time Budgets of Men and Women Shiftworkers, 1974 GDR Survey (in hours and minutes per day)

	All workers M	W	Daywork M	W	Two shifts M	W	Three shifts M	W	Continuous M	W
Working time	6.4	5.0	6.3	4.8	6.5	5.7	6.5	5.9	7.4	5.0
Time related to work	1.1	0.8	1.1	0.8	1.2	0.9	1.1	1.1	1.2	0.8
Time spent on household jobs	2.2	4.4	2.2	4.5	2.3	4.0	2.1	3.6	2.4	4.3
Time spent on care and upbringing of children	0.2	0.5	0.2	0.5	0.2	0.4	0.2	0.3	0.1	0.5
Physiological needs	10.0	10.2	10.0	10.2	9.9	10.2	9.9	10.1	9.6	10.2
Free time	4.1	3.1	4.2	3.2	3.9	2.8	4.2	3.0	3.3	3.2

Source: Helmut Hanke, *Freizeit in der DDR* (Berlin: Dietz Verlag, 1979), 64–65.

Table 5

Proportion of Workers Who Never Attend Events (%)

	Dayworkers (No. = 461)	Shiftworkers (No. = 372)
Sports events	47.6	59.3
Theater	50.7	65.1
Concerts	87.8	92.8
Dances and entertainment	16.5	28.2
General educational visits	62.4	74.0

Source: Stollberg, *Arbeitssoziologie*, 219.

that their type of work even lessens the amount of free time. The Halle-Wittenberg team attributed this kind of negative assessment to women's need for rest after the demands of work, family, housework, and travel.

The pattern of free-time activities pursued by GDR shiftworkers is similar to that found in other countries. Those activities associated with more flexible time schedules, for example, gardening, reading, walking, and handicrafts, are less affected than the time-constrained events such as visits to the cinema, theatre, concerts, and sports meets. Watching television is sometimes placed within the first category. Furthermore, the demanding nature of shiftwork tends to create a need for passive rather than active recreation. The Halle-Wittenberg researchers reported a lower participation by shiftworkers in time-constrained events but no difference in reading, listening to music, watching television, *Basteln*, or driving cars and motorbikes (see Table 5). However, significant gender differences emerged in both types of activity. Finally, the Halle-Wittenberg data show that shiftworkers were less likely than dayworkers to hold an office in the SED, the mass organizations, or the National Front. Once again, the hours of the afternoon shiftworkers, which coincided with most societal activities, acted as a serious constraint.[43]

Health

One of the most controversial issues is the impact of shiftwork on health. Although international research has shown that shiftworkers complain frequently about health problems (for instance, gastrointestinal disorders), many workers do adjust physiologically to their work schedules and many alleged ill-effects remain scientifically unsubstantiated. The research findings, well summarized by Sergean, Ruthenfranz, and Walker,[44] present the following picture. Certain groups of shiftworkers—those on nights or permanent shifts and former shiftworkers—are likely to complain more frequently about sleep disturbances than are dayworkers. There is, however, an overlap in the frequency of day- and shiftworkers' complaints. Common causes of disturbances are the telephone ringing and the noise of children and traffic. The possible deleterious effects of loss or disturbance of sleep include fatigue, irritation, and a decline in the performance of simple, uninteresting tasks; more complex, interesting tasks are less vulnerable. Some groups of shiftworkers have been affected by lack of appetite and eating disturbances as a result of their different working and social rhythms. Of about 1,000 workers examined in various studies, appetite disturbances were found among less than 5 percent of dayworkers and shiftworkers not on nights, 35 to 75 percent of workers whose schedules included nights, and about 50 percent of permanent shiftworkers. Not surprisingly, the literature reveals that gastric and intestinal dysfunctions are significant problems among permanent and former shiftworkers. The differences between those on days and other shift systems tend to be slight. If appetite disturbances and gastrointestinal problems are exacerbated by factors such as short meal breaks, heavy physical labor, and overtime, special health risks may arise. Indeed investigations of over 34,000 workers have shown that gastric ulcers were found among 2.5 to 15 percent of shiftworkers on nights and 10 to 30 percent of those who had given up shiftwork for health reasons. Once again, the evidence is not unequivocal. Two studies by Aanonsen and Thiis-Evensen discovered a lower ulcer frequency among shiftworkers on nights than among those on days; former shiftworkers, however, exhibited the greatest incidence of all groups. Finally, no significant medical evidence exists to link shiftwork with an above average incidence of cardiovascular symptoms or a higher mortality rate.

Because the GDR authorities regard shiftwork as a "societal requirement," many research projects and textbooks on occupational health and management have a tendency to play down some of the health problems outlined above. Considerable optimism prevails in most texts that any ill-effects can be prevented or at least controlled by adequate precautions such as regular medical examinations, a well-balanced diet, and frequent work breaks. Workers do not appear to share this optimism. The GDR national study of 5,503 women in nine branches of industry, conducted in the early 1970s, found that the second most important reason for rejecting shiftwork was the women's worry that their age or the state of their health would prevent them from coping with the demands of shiftwork.[45] At the Wolfen enterprise, only a small proportion of women believed that shiftwork did not have a negative effect, and in the Halle-Wittenberg survey of production workers the health burden was rated the second most important disadvantage by men and women on days and shifts.

GDR experts such as Quaas, Wullrich, and Karig are of the opinion that no significant differences are to be found in morbidity between day- and shiftworkers, especially if sufficient precautions are taken. In fact, a survey of 9,173 production workers in the textile industry found that in 1975 and 1976 shiftworkers were absent from work through illness less often and for shorter periods of time than dayworkers.[46] These findings were not corroborated by Brandt's earlier research in the 1960s, for which detailed results were made available at an international conference.[47] At a textile enterprise the men and women on the three-shift system were ill more frequently and for longer than those on "normal" hours. At a second enterprise, a foundry, the number of working days lost through illness over a period of three years was highest among workers on shifts. The frequency of illness was particularly high among the men aged 20 to 30.

Many studies have revealed serious sleep deprivation among shiftworkers. In the Halle-Wittenberg investigation the women, when on nights, enjoyed no more than four to five hours sleep, partly as a result of doing the housework after their return home from work in the early hours of the morning. Not surprisingly, 47 percent of the women shiftworkers regarded their sleep as insufficient in contrast to 32 percent of their daytime counterparts.[48] Shiftworkers with a partner on shifts enjoyed less sleep than those married to someone on "normal" hours. The situation was particularly serious for couples on different systems. These couples were the most likely to evaluate their general health as being impaired by shiftwork. This sleep loss was partly related to the tendency of wives on the late shift to get up with husbands on the early shift and of one partner, even when due to start work early next morning, not going to bed until the other's return home after the late shift.[49] GDR experts such as Stollberg and Quaas conclude that nervous problems, headaches, and irritability are consequences of sleep disruption; however, it should be noted that such judgments, also encountered in

Western inquiries, are not always scientifically proven. Professor Hecht is therefore quite correct to point out that international research has not managed to establish a clear and incontrovertible relationship between shiftwork and nervous disorders. Nevertheless, the existence of a problem is implied in his recommendations that positive attitudes to shiftwork should be developed in order to reduce fear and worry about this type of work.[50] Brandt's research, too, has demonstrated a cause for concern. On a three-shift system, women textile workers (12 percent), though not the men, exhibited a greater frequency of nervous disorders than did those on days (5.6 percent). At a motor vehicle works the men on three shifts were more prone to nervous illness than their colleagues on days and on the two-shift system.[51]

Social policy and shift schedules

GDR investigations demonstrate that shiftwork, especially the three-shift system with nights, is associated with gastrointestinal problems and sleep deprivation. There is a risk of nervous disorders and a higher accident rate than on "normal" daywork. Certain work schedules impose considerable strain on families with young children. Workers, quite rightly, have reservations about the introduction of shift systems. In order to overcome such doubts the SED attaches the utmost significance to political-ideological activities. Once workers have been persuaded to embark on shiftwork, it is hoped that they will perceive its advantages and that their fears and worries will be allayed. However, recruitment can be a problem. A trades union official at the electronic enterprise Grossenhain, with a relatively high female workforce, disclosed that the women were sometimes reduced to tears at the prospect of the changeover to a continuous three-shift system. The women were understandably reluctant to give up the workplace that they had occupied for twenty years and then to have to adjust to a new work collective.[52]

Management, trades union officials, and party functionaries are directly involved in overcoming workers' resistance to change.[53] The whole transition is usually organized by a special work group. Collective discussions at trades union and brigade meetings are encouraged. Tables and graphics depict the economic advantages of a more intensive utilization of expensive machinery. Experienced shiftworkers are drawn upon to inform dayworkers of the benefits of shiftwork. The *Polygraph* combine in Leipzig, the GDR's advisory center for matters relating to the continuous three-shift system, strongly recommends using well-integrated collectives as the spearheads for sorting out the teething problems of the changeover. When other workers see them adjusting to shifts they too may be willing to become shiftworkers. Another tactic, used with graduates, is to introduce them to shiftwork for a limited period. It is hoped that this experience will help to overcome their initial reservations and persuade them to remain permanently on shifts.[54] The key to the whole operation appears to lie in the discussions that representatives of the management and trades unions conduct with individual workers. The personal problems and anxieties of the workers can best be tackled at this level.

The task of persuasion encounters many difficulties, however. First, it is well known that workers tend to be insufficiently involved in the technological and administrative details entailed in the introduction of shiftwork. Gerhard Schellenberger, a sociologist at the University of Dresden, writing of the general process of intensification and rationalization, is highly critical of the procedure whereby the enterprise first sets the goals and only then informs the workers and seeks their approval.[55] Second, workers question the need for shiftwork when they experience frequent stoppages in the production process as well as a shortage of materials and tools. Third, plans for the introduction of shiftwork are sometimes inadequately coordinated between the enterprises and the local organs of state. Finally, workers are not easily persuaded to undertake the burdens of shiftwork when they realize that management, technical, and administrative personnel are able to avoid the inconvenient late and night shifts.[56]

The GDR has introduced a wide range of social measures not only to increase the participation rate in shiftwork but also to mitigate the burdens for those already on shifts. Preschool and *Hort* provision (afterschool child-care centers for pupils aged 6 to 10) has been extended, efforts are made to adjust the opening times of crèches, kindergartens, and shops to shiftworking hours, special theater performances have been organized and television programs may be repeated in the mornings for the benefit of the late shifts and some nightworkers. Enterprises are obliged to sign contracts with public transport authorities to reduce the time spent on traveling to and from work. Arrangements designed to prevent a deterioration in the well-being of shiftworkers include a shorter working week, longer holidays, priority in the allocation of housing, holiday places and cures, frequent work breaks, and a warm meal at night.

One crucial management task is to design shift schedules that minimize social inconvenience and psychological and physiological burdens. GDR occupational health experts such as Ackermann, Brandt, Sinz, and Quaas are extremely critical of the traditional three-shift system with a weekly changeover and three shifts of equal length. This *via media* between rapid rotation and permanent shift schedules involves sufficient nights for the workers' circadian rhythms to be disrupted but not time enough to adjust to the change in the sleep/wake cycle; a slower rotation of about four weeks at one shift, although requiring less frequent adjustment, suffers from similar drawbacks and entails a lengthier period on the burdensome night shift. The experts' preference is for rapidly rotating shifts with no more than two or three nights in a row and an unequal division of the length of shifts.

Shift premia and allowances represent an important and sometimes decisive incentive for the recruitment and retention of shiftworkers. Since 1975 a flat shift premium of 7 marks has been paid for each night shift. In addition, shiftworkers can usually expect an end-of-year bonus and on occasions an extra-wage bonus and other allowances. Considerable differences exist between enterprises and combines in the methods of assessment and in the amount paid. For example, at an enterprise in Stassfurt premia ranged, in 1975, from 250 marks on the continuous three-shift system to 85 marks on the discontinuous two-shift system.[57]

Summary and conclusions

The data presented in this essay have been gleaned from a wide range of GDR sources, including not only the blatantly propagandistic but also careful psychological, physiological, and sociological investigations. Although these investigations are not always representative of a particular population, and full details are sometimes lacking, the findings do not appear to differ significantly from those of Western researchers. It is also true that like other industrial societies the GDR cannot and will not dispense with shiftwork for a variety of economic, social, and technological reasons. In recent months SED leaders such as Erich Honecker, Günter Mittag, and Willi Stoph have made it quite clear that the party is seeking an increase of shiftwork in all sectors of the economy and the more intensive utilization of costly fixed assets. This policy involves the expansion of the controversial continuous three-shift system. Given the GDR's limited labor supply, its foreign trade burdens, a labor productivity considerably lower than that of France and the FRG, and the need for a more intensive operation of expensive machinery and plant, a powerful argument can obviously be advanced in favor of more shiftworking. As for the shiftworkers themselves, increased earnings enable their families to enjoy a higher standard of living and their health is not necessarily impaired by their type of work. Even if schedules include nights, care can be taken by workers who have a predisposition to gastrointestinal complaints or nervous disorders to ensure that they have adequate sleep and a balanced diet. Should problems continue, then it is advisable to transfer from nightwork to another system. Social isolation is certainly not the inevitable fate of shiftworkers. Leisure interests may be pursued which are family centered and whose timing is flexible. Hobbies—reading, angling, gardening—can be carried out without relying on other people. If the worker resides in a shiftworking community, it should be relatively easy to maintain friendships and to enjoy a variety of leisure activities. Furthermore, an individual's adjustment to the physiological requirements of shiftwork may be facilitated by the introduction of rapidly rotating shifts.

Nevertheless, the difficulties should not be understated. A growing number of people who dislike working at nights and on weekends will be affected by the increased incidence in the continuous three-shift system. Adequate medical precautions are essential in order to establish the suitability of workers for the more demanding work schedules. The strain on family life and marriage seems to be exacerbated by the relatively high proportion of women on shifts. We frequently encounter families that rarely meet as a unit. Childrearing, household tasks, and participation in societal activities also give cause for concern. These and other problems have prompted several GDR observers to call for restrictions on shiftwork. Irene Dölling, a cultural theoretician at Humboldt University, who is extremely worried about shiftwork's negative impact, under certain circumstances, upon sleep, leisure pursuits, and family life, has appealed for the introduction of shiftwork only when it is absolutely necessary.[58] Professor Wulfram Speigner, formerly a member of the Academy of Science's council "Die Frau in der sozialistischen Gesellschaft." has expressed a wish for restrictions on the participation of mothers with young children in the continuous and discontinuous three-shift systems.[59] A leading authority on shiftwork, the sociologist Rudhard Stollberg, advises against the three-shift system with weekend work, especially in the case of families with youngsters; it should be introduced only if it is technologically and economically necessary. In his opinion, increased national prosperity has to be balanced against the possible negative consequences for the shiftworkers themselves.[60] Finally, Professor Helga Wendt, of the *Technische Hochschule* "Otto von Guericke," Magdeburg, has speculated that the unmanned shift in completely automated production represents the ideal though distant solution to the problem of nightwork.[61] If we add to these critical voices the workers' subjective dislike of shiftwork, as it emerges from the studies cited in this essay, then the GDR authorities will need to proceed with the utmost care in their drive to expand shiftwork, especially where it involves nights and weekends. Since it also appears that no single optimum shift schedule can be designed, work schedules should be adjusted to suit the circumstances and the needs of the individual worker.

Notes

1. The term shiftwork applies to two- and three-shift rotating schedules. A two-shift program, usually of eight hours, is normally worked from 6.00 to 14.00 and 14.00 to 22.00 hours. Three-shift schedules in the GDR are traditionally divided into morning (early), afternoon (late), and night units, each eight hours in length and with the morning shift commencing at 06.00 hours. The shift change has normally taken place after one working week. A discontinuous three-shift system usually operates over five days and nights and a continuous three-shift system involves weekend work. However, hours of work and frequency of change are subject to considerable variations.

2. "FDJ-Auftrag X1. Parteitag der SED," *Junge Welt* (28 April, 1986): 6.

3. Jutta Bleibaum and Gudrun Nause, "Rechtzeitige Weiterbildung von Frauen für veränderte Arbeitsaufgaben," *Arbeit und Arbeitsrecht* 40, no. 11 (1985): 246.

4. Lawrence Whetten, *Germany East and West. Conflicts, Collaboration and Confrontation* (New York: New York University Press, 1980), 146.

5. Axel Bust Bartels, *Herrschaft und Widerstand in den DDR-Betrieben* (Frankfurt/ Main, 1980), 141–42, 149.

6. Rainer Sinz, Rudolf Schmitt, Hans-Joachim Selle, and Ruth Wiedemann, "Psychophysiologische Stress- und Beanspruchungsanalysen an rechnergestützten Arbeitsplätzen," *Zeitschrift für Psychologie*, supplement 3 (1982): 92.

7. "Auch an den Wochenenden im Betrieb gut umsorgt," *Tribüne* (8 June 1983): 1.

8. "Schichtarbeit und Interessenvertretung," Ibid. (13 June 1983): 2.

9. Marc Maurice, *Shift Work, Economic Advantages and Social Costs* (Geneva: International Labour Office, 1975), 47.

10. "Wachstum—und woher?" *Für Dich*, no. 12 (1983): 26.

11. Martina Lenz, "Bessere Nutzung des gesellschaftlichen Arbeitsvermögens durch Ausdehnung der Mehrschichtarbeit," *Sozialistische Arbeitswissenschaft* 26, no. 5 (1982): 424.

12. Claus Thiele, "Durchgehende Dreischichtarbeit stellt hohe Anforderungen an die Leitungstätigkeit," *Arbeit und Arbeitsrecht* 40, no. 10 (1985): 219.

13. Leonhard Kasek and Klaus Ulrich, "Hochschulabsolventen und Mehrschichtarbeit," Ibid., no. 8 (1985): 175.

14. "1986 National Economic Plan Act," *Documents on the policy of the German Democratic Republic* (Berlin: Panorama, 1985), no. 4, 23.

15. *Ökonomische Strategie der Partei—klares Konzept für weiteres Wachstum* (Berlin: Dietz Verlag), 99.

16. *Neues Deutschland* (18 April 1986): 6.

17. Hans-Dieter Jacobsen, "Die Aussenwirtschaftspolitik der DDR gegen den Westen zu Beginn der achtziger Jahre," *Die DDR vor den Herausforderungen der achtziger Jahre* (Cologne: Wissenschaft und Politik, 1983), 70; Maria Haendcke-Hoppe, "Probleme des DDR-Aussenhandels in den achtziger Jahren," *East Central Europe* 11, nos. 1–2 (1984): 70.

18. *Neues Deutschland* (18 April 1986): 5.

19. Alastair McAuley, *Women's Work and Wages in the Soviet Union* (London: Allen and Unwin, 1981), 197.

20. Robert Sergean, *Managing Shiftwork* (London: Gower Press, 1971), 151.

21. Dieter Voigt, *Montagearbeiter in der DDR* (Darmstadt: Luchterhand, 1973), 148–51. These results were not published in the GDR, only in the FRG.

22. Peter Armelin, "Bericht über eine Betriebssoziologische Fluktuationsuntersuchung," in Kurt Braunreuther, Fred Oelsner, and Werner Ott, *Soziologische Aspekte der Arbeitskräftebewegung* (Berlin: Akademie-Verlag, 1967), 130–31.

23. Petra Dunskus, et al., *Zur gesellschaftlichen Stellung der Frau in der DDR* (Leipzig: Verlag für die Frau, 1978), 135. This survey included 2,737 shift- and nonshiftworkers in state-managed industry. The women shiftworkers included a high proportion (72 percent) who had spent more than five years on shifts; they can be regarded as a survivor population and one that had adjusted to the work schedules.

24. Rudolf Sauerzapf and Anton Scheinpflug, *Probleme der Frauenschichtarbeit* (VEB Filmfabrik, Wolfen, Fotochemisches Kombinet, unpublished report, 1970), 22–23. This important investigation was carried out in 1969. Out of 6,411 women employed at the enterprise, 150 on days and 1,297 on shifts were questioned.

25. Werner Gerth and Heinz Ronneberg, *Jugend und Betriebsverbundenheit* (Berlin: Dietz Verlag, 1981), 87.

26. Jutta Stölzel, "Festgefügte Stammbelegschaften fördern Leistungswachstum," *Arbeit und Arbeitsrecht* 38, no. 5 (1983): 201. The survey was carried out between 1976 and 1981.

27. Dunskus, 136. The women's magazine reported the case of a husband's initial opposition to his wife's changing over from days to a two-shift system. The husband complained that difficulties would be created in taking care of their three children early in the morning and that the family's pigs and chickens would have to go. Sieglinde Hammer, "Eine Diedorfer Zeitgeschichte," *Für Dich*, no. 25 (1982): 14.

28. Renate Johne, "Zur Einstellung von Produktionsarbeitern zur Mehrschichtar-

beit,'' in Rudhard Stollberg, ed., *Schichtarbeit in soziologischer Sicht* (Berlin: Die Wirtschaft, 1974), 50.

29. Otto Eisenblätter, "Zur Arbeit der Frau im betrieblichen Dreischichtsystem," *Arbeit und Arbeitsrecht* 25, no. 19 (1970): 588.

30. Dunskus, 138.

31. Sauerzapf and Scheinpflug, 31–32.

32. James Walker, *Human Aspects of Shiftwork* (London: Institute of Personnel Management, 1978), 87, 91.

33. See, for example, Joseph Ruthenfranz, "Schichtarbeit—Arbeitsmedizinische Feststellungen zu Befindlichkeitsstörungen und Erkrankungen," in Friedhelm Farthmann, ed., *Landesforum Schichtarbeit* (Bonn: Verlag Neue Gesellschaft, 1979), 69.

34. The information in this section is derived from Martina Jugel, Barbara Spangenberg, and Rudhard Stollberg, *Schichtarbeit und Lebensweise* (Berlin: Dietz Verlag, 1978), 46–49.

35. "Wie wird die Fahrerlaubnis der Bäuerinnen genutzt?" *Für Dich*, no. 13 (1982): 11.

36. Manfred Hainich, "Schichtarbeit und Schule," *Elternhaus und Schule* 30, no. 2 (1981): 23.

37. Rudolf Sauerzapf, "Zu einigen Problemen der Frauenschichtarbeit in Betrieben der chemischen Industrie," in Stollberg, *Schichtarbeit* 43.

38. The Magdeburg results appear in Randi Stock, "Leistungsfähigkeit von Kindern berufstätiger und nicht berufstätiger Mutter" (Dissertation, Medizinische Akademie, Magdeburg, 1969), 17.

39. Their findings are in *Informationen des wissenschaftlichen Beirats "Die Frau in der sozialistischen Gesellschaft,"* no. 2, 1975.

40. Jugel, Spangenberg, and Stollberg, 53, 55–57.

41. Rudhard Stollberg, "Zum Einfluss der Schichtarbeit auf das Familienleben der Arbeiter," *Sozialistische Arbeitswissenschaft* 21, no. 3 (1977): 213.

42. *Schichtarbeit in beiden deutschen Staaten* (Bonn: Friedrich-Ebert-Stiftung, 1979), 40.

43. Rudhard Stollberg, "Grundlegende Forschungsaspekte zu den Wirkungen der Schichtarbeit auf die sozialistische Lebensweise der Werktätigen," in Stollberg, *Schictarbeit*, 21.

44. See Ruthenfranz, 59, 65–68; Sergean, 180–83, 190–92; Walker, 64–85.

45. Wulfram Speigner, "Die Lebensumstände und ihre Wirkung auf Denkweisen in der sozialen Gruppe der berufstätigen Frau," *Informationen des wissenschaftlichen Beirats "Die Frau in der sozialistischen Gesellschaft,"* no. 5 (1977): 27.

46. A. Brandt, "Über den Einfluss der Schichtarbeit auf den Gesundheitszustand und das Krankheitsgeschehen der Werktätigen," *Studia laboris et salutis*, no. 4 (1969): 130, 136, 139–46, 150.

47. An impressive review of recent Western publications is to be found in Sinz, 85–87.

48. Rudhard Stollberg, *Arbeitssoziologie* (Berlin: Die Wirtschaft, 1979), 216; Jugel, Spangenberg, and Stollberg, 68.

49. Ibid., 108–9.

50. Karl Hecht, "Altern Dreischichtarbeiter schneller?" *Arbeit und Arbeitsrecht* 32, no. 10 (1977): 303.

51. Brandt, 132, 134–35.

52. Wolfgang Haase, "Übergang zur Mehrschichtarbeit schliesst Sorge um den Menschen ein," *Arbeit und Arbeitsrecht* 40, no. 11 (1985): 243.

53. Examples of political-ideological activity are discussed in Jürgen Strassburger, "Ökonomische und soziale Probleme der Schichtarbeit," *Deutschland Archiv Sonderheft. Einheit von Wirtschafts- und Sozialpolitik. Anspruch und Realität. Elfte Tagung zum Stand*

der DDR Forschung in der Bundesrepublik (Cologne: Verlag Wissenschaft und Politik, 1978), 77–92.

54. Kasek and Ulrich, 176.

55. Gerhard Schellenberger, *Technische Neuerungen-sozialer Fortschritt* (Berlin: Dietz Verlag, 1980), 138–40.

56. Sauerzapf and Scheinpflug, 46–47; Horst Heintze, Grundfondsökonomie und Mehrschichtarbeit," *Arbeit und Arbeitsrecht* 25, no. 7 (1970): 213–14.

57. Gerhard Rosenkranz, *Mehrschichtarbeit* (Berlin: Verlag Tribüne, 1975), 38–39.

58. Irene Dölling, *Naturwesen—Individuum—Persönlichkeit* (Berlin: Deutscher Verlag der Wissenschaften, 1979), 121.

59. Wulfram Speigner, "Soziologische Untersuchungen zur weiteren Entwicklungen der gesellschaftlichen Stellung der Frau in der DDR" (Dissertation, Humboldt Universität, Berlin, 1972), 17.

60. Stollberg, "Zum Einfluss," 213; idem, *Arbeitssoziologie*, 213, 223–34.

61. "Rundtischgespräch," *Deutsche Zeitschrift für Philosophie* 31, no. 3 (1983): 325.

Part IV

Housing and the Environment

New Towns in the German Democratic Republic

The *Neubaugebiete* of Rostock

Marilyn Rueschemeyer

The new towns of Rostock are a result of planned social policy in the GDR in the 1960s which emphasized rapid and inexpensive housing construction. Based on empirical research in the new towns as well as an analysis of the East German sociological and architectural literature, this essay describes developments in housing that have taken place in the past twenty-five years—as well as some of the social responses of the inhabitants to their new living environment.

Rostock is a two-and-a-half hour ride north from Berlin toward the Baltic Sea (see Map 1). Over seven hundred years old, it has traditionally been a provincial city in the underdeveloped agricultural area of Mecklenburg. Shipbuilding and fishing play an important role in its economy. The University of Rostock, presently the Wilhelm Pieck University, was founded in 1419 and is one of the oldest universities in Northern Europe.

Before the outbreak of World War II, the population of Rostock was 120,000; in 1945, there were fewer than 90,000 inhabitants. Over half of the inner city was destroyed. During the last forty years, the population has more than doubled, reaching about 250,000, with an annual increase of 5,000 new residents. Sixty percent of the population now lives in the new residential areas begun in 1962 between old Rostock and Warnemunde, a popular seaside resort on the Baltic Sea. With the completion of the expanded international harbor and the building of a new chemical industry at the outskirts of the city, a further increase in population is expected. Of course, the construction industry has also developed enormously.

The first years after the war were characterized by a partial rebuilding of the

Map 1. **Cities in The German Democratic Republic.**

Source: Jiří Musil, *Urbanization in Socialist Countries* (New York: M. E. Sharpe, 1980), 102.

Figure 1. **The New Towns of Rostock.**

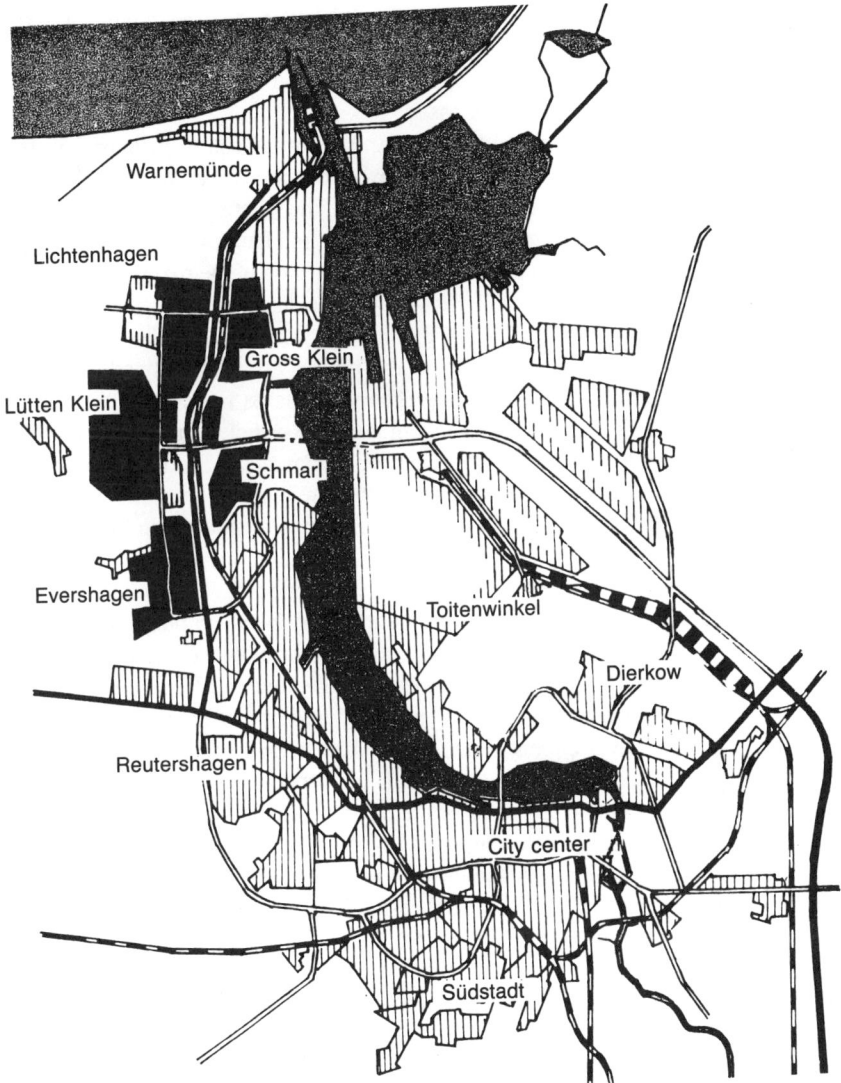

Source: *Bauen im Ostseebezirk* (Rat des Bezirkes Rostock, Bezirksbauamt), Band 7, 1982, 11.

main streets and important cultural monuments and buildings in the destroyed inner city. Then the residential areas of Reutershagen I and II (1953–60) and the Südstadt (1960–65) were built. New residential developments continued to be put up until they now represent 60 percent of all living quarters. The housing, which was erected in the primarily agricultural villages of Lütten Klein, Evershagen, Lichtenhagen, Schmarl, and Gross Klein (see Figure 1), was built on land considered generally poor—flat, unwooded, and wet, as well as windy. A sixth new community, Dierkow, currently is being built on the east bank of the river. In 1966, the first inhabitants moved into Lutten Klein, the oldest of the new residential developments discussed in this essay.

The settlements lie on both sides of the main traffic route, primarily in the northwest of the city, along the Unterwarnow. They are linked to each other by means of recreational zones, walks, and parks. The western boundaries of the new living quarters contain small, private gardens and fruit orchards, which also serve as some protection from the wind. On the east side of the main traffic route, both north and south, are large industrial complexes, as well as areas reserved for "nicht-störende Arbeitsstätten"—low-disturbance workplaces. New residential areas are being developed there as well. The houses are standardized constructions, built with prefabricated elements. The settlements were to be planned as quickly and as cheaply as possible to accommodate Rostock's increasing population. There are still 20,000 people without proper apartments, and the inner city's living quarters have yet to be modernized. After the renovation of the university center, the city planners expect to turn their attention to the many rundown houses in the city.

This essay, then, will address a number of issues revolving around the new settlements of Rostock. It will focus on the interplay between public policy and the experience of everyday life. The first section is a brief description of the goals and realities of urban development in the German Democratic Republic, of which Rostock is one manifestation; indeed it is considered one of the more successful examples of urban development in the GDR. The second section discusses new town design in Rostock and some of the learning processes in city planning. The third section deals with the reactions of the residents to their new living quarters, the social relations that have developed, as well as the role of political organizations and other institutions. Although the emphasis is on Rostock, the essay includes some comparisons to other new residential quarters, such as Marzahn, a huge new residential area around Berlin.

Reconstruction and urbanization in the GDR

The German Democratic Republic is the most industrialized of all the countries of Eastern Europe. Since it was highly industrialized as well as urbanized from its beginnings, it has not experienced change with the same degree of intensity and rapidity as has characterized other countries in the process of industrialization and urbanization. Already in 1975, about 70 percent of the population lived in urban communities and approximately 80 percent lived in urban regions,[1] while in the other countries of Eastern Europe, less than 60 percent of the population was urbanized.[2] However, the proportion of people living in really large cities is lower than in Poland, Hungary, or the USSR. Only one-quarter of the population of about 17 million lives in cities with over 100,000 inhabitants, while a little more than half lives in communities of 20,000 or less. The remaining quarter is in middle-size cities of 20,000 to 100,000 inhabitants. (See Table 1.)

The GDR, like other socialist countries, has tried to develop those areas that were industrially backward and has created a number of new industrial centers in the northern and eastern regions of the country while at the same time encouraging the expansion of already existing industries. General principles of development were first formulated at the Eighth Party Congress in 1971 where economic targets were set for the regions. In Rostock, as mentioned above, the port was enlarged, a shipyard expanded, and the fishing industry further developed. With the exception of Rostock, all cities with populations over 100,000 are south of Berlin. The small and medium-size towns in which people live are typically associated with huge industrial agglomerations. It has been estimated that a third of all employed people travel to work outside the town in which they live. Over 40 percent of the population lives in these industrial agglomerations with centers in Berlin, Leipzig-Halle, Karl-Marx Stadt-Zwickau, Dresden, and Magdeburg. Sixty percent of the total economic output is produced in only 15 percent of the territory of the GDR.[3] Concentrated investment in the major cities remained a part of GDR settlement policy since the 1950s. Between 1964 and 1975, 80 percent of the growth of cities with over 20,000 inhabitants was attributed to migration from small towns and communities. It is noteworthy that the strongest growth has taken place in towns with fewer than 100,000 inhabitants, continuing the pattern of urban decentralization in small urban centers.

In the territory that is now the GDR, more than half of the housing units in the inner cities were destroyed during World War II; 620,000 housing units were completely destroyed and another 200,000 were partially damaged.[4] As devastating as this was, in the immediate postwar period the availability of housing was greater than in West Germany where there was even heavier damage and higher rates of immigration.[5] Because of the GDR's economic policy goals as well as the reparations demanded by the Soviet Union, construction activity was concentrated primarily in the industrial sector. Although the reconstruction of the damaged houses began immediately, there were few funds allocated for new housing or for modernizing the existing housing stock. As late as 1981, only 35 percent of the housing units were built after 1945; 46 percent of all housing was built before 1919, while 19 percent was constructed between 1919 and 1945. In those buildings constructed before 1918, only 5 percent of living quarters have central heating and only 25 percent have an indoor toilet and bath.[6] By 1981, only a third of the living quarters had central heating while approximately two-thirds were equipped with a bath or shower and an indoor toilet.[7]

Rent is very low in the GDR, ranging from 3 to 10 percent of annual income, and even lower for those who are unable to afford these rates. Since over half of the old houses are in private hands, the low rents discourage extensive repair,

Table 1

Communities with 10,000 or More Inhabitants, Ranked by Size (end of 1983)

Community	Population	Community	Population	Community	Population	Community	Population
Hauptstadt Berlin	1,185,533	Wilhelm-Pieck-Stadt Guben	34,726	Ludwigsfelde	20,970	Klingenthal/Sa.	13,519
Leipzig	558,994	Weisswasser	34,624	Auerbach/Vogtl	20,837	Bischofswerda	13,490
Dresden	522,532	Aschersleben	34,303	Anklam	20,400	Gardelegen	13,462
Karl-Marx-Stadt	318,917	Saalfeld/Saale	34,141	Haldensleben	20,346	Eisenberg	13,159
Magdeburg	289,075	Sangerhausen	33,604	Markkleeberg	20,095	Taucha	13,060
Rostock	241,146	Naumburg/Saale	32,913	Werdau	19,986	Wolmirstedt	13,059
Halle/Saale	236,139	Rudolstadt	31,913	Mittweida	19,491	Lichtenstein/Sa.	12,922
Erfurt	214,231	Rathenow	31,896	Oschatz	19,318	Erkner	12,913
Potsdam	135,922	Senftenberg	31,796	Heidenau	19,270	Kleinmachnow	12,893
Gera	129,891	Wittenberge	31,053	Wurzen	19,120	Jüterbog	12,764
Schwerin	124,975	Arnstadt	29,916	Bernau b. Berlin	19,052	Ebersbach	12,663
Cottbus	120,723	Glauchau	29,697	Grossenhain	19,012	Flöha	12,649
Zwickau	120,486	Ilmenau	29,470	Königs Wusterhausen	18,951	Uckermünde	12,535
Jena	106,555	Quedlinburg	29,167	Zerbst	18,912	Bad Doberan	12,459
Dessau	103,738	Apolda	28,911	Blankenburg/Harz	18,763	Barth	12,407
Brandenburg/Havel	95,133	Sonneberg	28,827	Löbau	18,683	Pritzwalk	12,390
Halle-Neustadt	91,510	Aue	28,793	Kamenz	18,410	Olbernhau	12,296
Frankfurt/Oder	84,072	Coswig	28,696	Pössneck	18,222	Niesky	12,268
Neubrandenburg	82,450	Burg b. Magdeburg	28,216	Hohenstein-Ernstthal	17,943	Schmölln	12,255
Görlitz	80,216	Oranienburg	28,121	Ribnitz-Damgarten	17,817	Neuenhagen b. Berlin	12,187
Plauen	78,797	Delitzsch	27,866	Grimma	17,743	Sebnitz	12,151
Stralsund	75,335	Eisleben	27,346	Schmalkalden	17,440	Neustadt/Sa.	12,137
Hoyerswerda	70,698	Hennigsdorf b. Berlin	27,334	Oschersleben/Bode	17,372	Rüdersdorf b. Berlin	12,129
Weimar	64,007	Stassfurt	27,249	Demmin	17,301	Stollberg/Erzgeb	12,081
Greifswald	62,991						
Wismar	57,874						

City	Population
Gotha	57,662
Altenburg	54,999
Wittenberg	54,306
Eberswalde-Finow	53,473
Schwed/Oder	51,881
Suhl	51,731
Freiberg	51,290
Riesa	51,285
Eisenach	50,895
Bautzen	50,502
Eisenhüttenstadt	49,491
Merseburg/Saale	49,219
Pirna	48,253
Nordhausen	47,203
Halberstadt	47,115
Stendal	45,792
Freital	45,199
Schönebeck/Elbe	44,876
Zeitz	43,716
Mühlhausen	43,656
Wolfen	41,229
Bernburg/Saale	41,090
Zittau	40,554
Weissenfels	39,044
Gustrow	38,931
Meissen	38,710
Greiz	36,228
Wernigerode	36,166
Fürstenwalde/Spree	35,240
Radebeul	34,928
Kothen/Anhalt	34,728
Luckenwalde	27,039
Neustrelitz	27,028
Döbeln	26,751
Forst/Lausitz	26,709
Annaberg-Buchholz	26,514
Neuruppin	26,294
Meiningen	25,907
Strausberg	25,576
Crimmitschau	25,539
Reichenbach/Vogtl	25,446
Lauchhammer	24,438
Spremberg	24,166
Waren	24,101
Finsterwalde	24,082
Falkensee	23,794
Prenzlau	23,702
Sondershausen	23,667
Parchim	23,374
Sömmerda	23,251
Borna	23,221
Salzwedel	22,850
Limbach-Oberfrohna	22,573
Hettstedt	22,112
Bitterfeld	21,768
Eilenburg	21,724
Schneeberg	21,689
Meerane	21,677
Lübbenau/Spreewald	21,401
Torgau	21,291
Bad Salzungen	20,996
Wolgast	17,039
Schwarzenberg/Erzgeb	16,967
Genthin	16,910
Thale/Harz	16,605
Bad Langensalza	16,596
Radeberg	16,288
Heiligenstadt	16,110
Pasewalk	15,815
Sassnitz	14,813
Teltow	14,795
Grimmen	14,760
Zeulenroda	14,741
Leinefelde	14,686
Perleberg	14,538
Rosslau/Elbe	14,469
Lübben/Spreewald	14,209
Hagenow	14,208
Waltershausen	14,198
Torgelow	14,166
Bergen/Rügen	14,128
Calbe/Saale	14,091
Schkeuditz	14,010
Zella-Mehlis	14,008
Burgstädt	13,991
Bad Dürrenberg	13,951
Frankenberg	13,768
Ludwigslust	13,734
Oelsnitz	13,733
Wittstock	13,646
Templin	13,636
Oelsnitz/Erzgeb	13,554
Boizenburg/Elbe	12,059
Hildburghausen	12,049
Angermünde	11,877
Grevesmühlen	11,825
Tangermünde	11,814
Meuselwitz	11,796
Zehdenick	11,773
Grossräschen	11,736
Nauen	11,721
Teterow	11,695
Premnitz	11,623
Falkenstein/Vogtl	11,560
Zwönitz	11,503
Marienberg	11,473
Wilkau-Hasslau	11,426
Bad Freienwalde/Oder	11,143
Lugau/Erzgeb	11,040
Weida	10,907
Coswig/Anhalt	10,899
Werder/Havel	10,860
Neustadt/Oria	10,822
Hermsdorf	10,712
Elsterwerda	10,671
Aken/Elbe	10,651
Malchin	10,629
Bützow	10,610
Gröditz	10,585
Zschopau	10,555
Waldheim	10,540
Kyritz	10,197
Thalheim/Erzgeb	10,104

Source: *Statistisches Jahrbuch der DDR 1984*, Berlin: Staatsverlag der DDR, 1984, 12.

although it is possible to obtain low-interest credit loans, on which the landlord pays only .5 percent interest. But repair also is a problem because necessary parts and materials are very difficult to obtain. As late as 1971, per capita living space (79 feet) was one-fourth less than in the Federal Republic and the lowest among the European communist states.[8]

Construction began in the 1950s with the elimination of the worst destroyed houses and the rebuilding of those that were salvageable. The state began to rebuild its most important institutions and cultural monuments; Stattsoper Berlin and Zwinger Dresden were started at that time. Also begun during this period were the building of the industrial towns as well as the repair of major streets in the old cities. Traditional elements of the eighteenth and nineteenth centuries were used quite extensively in the renovation. In addition, a few new housing projects were completed in Berlin and in other important centers. During the sixties, the use of prefabricated materials increased. The housing projects that were built were generally considered monotonous and inadequate.

Throughout the GDR, there were serious complaints about the condition of the housing. The low birth rate was in part attributed to the poor living conditions. Furthermore, the regime was unable to sufficiently increase the mobility of its workforce because it was difficult to attract workers to an industrially developing area where the housing was poor. Many skilled workers refused to take on better jobs in exchange for poorer housing. The political leadership widely recognized that the condition of housing had a significance that reached far beyond living areas and working spaces to also affect identification with the country as well as with the political system. The location of housing and the living conditions in the area were considered important for motivating workers as well as for promoting a positive atmosphere in the work collective itself. Peter Voigt, head of the Sociology section at the Wilhelm Pieck University emphasizes this comprehensive aspect of territorial planning: "Whereas social planning within the place of work is aimed at increasing productivity at work, territorial social planning embraces the way of life of the collective as a whole."[9]

Under the Honecker administration, expenditures for housing doubled, and systematic goals and plans were established for the improvement of housing conditions in the GDR. The overall goal was to provide decent housing for all citizens by 1990 and to eliminate housing as a social problem in the GDR. The long-term housing program adopted by the Eighth Congress of the SED (Socialist Unity Party—Sozialistische Einheitspartei Deutschlands) in 1971 is considered the basis of its social policy. It is seen as fundamental to the further development of the material and spiritual-cultural life of the citizens and intimately connected with the development of all aspects of the quality of life. The objectives specified at the Eighth Party Congress with respect to housing were:

—to provide all families with an apartment
—to improve housing conditions, notably those of workers, cooperative farmers,

and large families, and to assist young couples in the procurement of housing
—to gradually eliminate the historically based social and regional differences in
housing conditions
—to provide neighborhoods with the necessary cultural and social facilities so
that more leisure time will be available for recreation and education.[10]

Much attention has been given to the technical and economical aspects of these
goals. At the Ninth Party Congress in 1976, housing received the highest social
priority. Plans were made to build or modernize 2.8 to 3 million apartments
between 1976 and 1990. From 1971 through 1982, 1,794,300 living units were
created. Of these, 1,207,100 were newly built; the remaining units were created
through renovation and modernization. It was anticipated that by 1980, 40 percent of the population would live in buildings that were newly constructed or
renovated, and by 1990, 10 out of approximately 17 million GDR citizens would
have their housing conditions improved.[11] These goals laid out at the Congress
were long prepared for; the construction industry had already been greatly expanded. Until 1980, building constituted 17 percent of the total investment of the
GDR.

Because of the desperate need for housing, the GDR has tried to construct apartments as quickly and as cheaply as possible. Already in 1960, 49 percent of apartments were industrially constructed with prefabricated parts. By 1974, the percentage of industrial housing rose to 84 percent and then to its present level of 96
percent, which compares with only 8 percent in the Federal Republic. The GDR
now produces its own prefabricated parts, and the time required to build an apartment has been enormously reduced. In the 1950s, workers took 2,000 hours to
complete an average housing unit; now the average has been lowered to 600 hours.

At the same time, architects, engineers, and planners have introduced many
other considerations that go far beyond giving each family a warm and comfortable apartment. Since 1966, with the reorganization of the Bauakademie der
DDR (Academy for Housing and City Planning), aesthetic principles were taken
more seriously into consideration, at first with attention to the centers of important cities and, after the death of Ulbricht, to the new residential quarters. Despite
economic constraints, architects are concerned with many of the same issues as
Western architects, and they want to construct good architectural forms while
developing a particular style that is expressive of East German society and of
local traditions. One interesting reaction from at least some GDR architects has
been the rejection of the postmodern architecture that has characterized much of
the new building in the West as well as in the GDR. While cherishing the past and
advocating the preservation of old buildings, architects also express concern
about simply turning back to historical elements instead of creating something
new.[12]

Thousands of scientists, technicians, architects, and planners are involved in
planning and construction. Aesthetic as well as social goals are discussed and

planned for, but economic considerations remain paramount. The architectural plans as well as the social arrangements of the new living quarters are compromised by the need for economic budgeting. From the point of view of the sociologists, construction can never become an end in itself but always has to be oriented to the living of the people and progress in the development of a "socialist way of life." The planners and architects are asked to establish the preconditions for a successful family life, for the equal participation of the women in society, for the education and socialization of the young, and for the care of the elderly and disabled.

New residential areas are designed with public or communal facilities and services. The building program typically includes plans for homes for the aged, clinics, markets, restaurants, pubs, and buildings for culture and recreation, libraries, youth clubs, sports facilities, and necessary services. However, new towns vary enormously in the realization of these plans, and in how the residents in the new living areas perceive the adequacy of public facilities and services. One Rostock architect indicated that for every 1,000 residents, the average goals are 108 school places, 76 kindergarten places (for children under 6), and 58 places in the nurseries (for children under 3). These figures necessarily vary from area to area. Sixty percent of the cost of an apartment is used for its construction, 18 percent for the public facilities, and 22 percent for traffic and other technical expenses.

Housing in the GDR is either built and administered by the state, by cooperatives (Genossenschaften), or it is privately owned. In the new developments of Rostock, the state owns 60 percent of the housing and the Genossenschaften 30–40 percent. Cooperative apartments receive state credit and subsidies by production enterprises but the members are expected to pay a large sum for the common stock, 1,500 marks for a room. The deposit goes into the stock and is at the cooperative's disposal. Some of the costs are paid for by actual participation in the construction of the housing by the future residents, and it is not infrequent for friends, colleagues, or students to lend a hand. While these time demands and the additional expense may be considered a disadvantage, members of the Genossenschaften are fairly certain of being able to move into their apartment in two to three years, and exert more control over such things as repairs than residents in state-owned housing. Workers can apply for low-interest loans for the required amount from their production enterprises; afterward, the rents are somewhat lower than in the state-owned apartments.

Private housing in the new residential quarters is primarily for families with many children, although workers responsible for construction as well as families with access to West German marks may also acquire their own small houses. The percentage of private, newly built houses is low compared to other East European countries: GDR—12 percent; Romania—20 percent; Poland—30 percent; Hungary—70 percent.[13] Possibilities for obtaining credit provisions (3.25 percent for loans) and material allocations for the private construction of new housing have increased. However, state expenditures for housing have also grown,[14] and at present the state sector is responsible for about two-thirds of all new housing reconstruction and renovation.

Urban planning has a complex structure. The Socialist Unity Party (SED) has developed general principles and guidelines for territorial and city planning in its programs of the Eighth and Ninth Party Congresses of 1971 and 1976 and it also maintains, at each level of organization, officials and committees concerned with housing and urban development. Operative planning and implementation, however, are in the jurisdiction of the state. Here we find a differentiation by time horizon (from five-year plans to long-term perspectives of up to thirty years), by economic branch (construction industry, transportation), and by territorial level (from city through district to the whole republic).

The longest-term plans, working with periods from fifteen to thirty years, concern general urban development, location of industry, supply of the area, and changes in transportation as they relate to perspectives on economic development. Long-term plans covering ten to fifteen years deal with shifts in industrial distribution and the broad articulation of demand and supply in different aspects of urban development. The plan to deal with the deficit in housing by 1990 belongs in this category. Finally there are the five-year plans that take the form of enacted law and which quite concretely determine what is to be produced in different areas and by whom.

The State Planning Commission is the central organ of the Council of Ministers for developing these plans. It cooperates, with respect to urban planning, with the relevant ministries of Construction and of Transportation. All three of these national bodies have also offices at the district and city levels. Thus, at the city level the Bureau for City Planning, the City Construction Office, and the Department of Energy, Transportation, and Mass Transit have to cooperate with each other. These lower-level offices are of considerable importance. Jiří Musil writes of the GDR:

> The long-range strategy for settlement development . . . differs somewhat in character . . . from the Czechoslovak, Polish, and Hungarian strategies. The concept for settlement developments is not drafted as a national physical plan but rather in the form of general principles and guidelines.[15]

Planning is increasingly based on research. The Institute of Geography and Geoecology at the Academy of Sciences does basic research, while the Research Station for Territorial Planning (Forschungsleitstelle für Territorialplanung), which is attached to the State Planning Commission, concerns itself with more applied research directly relevant for planning. The Institute for City Planning (Städtebau) and the Bauakademie der DDR contribute to the development of plan guidelines which the national organs give to the districts and cities. At the city level local research projects or specially commissioned studies by such institutes as the Hochschule für Architektur und Bauwesen in Weimar have some impact on detail planning. The operational planning is accomplished jointly by the construction firm (Wohnungsbaukombinat) and the Bureau for City Planning, which employs architects, engineers, and other specialists.

There are several alternative routes to take in order to obtain an apartment. Individuals may advertise in the newspapers, offering to exchange apartments with someone in another part of the city or with a family living in a different city altogether, or simply stating the need for an apartment. There are centers (Wohnungskommissionen) for apartment changes with lists of people who are moving out of their apartments and lists with requests from people needing housing. Most people are able to arrange for a new apartment at their place of work.

The actual provision of housing falls mainly into the competence of regional local councils which lay down the criteria by which apartments are allocated, according to the aforementioned principles established by the Eighth Party Congress (priorities include newly married couples, families with several children, workers needed in a particular enterprise). The Wohnungsamt decides which enterprises are allocated apartments and these apartments are then distributed by the trade union (Betriebsgewerkschaftsleitung BGL). The union leadership distributes old as well as new housing, which is administered by the Volkseigene Kommunale Wohnunsverwaltung. The cooperative apartments are distributed by the Arbeiterwohnungsbaugenossenschaften (AWG). Part of the payment involves participating in construction. Residents claim that they received their housing quicker and that the quality was somewhat better.

Despite the enormous number of new apartments, there remain many problems. Even if we exclude the condition of the older housing in the inner city, which is just beginning to be addressed, the location of the apartment is not always where it is most needed and the size of the apartment may be too small for its inhabitants. Nearly half of the apartments are one- and two-room flats, a flat containing a living room, bedroom, kitchen, and bathroom.

There are some characteristics of the population that present particular problems. As of 1981, 18.9 percent of population of the GDR (16,739) was under 15; 63 percent was of working age, and 18 percent were pensioners. The GDR has a high population of retired people compared to other developed countries. About 10 percent of the elderly continue to work for at least part of the work week. Nearly half of them live alone. Furthermore, due to the high divorce rate (about one in every three marriages ends in divorce)[16] there is a high percentage of one-parent families. Altogether, 3 million people—23.1 percent of the adult population over the age of 18—live on their own in the GDR.[17]

The construction of the new towns of Rostock

Primarily because of the development of new industries, the population has been increasing at the rate of about 5,000 inhabitants a year. About 17 percent of the

Figure 2. **The Town of Lütten Klein.**

Apartments (planned)	10,270
Apartments (existing as of 31 December 1980)	10,270
Residents (planned)	37,000
Residents/hectare	273
∅ m² floor space/apartment	50.0

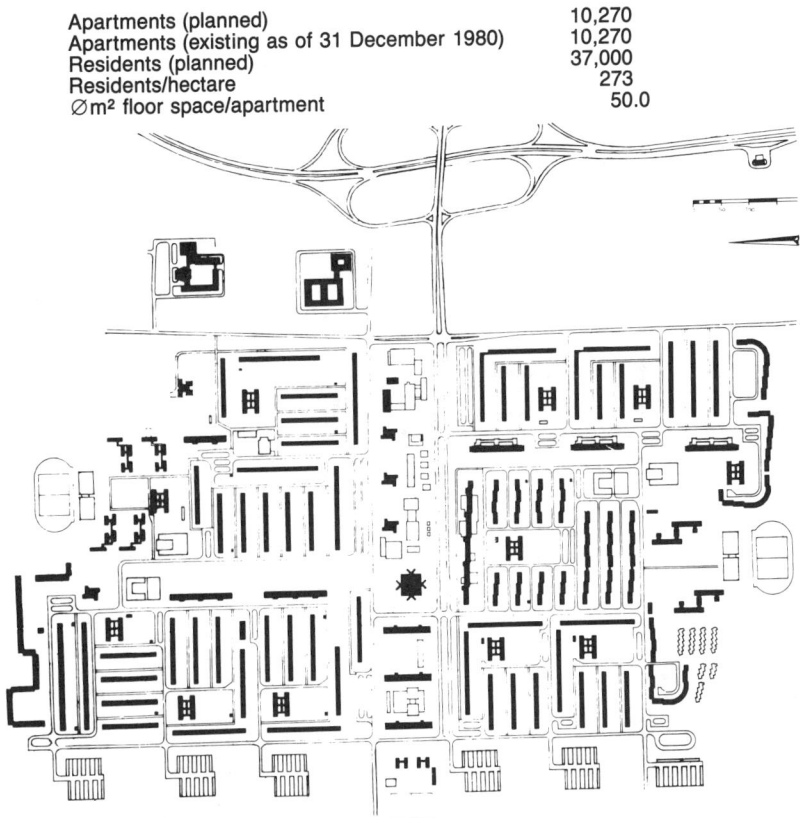

Source: Bauen im Ostseebezirk, 36.

population has lived in Rostock less than 15 years. If we look at the recent new towns of Schmarl and Lichtenhagen, 20 percent of the population has been in Rostock for 6 years or less. Many of those who come are between 18 and 40; they migrate from other areas of the GDR, frequently from cities in the south or from the countryside. In 1972, 41.6 percent of the population of Rostock was 25 or under (compared to 37 percent in the GDR); in the settlement of Lütten Klein, it was 48.9 percent. In the years from 1971–1981 Rostock ranked first in the growth of housing: Rostock—16.8 percent; Frankfurt/O.—12.1 percent; Berlin—11.8 percent; Erfurt—11.7 percent; Gera—11.1 percent; Schwerin—11.1 percent.[18]

The new towns in Rostock were designed as more than mere aggregates of apartments. There were careful plans regarding access to the main traffic routes, the kind and number of public institutions necessary (schools, clinics, etc.), retail

Figure 3. **The Town of Evershagen.**

Apartments (planned)	8,224
Apartments (existing as of 31 December 1980)	8,224
Residents (planned)	28,500
Residents/hectare	282
Øm² floor space/apartment	54.5

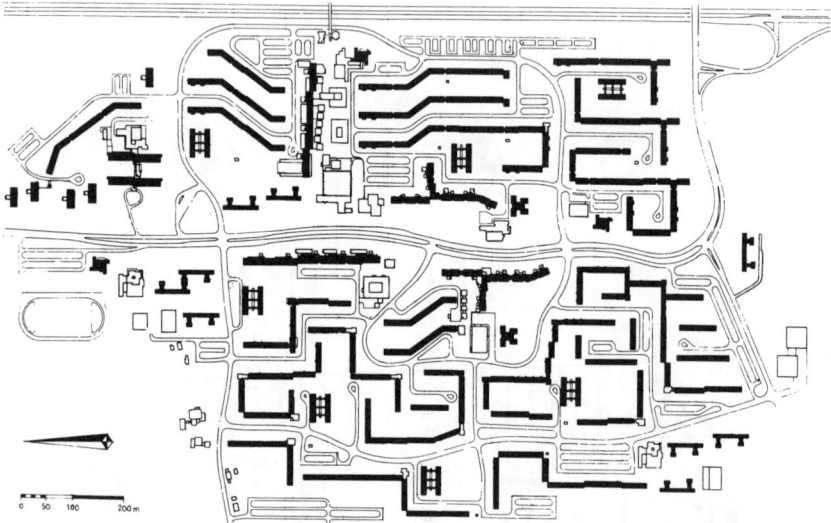

Source: *Bauen im Ostseebezirk*, 54.

and service shops, and spaces for recreation of all sorts. In the first phases of construction, only the most essential features were realized. Nevertheless, given the scarcity of apartments, many people were only too happy to finally have a private and comfortable place in which to live. Later, technological advances and a greater understanding of the needs of the population resulted in considerable modifications of the new towns.

As previously stated, the use of industrial material and parts and the necessary concentration of living functions resulted in similarity and monotony. Multistory blocks are prevalent in all the settlements. High-rise buildings are used to identify centers, underline green areas, and represent an orientation to the train stations.[20] Architectural variation seeks to give a distinctive character to the different town developments. While Lütten-Klein is characterized by typical block projects, in Evershagen a somewhat freer design application was used through the construction of segmental projects, completed in sequence, allowing new possibilities for adjusting the building plans (see Figures 2 and 3). The newer settlement designs included a kitchen with an outside view, a partial separation of toilet and bath, an eating place in the kitchen, and a wind-protected balcony inset (loggia). Evershagen represents a more court-forming, meandering-like design. Lichtenhagen

Figure 4. **The Town of Lichtenhagen.**

Apartments (planned)	6,611
Apartments (existing as of 31 December 1980)	6,324
Residents (planned)	22,350
Residents/hectare	264
∅m² floor space/apartment	54.0

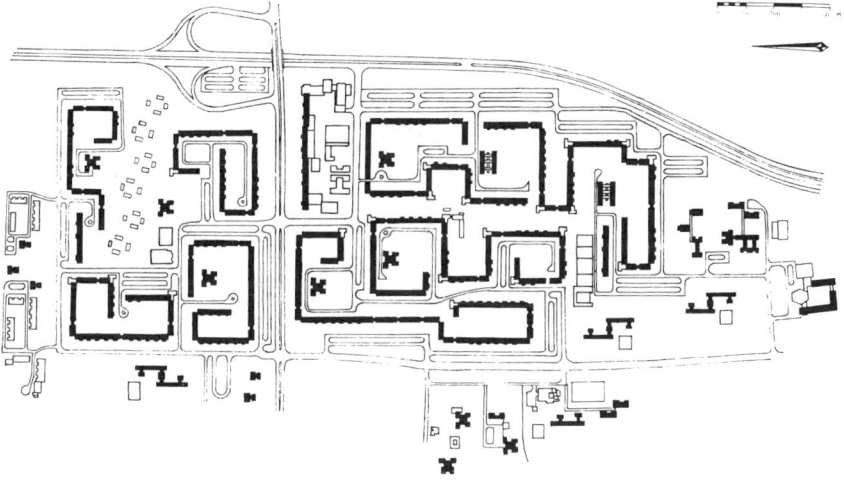

Source: *Bauen im Ostseebezirk*, 72.

(Figure 4) constitutes a large space with a closed rambling structure with cars parked outside. Schmarl (Figure 5) closes itself to the outside and to the characteristic winds through large-scale rounded blocks. There are also attempts to relate the new towns to the nonurban environment—provision of easy access to the harbor, fruit orchards, or to a nearby village or restaurant in a more traditional style. Lütten Klein and Evershagen, for instance, share a little restaurant, Fischerdorf. The hope is to avoid having the residents completely enveloped by an environment of cement. Still, the overwhelming impression is not one of an intimate, warm living quarter; even with only 28,500 residents in Evershagen or 17,568 in Schmarl, it takes quite a while to walk away from the buildings themselves. Of course, compared to Marzahn, one of the satellite cities outside of Berlin, with a population of 150,000, the housing developments in Rostock appear less formidable. The little village near the Marzahn development is completely dwarfed by the huge residential complex.

Aside from the differences in the architectural form of the new towns, each Neubaugebiet usually includes some special public institution which is shared by one or more towns—such as a large gymnasium, swimming pool, a polytechnical school, a home for the aged, or a medical clinic. The shopping complexes also vary in kind as well as adequacy. Each new residential area that is built is

Figure 5. **The Town of Schmarl.**

Apartments (planned)	5,352
Apartments (existing as of 31 December 1980)	4,356
Residents (planned)	17,568
Residents/hectare	262
Ø m² floor space/apartment	57.1

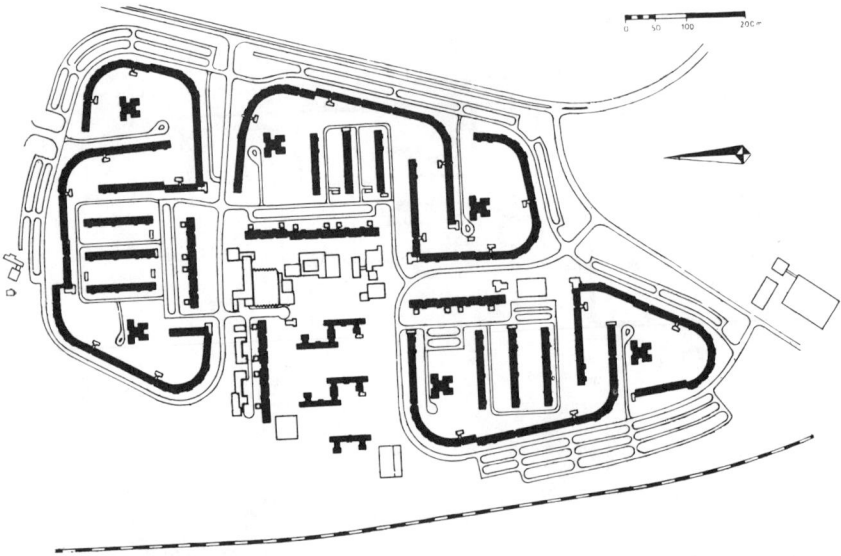

Source: *Bauen im Ostseebezirk*, 90.

purposefully arranged differently, and the social services that are introduced as well as the changes in spatial arrangement stem at least in part from the difficulties encountered in older settlements. For example, parents in many of the older high-rise apartments were neither able to see their children in the little playgrounds nor call to them from their apartments. Consequently, the newer residential areas were built with a larger number of smaller (though still five- and six-storied) apartment houses. Furthermore, since children were frequently unable to find their way back to their apartment because the houses were so similar, within the settlements themselves the entrances had to be painted with different colors.[21] In the newer settlements, increasing differences in the design of the facades were introduced (Figure 6). The smaller apartment houses were to facilitate neighborly relationships. Schmarl has several little park areas, some with concrete ping pong tables, a response to the need for intimacy and for activities for young people. The more rounded buildings were intended to create a more communal and intimate atmosphere as well. It was anticipated that the provision of land adjacent to the residential areas for small family gardens and tiny bungalows would

Figure 6. **Facade with Traditional Brickwork.**

Source: *Bauen im Ostseebezirk*, 97.

increase the satisfaction of many residents with their new living quarters.

More debate greeted the reaction of the Kombinat to changing demographic conditions in the GDR. With an increase in divorce, more 1½ room apartments were planned, for example, in Dierkow an increase from 18 percent to 28 percent. (Another reason for this increase may be the crude incentive system by which the building firm receives premiums for the number of apartments constructed, independent of apartment size.) Sociologists strongly advocated anticipating the use of a stable mix of apartments with a changing population, just as public institutions can be used differently during the history of a residential area. After a few years there may be less need for schoolrooms and they then could be converted to club spaces or eventually for use by an increasing older population. Sociologists advocated providing space from the beginning for a mixture of age groups and family sizes as well as functions.

Sociologists and city planners both in Rostock and in the Hochschule für Architektur und Bauwesen in Weimar have been involved in a number of studies of Rostock's new living quarters. Using information from the research done in the GDR together with my own interviews has made it possible to gain some understanding of the reactions of the residents to the new residential areas as well as of the social relationships and supports that have developed over the years.

An unofficial estimate is that a quarter of the population of Rostock's new residential areas would like to live elsewhere. Part of the dissatisfaction stems from the small size of apartments and the inadequate number of rooms; indeed those who are crowded plan to move out of their apartments as soon as they are able. At present, five out of eight households with more than three people live in two- and three-room apartments.[22] Many of the young couples with children dream of a one-family house of their own. Still others who are uncomfortable in their new surroundings are unused to an urban life-style; having migrated from the countryside, they experience difficulty adjusting to a more anonymous and built-up environment. While the inhabitants of the new living areas acknowledge the housing shortage and appreciate the innovations and responses of the architects and city planners (for example, the differences in the form and facade of Schmarl or the Lichtenhagen Brink, a gardened mall, as a center of activity), nevertheless they complain that despite their increased comfort and despite the innovations, the environment of the residential quarters is monotonous. They are further away from the center of the city than they had anticipated, and within the new towns there are neither enough cultural activities nor sports' opportunities for their families. There are few cafes and little restaurants to make their town warm, inviting, and an interesting place to be. Of course, despite a tendency for a predominance of younger couples and single parents with children in each new settlement, the inhabitants of the new towns are at different life stages and social levels so that their dissatisfactions and complaints vary. The higher the occupational qualification of the inhabitant, for example, the greater the expectations are for the quality of life in the residences.

Approximately a third of the population of the new towns travels 45 minutes or more to work, longer than originally anticipated. Even for the 38 percent of the residents who arrive at work in 30 minutes or less,[23] the ride is typically on overcrowded streetcars that are difficult to negotiate during work hours, and that along with trains come too infrequently (although the situation has improved in the past two years). Although 50 percent of the residents of the new towns own cars, not everyone is able to drive to work; husbands and wives may have completely different schedules.

Women, especially, may decide to take work that is below their level of qualification in order to remain closer to their apartment and to the nurseries or kindergartens of their children. At present, about a third of the residents travel to the inner city for work and 18 percent work in the residential area itself. As the local services increase in number, it is expected that even more will seek employment within the residential area. Ironically, when a study of Lütten Klein and Evershagen was done in 1974, there were women trained to work in the services, in tailoring for example, who were not doing so and were even unemployed. One reason was that much of the work was defined traditionally as women's work, neither well respected nor well paid.[24] Thirty-five percent of the women interviewed in that study were working at jobs that did not correspond to their training. University-trained women, more than others, were willing to travel longer to do work that was appropriate to their qualifications.[25]

The dispersion of many specialized shops all over the city forces men and women to do considerable traveling to buy what they need for their wardrobe or their home. Despite complaints over the years from the residents of Evershagen, for example, and the empty space already allocated for small shops at a central crossing, the shops are not being constructed. Where they are introduced as part of a newly built town, the residents express more satisfaction with their housing arrangements. At the same time, food shopping for everyday needs is easier in the residential areas than in many parts of the inner city because of the number of markets in the towns, and most of the people do their shopping there in the afternoon, after work. Especially coveted items, fresh fruits for example, may not be found in the local market and so it is not unusual for someone to be seen traveling with an enormous bunch of bananas to distribute to friends and colleagues. Within recent years, there has been an expansion of nurseries and private gardens to meet the demands of residents for fruit and flowers.

The construction of the new towns was to involve more than giving GDR citizens an apartment and necessary services; ideally, the social relations in the new settlements and the active involvement of the residents should lead to a socialist way of life. In the new towns around Rostock, less attention has been devoted to these aspects of the community than to its physical construction. Such national organizations as the Democratic Women's League (Demokratischer Frauensbund Deutschlands) and the People's Solidarity Movement (Volkssolidarität) maintain some activities in the new residential areas, but the degree of involvement and influence varies from town to town and especially within any particular area with age and social level. The Democratic Women's League plans some role in advising local councils and planners on the needs of women and may act as a pressure group under certain conditions, relocating a playground, for example, or having the hours of local shops arranged so that women on shift work have access to them. Most recently, a new ramp in Evershagen was constructed so that parents can more easily get their baby carriages to the train. Volunteers of Volkssolidarität visit the elderly regularly, delivering meals and doing small errands; many of the active workers are themselves retired.

Families in the new towns as well as in the inner city's apartment houses are organized into Hausgemeinschaften (house organizations) and send representatives to the leadership board of the residential area. The ideal house organization comprises no more than twelve families and contains a mixture of apartment sizes to encourage mutual help among people of different ages.[26] The functions of the organization are to ensure that order and cleanliness prevail, to care for repairs, and to organize social activities. The success of these Hausgemeinschaften varies enormously; when people are from very different social backgrounds, when they do not adhere to the apartment houses' standards of cleanliness and orderliness, when there is a lack of leadership due to families being involved in shift work or sea travel, or when the Gemeinschaft is not well defined, the residents may come together primarily to decide on necessary repairs or to take care of any emergency that may arise in the apartment house. The Hausgemeinschaft receives money from the city administration for repairs. When responses to complaints from the residents take a long time to be resolved, when money for repairs is not forthcoming, when equipment parts are nearly impossible to acquire, people become discouraged, less active in the Hausgemeinschaft, and less willing to respond to campaigns to clean up, make repairs, or care for the grounds. At the same time, at least in the new towns I observed, the hallways were undamaged, and at least in moderately good condition. Once a year at least the Oberbürgermeister (mayor) or city deputies come and a "town meeting" is held which many of the residents attend. The city administration also has a permanent office in each Neubaugebiet.

From the observations of the sociologists involved in the study of city life, it became clear that there was more individual activity and mutual support than indicated by the statistics of the Hausgemeinschaft leadership or the district committees of the National Front (Wohnbezirkausschusse).[27] People in the apartment buildings establish standards and norms for behavior and security, as well as for the common care of the house. Among the residents, researchers found a great deal of informal mutual support and neighborliness, which was not defined as close friendship except for a minority of residents. In a study of Marzahn, the large residential town built on the outskirts of Berlin, sociologists observed an interesting change in social patterns which also seems to apply to Rostock. Generally, as in the United States, workers spend their free time primarily with relatives, and to a lesser extent with friends; among professionals, this tendency is reversed. Third on the list of both groups were colleagues at work, and last were neighbors in the house. After some time in the Neubaugebiet, more and more people turned to their neighbors, who were then ranked third on their list, followed by work colleagues. The explanation given was that it was complicated to travel to meet people after a long day's work. Some neighborliness develops very quickly. Residents were asked if they had neighbors they would trust with their keys. Of those who lived in Marzahn less than three years, 90 percent of the respondents had at least one other family they would trust with their keys; 50 percent of those interviewed felt comfortable enough with five or six families to give them their keys.

With time, the inhabitants of the new towns are generally more satisfied with their residences. It takes a while to develop a community; many of the residents in Rostock's new towns have only lived in the city for a few years. Friendships in Lütten Klein, one of the older settlements, are stronger than in other towns. At the same time, in the newer settlements, more often both parents are at work and the children are educated in nurseries and kindergartens. There is little that people share to bring them together beyond the minimal participation needed to keep the housing in good repair and an occasional common celebration. Where several work colleagues live in a house together, there is more the residents can share, though they are not necessarily intensely involved with each other after work. Generally, the researchers believe that the kind of participation that exists in successful work collectives is in its infancy in the residences and that people are not involved in a way that is comparable with their involvement in the workplace.

Niederländer suggests that the reason people are not involved in their residential communities has less to do with their desire to retreat from the outside world than with the lack of opportunities to engage in social activities.[28] In a research project on the new towns in the GDR, workers indicated that little free time after work is spent in the residential area itself (outside of the private apartment), and that during the weekend the communities are deserted, with the exception of very few of the new towns. Warnemünde, the seaside resort, is an easy ride, even with public transportation. Workers and employees at different levels and in different cities in the GDR indicated the following preferred activities: television—73 percent; work in house and garden—56 percent; sports, hiking, walking—52 percent; reading—47 percent; meeting friends and acquaintances—44 percent.[29] Fewer respondents expressed interest in hobbies, going to the theater, concerts or films, and artistic activity. Most of the preferred activities reflect a strong desire for privacy.

In a study of different areas of Rostock, residents interviewed in the new towns were asked where they typically spent their time after work: 62 percent were in their apartments, 8 percent remained in the residential area itself, and 30 percent left the residential area altogether. During the weekend, 11 percent were in their apartments, 7 percent remained in the residential area itself, and 82 percent left the residential area altogether.[30] Several of my respondents indicated that there was little need to become involved in the towns, that they could easily drive to the city to see friends, that they had activities with colleagues at work or afterward, and that they looked forward to the privacy of their own homes. Nearly three-quarters of the residents between 25 and 55 want a garden of their own. Though in 1983 only a quarter of the families had their own garden (either on land adjacent to the town or some distance away), a standing joke in the GDR is that there are more dachas than mushrooms. These include little, very simple country houses as well as one-room structures in the garden itself. Studies indicate that a garden considerably increases the satisfaction of the residents and relieves in part the yearning for a private house.[31] It is interesting to observe that people prefer their own private gardens, and in one study of Rostock's new towns the residents were not enthusiastic about sharing a garden with other tenants directly adjacent to the apartment house. There were several reasons for their response; two primary ones were the desire to leave the residential area and the wish to have private time, unobserved by others.

Even those who look forward to the privacy of the apartment and garden would like to increase the possibilities for more family activities in the residential area. Activities are primarily geared to families with young children, and the organization of the few that exist may be poor. In Schmarl, for example, the cinema program begins between seven and eight, a very difficult time for parents with young children. At the same time, there are an impressive number of playgrounds for little children, and in Schmarl, the concrete ping pong tables are used by the older ones as well.

The lack of opportunities is especially problematic for the elderly, most of whom do not own cars and are not able to travel on crowded streetcars. During the weekends, they tend to remain in the residential area, though they too express the wish to leave to visit friends, etc. One elderly man complained that they were promised a cinema for their residential community for years but that he still had to travel "to visit the mistress in order to see a film." The problems of loneliness are acute for many of the elderly. They would like to live within walking distance of their children, but it seems that a number of tiny apartments interspersed with larger ones that were reserved for them have been given to families. Although there are a few homes for the retired and elderly in the residential areas, both a better age mix and an increased variety of housing were recommended by planners. One architect maintained that it was impossible to take for granted one housing preference for the elderly—some prefer quiet living spaces, while others find it important to be near a train station; some very much enjoy living near young children while others prefer to be surrounded by people their own age.

Single parents with children, and these tend to be mostly women, also have difficulties with social isolation in the new towns. In the GDR as a whole, a third of the births are to unmarried mothers. Since the divorce rate is also high, families headed by women are further increased in number. Such women have special social supports; indeed when there is housing available, their needs have priority. At the same time, if they work far away from their residential community, it is not easy to return quickly if they have to, and it is difficult to leave the children at night and travel into the city. Parents do support each other with baby-sitting and other forms of help, but many expressed a desire for more clubs and cafes in the residential quarters, more activities, and more possibilities for meeting other adults.

Perhaps the group that is considered the greatest problem, and the least catered to in the new towns, are young people under 25 who have not yet embarked on a life of their own, either personally or professionally. In a GDR film, "The Island of Swans," a fourteen-year-old from the countryside living in one of the new residential areas on the outskirts of Berlin had great difficulty adjusting to his new environment. The youngsters in the town left a note on their community bulletin board announcing that they have had enough of cement! The film was strongly criticized by the Party and the Free German Youth newsletter, though even the Party itself at times has leveled accusations at the quality of the projects.

Everyone seems to agree that the young people need much more to do in the new towns, more clubs and cafes, increased sports facilities, perhaps working spaces where they can increase their skills while repairing bicycles, record players, etc. Sometimes, they are paid to work on the grounds or on the care of the apartment house but their activities for the most part are in their apartments or outside their residences, away from the town. They like to go dancing or hang out in places where they can talk; they enjoy the movies and beer drinking; they like to be with their friends. While over 80 percent of the retired people in the new towns preferred their free-time activities to take place in their residence, almost 50 percent of the young preferred these activities outside the community.[32]

Only 10 percent of the young workers in a study done in Rostock indicated that the Free German Youth leadership concerned itself with the leisure time of the youngsters in the town and only 4.9 percent indicated that the National Front was concerned; only 6.8 percent believed the enterprise showed concern. More than half of the youngsters did not conceive of the possibility of spending time in their residences in an interesting and stimulating way.[33] Researchers in Berlin found tensions among some of the families because property, destroyed supposedly by youths, took so long to repair that the condition of the housing deteriorated. People were reluctant to criticize each other because they were uncertain of who was actually at fault. Young people are seen as not having the same attitudes as their parents; they are not as orderly and they typically are not interested in the lectures and activities at their school or youth organization. Since young people represent, at least during a certain stage of the history of a new town, a large percentage of the population, the lack of activities and the response of the youngsters is seen as a severe problem.

Conclusion

It is difficult at this time to evaluate the success or failure of the new towns of the GDR. They were a response to complaints about the lack of housing and about the miserable conditions of the existing housing stock. Typically, each succeeding town contains some elements that are a response to previous difficulties and in turn, with time, reveal new issues that have to be addressed.

Needs vary according to age, stage of life, occupation, etc., and with limited resources and differences over where these resources should be channeled, it is difficult to meet all these demands. In a comparative study of the older parts of cities and new residential quarters, people living in the older quarters were still found to complain about the condition of the housing while leisure time activities, the distance to work, and difficult access to the shops and other public institutions of the inner city were complaints from those living in the new residential quarters.[34] GDR research on Rostock's residential areas and my own work confirmed these differences. Overall satisfaction with the new residential quarters of Rostock is greater than in some of the other new developments in the GDR. In part, this is due to the access to the sea and somewhat more innovative construction.

City officials, architects, construction firms, and different resident groups view the towns from varying perspectives. However, since over 60 percent of Rostock's population lives in the new residential quarters, many of the officials, architects, and planners live there themselves. Administrators consider maintaining a relatively contented population as crucial not only for the relations in the community itself, but for continuity in the process of production.

The varying reactions to the new towns are not simply determined by the architecture of the settlements. Rather, the architecture and the overall design are one important element in the lives of the inhabitants whose world is equally shaped by the settlement's relation to the city, workplace, and essential services— and the ease of transportation to these, by the structure of political life and its concomitant political culture, by work organization and work satisfaction (or lack thereof), and by the ability to realize family and personal goals. The role the settlements play in this broader social constellation provides a critical dimension for our understanding of the quality of life in the GDR.

Notes

The author is very grateful to the Joint Committee on Eastern Europe of the American Council of Learned Societies and the Social Science Research Council, financed in part by the National Endowment for the Humanities and the Ford Foundation, which supported her with a research grant during the preparation of part of this study, as well as to the sociologists at the Wilhelm Pieck University, Rostock, for their help with this project. She also wants to thank Duncan Smith, director of the exchange program between Brown University and the University of Rostock, for his continuing support and encouragement of her work. Dietrich Rueschemeyer's comments on this chapter are very much appreciated.

1. Jiří Musil, *Urbanization in Socialist Countries* (New York: M.E. Sharpe, 1980), 100.

2. Phillip Bryson, "The Quality of Socialist Life in the GDR" (paper presented to the Wingspread Conference, "The German Democratic Republic in Comparative Perspective," Racine, Wisconsin, 1983), 10.

3. Musil, 103–4.

4. Jutta Gysi and Wulfram Speigner, "Changes in the Life Patterns of Families in the

German Democratic Republic," (Academy of Sciences of the GDR in Institute of Sociology and Social Policy, Berlin [East], 1983), 41.

5. C. Bradley Scharf, *Politics and Change in East Germany* (Boulder, Colorado: Westview Press, 1984), 112.

6. Manfred Melzer, "Bau- und Wohnungswesen," in *DDR Handbuch*, ed. Hartmut Zimmermann, Horst Ulrich, and Michael Fehlauer (Köln: Verlag Wissenschaft und Politik, 1985), 156.

7. *Statistiches Jahrbuch der DDR 1984* (Berlin: Staatsverlag der DDR, 1984), 170.

8. Scharf, 112

9. Peter Voigt, "Zu einigen konzeptionellen Aspekten in der territorialen Sozialplanung" (Wissenschaftliche Zeitschrift der Universitat Rostock—22 Jahrgang, 1973), Heft 7, 625.

10. Gysi and Speigner, 41.

11. Melzer, 157.

12. "Architektur der DDR," *DDR Report* (10/84) (Bonn: 17 Jahrgang), 623.

13. For a further discussion of estimates, see "Rolf Linke: Eigenheimbau-internationale Einschätzungen, Vergleiche und Tendenzen," *DDR Report*, vol. 18, 1/85: 51.

14. Scharf, 114.

15. Musil, 105.

16. Gysi and Speigner, 93.

17. Alice Kahl and Steffi Riedel, "Wohnverhältnisse, Wohnweise und Wohnverhalten in der sozialistischen Grossstadt," *Jahrbuch für Soziologie und Socialpolitik* (Berlin: Akademie Verlag, 1985), 152.

18. Ibid., 41.

19. G. Beier, "Zu einigen sozialen Problemen der Entwicklung von Jugendlichen in städtischen Neubaugebieten und sich daraus ergebenden Konsequenzen fur die territoriale Sozialplanung," *Leitung und Planung Sozialer Prozesse im Territorium*, Part 1 (Rostock: Wilhelm Pieck Universität, 1975), 71.

20. *Bauen im Ostseebezirk* (Rat des Bezirkes Rostock, Bezirksbauamt, 1982), Band 7, 14.

21. For a more detailed architectural description of the new towns, see Derek Bradford and Marilyn Rueschemeyer, "The New Towns Around Rostock: Housing as Political Policy in the German Democratic Republic," *The Journal of Architectural and Planning Research* (forthcoming).

22. Fred Staufenbiel et al., *Soziologische Untersuchung von Wohngebieten der Stadt Rostock* (Weimar: Hochschule für Architektur und Bauwesen, 1983), 22.

23. Ibid., 36.

24. M. Wiesener, "Zu einigen Problemen des Einflusses hauswirtschaftlicher Dienstleistungen auf die Entwicklung der sozialistischen Lebenweise," *Leitung und Planung Sozialer Prozesse im Territorium* Part 1 (Rostock: Wilhelm Pieck Universität, 1975), 63.

25. S. Hinz, "Zu einigen mit der Wege-Zeit-Beziehung zwischen Wohnung und Arbeitsplatz verbundenen Problemen unter dem Gesichtspunkt der Teilzeitbeschäftigung der Frau," *Leitung und Planung Sozialer Prozesse im Territorium* Part 1 (Rostock: Wilhelm Pieck Universität, 1975), 32.

26. Staufenbiel, 130.

27. Kahl and Riedel, 150.

28. Loni Niederländer, *Arbeiten und Wohnen in der Stadt* (Berlin: Dietz Verlag, 1984), 72–74.

29. Helmut Hanke, *Freizeit in der DDR* (Berlin: Dietz Verlag, 1979), 75.

30. Staufenbiel, 38.

31. Ibid., 137.

32. Ibid., 39.

33. M. Klohr, "Entwicklung und Befriedigung der geistig-kulturellen Bedürfnisse junger Arbeiter als Objekt der Sozialplanung," *Leitung und Planung Sozialer Prozesse im Territorium* Part 1 (Rostock: Wilhelm Pieck Universität, 1975), 104–5.

34. Rolf Kuhn, "Vergleichende stadtsoziologischer Analyse von Alt- und Neubau Wohngebieten in Karl-Marx-Stadt und Erfurt," *HAB Informationen* (Hochschule für Architektur und Bauwesen Weimar, 1984), Sonderreihe Soziologie, 6.

References

"Architektur der DDR." *DDR Report.* Bonn: 17 Jahrgang, October 1984.

Bauen im Ostseebezirk. Rat des Bezirkes Rostock, Bezirksbauamt, Band 7, 1982.

Beier, G. "Zu einigen sozialen Problemen der Entwicklung von Jugendlichen in städtischen Neubaugebieten und sich daraus ergebenden Konsequenzen für die territoriale Sozialplanung." In part 1 of *Leitung und Planung Sozialer Prozesse im Territorium.* Rostock: Wilhelm Pieck Universität, 1975.

Bryson, Phillip. "The Quality of Socialist Life in the GDR." Paper presented to the Wingspread Conference on "The German Democratic Republic in Comparative Perspective," Racine, Wisconsin, 1983.

Grundman, Siegfried. *Das Territorium Gegenstand Soziologischer Forschung.* Berlin: Dietz Verlag, 1981.

Gysi, Jutta and Wulfram Speigner. "Changes in the Life Patterns of Families in the German Democratic Republic." Academy of Sciences of the GDR in Institute of Sociology and Social Policy, Berlin (East), 1983.

Habermas, Jürgen. *Theorie des Kommunikativen Handelns.* Frankfurt: Suhrkamp, 1981.

Hanke, Helmut. *Freizeit in der DDR.* Berlin: Dietz Verlag, 1979.

Hinz, S. "Zu einigen mit der Wege-Zeit-Beziehung zwischen Wohnung und Arbeitsplatz verbundenen Problemen unter dem Gesichtspunkt der Teilzeitbeschäftigung der Frau." In part 1 of *Leitung und Planung Sozialer Prozess im Territorium.* Rostock: Wilhelm Pieck Universität, 1975.

Kahl, Alice and Steffi Riedel. "Wohnverhältnisse, Wohnweise und Wohnverhalten in der socialistischen Grossstadt." In *Jahrbuch für Sociologie und Sozialpolitik*, 136–52. Berlin: Academie Verlag, 1985.

Kuhn, Rolf. "Lösung der Wohnungsfrage als soziales Problem in ihrem Einfluss auf Lebensweise und Stadtgestaltung," HAB dissertation, 1985.

Kuhn, Rolf. "Vergleichende stadtsoziologischer Analyse von Alt und Neubau Wohngebieten in Karl-Marx-Stadt und Erfurt." *HAB Informationen.* Hochschule für Architektur und Bauwesen Weimar, 1984. Sonderreihe Soziologie.

Leptin, Gert and Manfred Melzer. *Economic Reform in East German Industry.* Oxford: Oxford University Press, 1978.

Melzer, Manfred. "Bau- und Wohnungswesen." In *DDR Handbuch,* ed. Hartmut Zimmermann, Horst Ulrich, and Michael Fehlauer, 152–60. Köln: Verlag Wissenschaft und Politik, 1985.

Musil, Jiří. *Urbanization in Socialist Countries.* New York: M. E. Sharpe, 1980.

Niederländer, Loni. *Arbeiten und Wohnen in der Stadt.* Berlin: Dietz Verlag, 1984.

Rueschemeyer, Marilyn. "Integrating Work and Personal Life. An Analysis of Three Professional Work Collectives in the German Democratic Republic." *GDR Monitor,* no. 8 (Winter 1982/83).

Rueschemeyer, Marilyn. *Professional Work and Marriage: An East-West Comparison.* London: Macmillan & Co.; New York, St. Martin's Press, 1981.

Rueschemeyer, Marilyn and Bradley Scharf. "Labor Unions in the German Democratic Republic." In *Trade Unions in Communist States,* ed. Alex Pravda and Blair Ruble.

London and Boston: Allen and Unwin, 1986, 53–84.

Scharf, C. Bradley. *Politics and Change in East Germany.* Boulder, Colorado: Westview Press, 1984.

Staemmler, Gerlind. "East Germany." In *Housing in Europe,* ed. Martin Wynn. London: Croom Helm; New York, St. Martin's Press, 1984.

Statistiches Jahrbuch der DDR 1984. Berlin: Staatsverlag der DDR, 1984.

Staufenbiel, Fred et al. *Soziologische Untersuchung von Wohngebieten der Stadt Rostock.* Weimar: Hochschule für Architektur und Bauwesen, 1983.

Staufenbiel, Fred et al. *Stadtentwicklung und Wohnmilieu: Halle/S., Halle-Neustadt.* Weimar: Hochschule für Architektur und Bauwesen, 1985.

Voigt, Peter. "Zu einigen konzeptionellen Aspekten in der territorialen Sozialplannung." *Wissenschaftliche Zeitschrift der Universität Rostock.* XXII Jahrgang, Heft 7, 1973.

von Beyme, Klaus and Hartmut Zimmerman, eds. *Policymaking in the German Democratic Republic.* New York: St. Martin's Press, 1984.

Weber, Hans. *Einzug ins Paradies.* Berlin: Verlag Neues Leben, 1979.

Wiesener, M. "Zu einigen Problemen des Einflusses hauswirtschaftlicher Dienstleistungen auf die Entwicklung der sozialistischen Lebenweise." In part 1 of *Leitung und Planung Sozialer Prozesse im Territorium.* Rostock: Wilhelm Pieck Universität, 1975.

Wynn, Martin. *Housing in Europe.* New York: St. Martin's Press, 1984.

Zimmermann, Hartmut, Horst Ulrich, and Michael Fehlauer, eds. *DDR Handbuch.* Köln: Verlag Wissenschaft und Politik, 1985.

"The Future Has Already Begun"

Environmental Damage and Protection in the GDR

Joan DeBardeleben

On ten days during January and February 1987, the authorities in West Berlin issued "smog warnings" or "smog alarms."[1] In the surrounding GDR, East German citizens also learned of the extreme air pollution levels from West Berlin broadcasts; the GDR authorities remained silent, explaining the unusual atmospheric conditions with forecasts of foggy weather. On these days, an estimated 80 percent of the sulfur dioxide (SO_2), a major component of West Berlin's smog, originated in the GDR. (Under normal conditions West Berlin "imports" an estimated 45 percent of its SO_2 pollution and two-thirds of its dust pollution.)[2] Some days in Berlin one smells the bad air; on other smoggy days the air seems surprisingly fresh, as some harmful pollutants are hard to detect without appropriate air quality control equipment. In the highly industrialized southern regions of the GDR, residents know that the air is polluted: they see the dust on their laundry and smell it in the air.

Only by arduous scrutiny of GDR scientific publications can one begin to garner enough information to roughly assess pollution levels in East Germany. The popular press assures the public about continued progress in overcoming the few deficiencies. On November 16, 1982, the Ministerrat adopted an official "Order for Ensuring the Secrecy [*Geheimschutzes*] of Environmental Data."[3]

The author wishes to thank McGill University, the International Research and Exchanges Board, and the Canadian Social Sciences and Humanities Research Council for support in carrying out this research.

The order itself was never publicized, but its effects on public information policy are obvious to any concerned citizen. Virtually no information is published on actual pollution levels, except for occasional indirect references in scientific sources.

Despite official reassurance, public awareness is growing in the GDR, although its extent is only a matter of speculation. The nuclear accident at Chernobyl in the USSR in April 1986 gave an additional impetus to the growing popular concern. By 1986 some 60,000 GDR citizens were members of the officially sponsored Society for Nature and Environment and at least several hundred were active in the more challenging unofficial environmental groups connected to the GDR Evangelical Church. In recent years these unofficial groups have held "environmental worship services" in heavily polluted areas, such as the small town of Möblis some 20 kilometers south of Leipzig.[4] The motto "In Möblis the future has already begun" provides a warning—if more isn't done now, the future will look as grey and smell as foul as towns like Möblis do now.

The problems

The GDR citizen suffers the effects of numerous kinds of environmental damage, but controls on public information prevent awareness of the dimensions and implications. Although people complain about the bad air, environmental deterioration may not be a major source of discontent, for its effects and scope are often hidden. Nonetheless, the hazards to health and well-being are very real.

Brown coal

Air pollution is the most serious, pervasive environmental problem in the GDR. The major source of air pollution is the burning of the GDR's domestic brown coal for heat and energy. The coal, while varying from area to area, has high sulfur and ash content, and therefore produces high sulfur dioxide and dust emissions.

Brown coal is the GDR's only significant energy resource, other than uranium ore which can be processed for use as fuel for nuclear reactors. In the early 1980s, GDR leaders increased reliance on domestic brown coal as the primary energy source, reversing the shift of the 1970s to imported oil. Confronted by rising foreign debt and oil prices in the late 1970s, import of fuel seemed increasingly untenable. Beginning in 1975, imports of Soviet oil above negotiated annual quotas had to be paid for in hard currency, and in 1982 these quotas were reduced by about 10 percent. Since that time Soviet oil imports have stabilized at around 17 million tons and gas imports at just over 6 million tons annually. Much of the oil is, however, utilized in the petrochemical industry, not as fuel. By 1985, 82.7 percent of electrical energy production was based on brown coal.[5] The increased

Map 1. **Levels of SO₂ Emissions in the GDR, 1982**

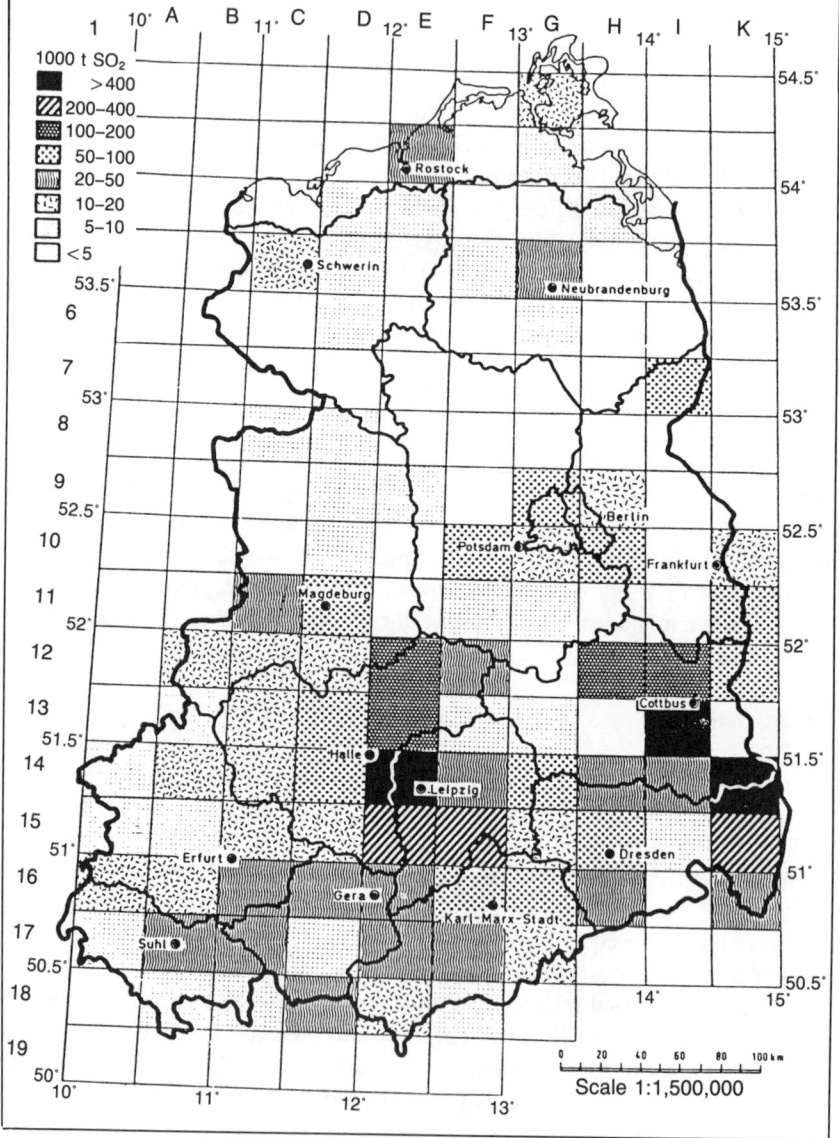

1000 t SO₂
- ■ >400
- ▨ 200–400
- ▥ 100–200
- ▦ 50–100
- ▥ 20–50
- ▦ 10–20
- □ 5–10
- □ <5

Rostock

Schwerin

Neubrandenburg

Berlin

Potsdam

Frankfurt

Magdeburg

Cottbus

Halle

Leipzig

Erfurt

Dresden

Gera

Karl-Marx-Stadt

Suhl

0 20 40 60 80 100 km

Scale 1:1,500,000

Source: "Luftverunreinigung in der DDR: Die Emissionen von Schwefeldioxid und Stichoxiden," *DIW Wochenbericht*, 25 July 1985 (vol. 52), p. 339.

reliance on this fuel has helped to lower imports and thus the GDR's foreign debt, but at the same time has produced intensified air pollution. Emissions from large power plants are accompanied by smoke from residential coal ovens and from small outdated furnaces supplying individual factories. At the end of 1982 about 4.8 million apartments were still heated by coal ovens.[6] Western experts estimate that total SO_2 emissions for the GDR in 1985 were about 5.8 million tons, the highest in Europe (e.g., compared to about 3 million tons for West Germany, which has over three times the population and more than twice the land area of the GDR).[7] This pollutant contributes both to smog and to acid rain, although the latter often falls far from the source, affecting neighboring countries more than the GDR itself. High smoke stacks (200–300 meters) reduce intense pollution in the immediate vicinity but distribute it over a wider area. While the GDR's SO_2 pollution is high, some other pollutants, most notably nitrogen oxides, are emitted in the GDR in much lower quantities than in the FRG.[8]

The air in the industrial south of the GDR is the worst (see Map 1). Half of the SO_2 emissions from the large brown coal energy plants come from the district of Cottbus.[9] Cities such as Leipzig, Bitterfeld, Karl-Marx-Stadt, and Halle are also highly polluted; the chemical industry, concentrated in the area around Halle, adds to the problem. Already in 1970 one GDR scientist estimated that in these heavily polluted areas a reduction of 50 percent in emissions could extend life expectancy by 3 to 4 years, reduce heart and circulatory disease by 10–15 percent, and bring a long-term decline of 25 percent in respiratory malignancies.[10] Life expectancy in the Halle area is reportedly five years less and the incidence of heart and respiratory disease ten to fifteen percent higher than elsewhere in the GDR.[11] Some GDR scientists acknowledge that increasing cancer rates in the Cottbus area are at least partly due to high air pollution levels.[12]

Human health is not the only victim of air pollution. An emigre expert estimates that some 90 percent of the GDR's forests are damaged and about 500,000 hectares (between 15 and 20 percent) of the forests are already dead or dying.[13] The Erzgebirge, near the Czechoslovakian border, leaves a horrifying impression on visitors and local residents alike. Air pollution from neighboring Czechoslovakia, Poland, and West Germany contributes to the damage. GDR policy emphasizes replanting damaged areas with "smoke-resistant" varieties (e.g., maple, beech, birch, aspen, mountain ash) to replace the more sensitive spruce and pine.

Research into technological processes for neutralizing harmful pollutants from power plant emissions is advanced in the GDR, but practice is less satisfactory. For example, the lime-additive process, often mentioned in GDR sources, involves binding sulfur with lime, but generally results in only a 30 percent reduction in SO_2 emissions. High expenditures are required to transport the very large quantities of lime and waste ash, so that only selected and intermittent use of this method is deemed feasible (e.g., in heavily populated areas or on extremely polluted days). So far this technology is operating on a trial basis at the Vockerode plant (Bezirk Halle, 385 MW), although it is soon to be introduced at three additional plants.[14] Import of expensive desulfurization equipment from Western firms requires the expenditure of valuable hard currency, and its effectiveness in GDR plants is not proven. As a test project the British have loaned the GDR some 40 million pounds to finance import of smoke-desulfurization equipment (applying the Wellman-Lord-Process) for the relatively small Rummelsburg power plant (180 MW) in Berlin.[15] Existing equipment designed to remove dust particles from emissions is not always cleaned regularly, thus its effectiveness is impaired.

Despite these difficulties, at the 1985 meeting on the environment of the United Nations Economic Commission for Europe (ECE) the GDR joined other nations in an agreement to reduce SO_2 emissions by 30 percent (in relation to 1980 levels) by the year 1993. Some Western experts question the economic feasibility of achieving this goal, especially since no apparent progress had been made by the end of 1986. GDR spokespersons point to more efficient energy use, improved desulfurization of emissions, increased reliance on nuclear energy, and expanded use of centralized heating stations as the main methods to realize the commitment.[16]

Even before it is burned, brown coal leaves a permanent mark on the landscape and on human lives. Mining the fuel is increasingly expensive as reserves are deeper in the ground and lie under established settlements. Between 1960 and 1980 at least seventy villages or parts of villages were sacrificed, and 190 kilometers of road as well as 60 kilometers of waterway had to be moved to accommodate brown coal strip mining.[17] Several other villages, especially in Bezirk Cottbus and south of Leipzig, face the same fate in the future, as mining is to increase from about 260 million tons in 1980 to a planned level of 335 million tons in 1990. The residents are resettled, as tons of ground water and earth must be brought to the surface to allow access to the coal. GDR spokespersons claim that recultivation means a positive transformation of the landscape in the affected areas, through development of new lakes and recreational areas, along with an improvement in soil conditions through careful attention to the character and quality of the soil as it is replaced. In most cases this promise still awaits fulfilment. The economic and ecological costs are enormous: agricultural land must be removed from cultivation; ground-water levels fall; water becomes polluted with sulfates, phenols, sulfuric acid, and particulate matter;[18] animal and plant habitats are disrupted; trees are felled; new housing, schools, and other facilities must be provided for the resettled population. As the GDR already suffers a housing and labor shortage, these demands strain even further the limited resources available for improving the sociocultural environment. Nonetheless, GDR economists believe that continued exploitation of domestic brown coal is still the most economical alternative.

A nuclear future?

In the long run, the GDR plans to turn to nuclear energy. At present only some 11 percent of the GDR's electrical energy comes from nuclear plants, and the GDR has only one large reactor complex, Griefswald (four reactors, 440 MW each), located near the northern sea town of Lubmin. In addition a small 70 MW plant, also used for research and education, is located about 30 kilometers north of Berlin near Rheinsberg. By 1990, 15 percent of electrical power should come from nuclear energy; longer term projections set a target of 54 percent by 2020, as brown coal reserves approach depletion.[19] Immediate plans for expansion include a doubling of capacity at Griefswald and completion of a new complex near Stendal (Bezirk Magdeburg), some 100 kilometers west of Berlin and less than 50 kilometers from the West German border. The first reactor (1000 MW) is to commence trial operation by 1990.

Like the other East European countries, the GDR uses Soviet-designed pressurized water reactors (VVER), not the Chernobyl-type channel graphite-moderated reactor. Major components for the newer generation of VVER reactors in the GDR will be produced at the Skoda works in Czechoslovakia. Despite reports of a small accident at the Griefswald plant in 1976,[20] the East German safety record thus far has been good. However existing reactors are not outfitted with the concrete containment structures characteristic of most pressurized water reactors in the West. The new ones probably will be. GDR leaders may find it necessary to reconsider their nuclear commitment, due to the high investment costs associated with nuclear power development. Economic considerations, not ecological concerns, probably explain the consistent lag in plan fulfilment in the past ten years.[21] However, since the Chernobyl accident, there is increasing evidence that the GDR leadership may be reevaluating the scope of its commitment to nuclear power, and that certain aspects of reactor safety are also being studied.[22]

The citizen hears little from the GDR media about the possible hazards of nuclear power. However, access to West German broadcasts assures most East Germans exposure to the full gamut of information. From April 29 to May 6, 1986, the major East German daily, *Neues Deutschland*, did publish several articles about the Chernobyl accident.[23] Radiation levels in the GDR on the peak days of April 30 and May 1 were printed on page one of the newspaper, but in a form of little use to the average citizen.[24] The media offered reassurance that no danger to health existed at any time, also citing West German sources. On May 5 and 6 additional articles in *Neues Deutschland* cited past nuclear accidents in the USA. While these reports might reassure citizens that Soviet plants are little worse than their Western counterparts, they might also raise doubts about the overall safety of the technology (if even Western technology is unsafe!). To counter these doubts, GDR sources subtly hinted that GDR plants are more reliable than their Soviet counterparts.

Table 1

Supply of Crop Protection Agents and Chemical Weedkillers

Year	Supply of agriculture with crop protection agents	
	Total tons of active substances	Of which, herbicides
1965	8,219	6,197
1970	18,567	13,758
1971	18,037	13,979
1972	21,901	15,346
1973	21,957	12,150
1974	22,090	14,694
1975	22,480	15,004
1976	23,665	16,243
1977	24,502	16,915
1978	25,298	17,080
1979	26,715	17,999
1980	27,009	18,067
1981	26,951	19,277
1982	26,744	19,432
1983	25,951	18,773
1984	25,985	18,758
1985	26,731	18,179

Source: *Statistisches Jahrbuch der DDR*, Berlin: Staatsverlag der DDR, 1986, 191.

It seems doubtful whether any milk or other food products were withheld from sale immediately following the accident (as was the case in some neighboring countries like West Germany, although presumably radiation levels were similar in at least some parts of the GDR). Reportedly, East German shoppers were glad to buy fresh Polish vegetables exported to the GDR after their rejection by the FRG due to unacceptable contamination levels. One Western report indicates that some dry feed was withheld from use for dairy and slaughter cattle early in 1987.[25] No information has been made available to the GDR citizen, however, regarding post-Chernobyl radiation levels in food items, whereas more than a year after the accident some newspapers in West Berlin continue to publish measurements daily. GDR citizens could view a Soviet film production on the accident, aired on GDR television just a few days after its debut on Soviet TV on February 25, 1987. (The film, called "The Warning," emphasizes how unthinkable nuclear war is, given the catastrophic effects of Chernobyl.) On February 8, 1987, apparently for the first time, experts from the GDR State Office for Atomic Safety and Radiation Protection met with about 100 "environmentalists" (it is

Table 2

Supply of Agriculture with Mineral Fertilizers

Calendar year	Nitrogen (N)	Phosphate (P$_2$O$_5$)	Potash (K$_2$O)	Lime (CaO)
		kg per hectare of agricultural area		
1950	28.7	15.4	59.7	84.5
1955	32.4	20.5	65.6	109.6
1960	36.7	34.0	77.4	121.0
1965	65.1	49.3	92.1	212.2
1970	81.3	65.2	97.7	186.8
1975	107.7	70.1	112.2	206.3
1976	120.0	67.5	99.1	202.6
1977	122.5	67.9	75.0	172.5
1978	124.8	68.6	72.4	170.0
1979	119.0	66.3	87.3	151.1
1980	119.9	62.0	79.2	197.8
1981	119.7	59.8	96.0	198.3
1982	97.1	48.6	79.3	192.7
1983	111.0	53.3	67.9	222.4
1984	111.6	51.1	88.1	221.6
1985	123.7	51.2	88.4	228.8

Source: *Statistisches Jahrbuch der DDR*, Berlin: Staatsverlag der DDR, 1986, 191.

not clear who was included in this group) and members of a mass women's organization (Demokratische Frauenbund) to allow airing of questions about nuclear power safety.[26] What the effect of a more open information policy would be is hard to know. The hypothetical and completely invisible dangers of nuclear power may well seem worth the risk, if nuclear power can assure an improved standard of living. Furthermore, these dangers may seem preferable to the demonstrable disadvantages of a brown-coal economy. The average GDR citizen may well affirm Erich Honecker's sentiment, stated at the 11th Party Congress of the SED just before the Chernobyl accident in April of 1986: Nuclear power should be expanded, "not the least for the sake of the environment."[27]

Land, food, and water

Agriculture is one of the worst sources of environmental damage in the GDR; ecological consciousness among agricultural practitioners is considerably behind that of industrial managers. Fertilizers and pesticides are employed extensively to increase crop yields, although there was a slight reduction in the early 1980s compared to the upward trend in the 1960s and 1970s (see Tables 1 and 2).[28] Some of these pesticides contain DDT and mercury compounds. Although the use of DDT is gradually declining, it is still available to the average citizen for use in private gardens and is also a component in widely available wood preservatives. Disturbing concentrations of DDT have been measured by GDR scientists in mothers' milk, birds, and plants; high levels of mercury have been found in some birds and fish. Likewise, excessively high (and in some cases rising) nitrate levels make water unsafe for drinking in some, especially rural, areas. Nitrate consumption through food and water in the GDR almost doubled between 1970 (78 mg per capita per year) and 1983 (150 mg per capita per year).[29] In some cases, scientists have advised mothers to nurse their infants or use bottled mineral water for infant feeding. Levels of these and other contaminants in the food and water supply are not generally available from GDR sources, but presumably they are significant enough to pose some health hazard, particularly for young children.[30] The average GDR citizen knows nothing of these dangers, even when they affect produce from his or her own small garden.

Agricultural chemicals are increasingly sprayed from airplanes, not always with appropriate care to wind conditions. Rivers, streams, and nearby livestock may be inadvertently contaminated. Local residents, unaware of the spraying, sometimes gather contaminated berries and mushrooms from the woods in the springtime. Unofficial channels have reported several cases of human illness and livestock deaths.[31] Fertilizer is often unloaded in loose, unpacked form, resulting in heavy dust pollution, contamination of soil and water, and chemical burns on vegetation.[32] Several plant and animal species are now extinct or threatened with extinction in the GDR, in large part as a result of the heavy use of chemical fertilizers and pesticides, as well as the extensive land drainage programs of the 1960s and 1970s.[33] While most of these problems are not unique to the GDR, the lack of open debate makes their solution more difficult. Nature protection zones have, however, been expanded, and in 1985, 856 animal species and 136 plant species were under special protection.[34]

Because the GDR has a limited natural water endowment, contamination of ground water with nitrates and other chemical pollutants is especially serious. In many areas water must be reutilized many times by various industrial and agricultural producers. Enterprises are encouraged to introduce technological processes that reduce water waste and improve purification to allow recycling in the production process. Much of the ground water now requires purification before drinking. In 1970, some 80 percent of the surface waters already were classified as polluted or heavily polluted, unsuitable for fishing, sport, or drinking (without treatment).[35] Many rivers (notably the Elbe, Pleisse, Salle, and Werra) are heavily polluted from the chemical, textile, paper, metallurgical, and potash industries, especially in the industrial south, and reports of significant fish kills occasionally reach the West. Despite these problems, in the past few years the situation appears to have stabilized and in some cases improved.

Waste and recycling

GDR policy has been remarkably ambitious and quite successful regarding reuse of waste products as "secondary raw materials." Enterprises are required to include measures in their economic plans, and in accordance with *Verursacher-verantwortung* (responsibility of the producer) are sometimes even expected to organize the recycling of worn-out consumer items they produce. For example, the VEB Petrochemical Combine Schwedt is responsible for recycling used motor and industrial oil, and the VEB Tire Combine Furstenwalde is responsible for used tires.[36]

The Combine Secondary Raw Material Recovery *(Sekundärrohstofferfassung)* organizes popular involvement in recycling through the establishment of collection centers where citizens can return waste for payment. (For example, .3 mark is paid for each kilogram of newspapers, .2 to .3 mark for recycled glass containers, and .5 mark for each kilogram of old textiles.)[37] The Free German Youth also organizes voluntary collection initiatives. Supermarkets have large bins for collection of old plastic containers, and cans on the streets are for collection of table waste for pigs. Nonreusable glass bottles no longer exist in the GDR. Some 50 percent of paper production is based on old paper; scrap metal provides about 75 percent of the raw material for iron and steel production; 35 percent of the raw material for copper production comes from scrap, 40 percent for lead, and 20 percent for aluminum production. In 1980 some 916,000 tons of kitchen waste were collected from the population. Overall, reuse of industrial waste for secondary raw materials increased from 12 million tons in 1975 to 30 million tons in 1983.[38] These achievements are important to the GDR leadership primarily for the economic savings realized; ecological motives may be secondary. Nonetheless, the environmental benefits are significant.

An enterprise must receive authorization from the responsible local organ before deposition of waste products; such authorization follows only after the enterprise provides sufficient evidence that the waste cannot be reutilized as secondary raw material. Once this is forthcoming, the local authority approves deposition of the material at a specified dump.[39] Nonetheless, *Wilddeponie* (unregulated dumps) are still common in the countryside, with average citizens often the worst offenders. Storage of toxic waste occurs at specially regulated sites and until now there have been no reported incidents in this regard. The GDR also accepts waste from the Federal Republic of Germany and West Berlin in exchange for hard currency payment. Some is recycled (e.g., old glass and paper), while the remainder is deposited at state dumps, such as the one in the northern GDR at Schönberg.

The policies

If one were to judge the GDR by its legal enactments, it would be considered an environmental leader. Already in 1970 a comprehensive environmental policy act (*Landeskulturgesetz*)[40] was enacted. Numerous implementation decrees and additional legislation since then have addressed specific issues in more detail.[41] These documents specify the legal rights and obligations of the various state bodies and establish the basis for emission limits of various pollutants as well as sanctions for their violation. Environmental law is in constant evolution in the GDR; leading legal experts in scientific institutions cooperate with central state agencies in drafting and amending legislation.

A basic principle underlying state policy is that the use, protection, and transformation of nature are inextricably linked. Environmental protection is not an end in itself; natural resources are for human use. Therefore, the relationship between environmental protection and economic policy becomes pivotal. Most GDR citizens probably place a higher value on an improved material standard of living than they do on environmental protection, for compared to West Germany, East Germans still suffer a conscious sense of deprivation with respect to consumer goods and diet. Probably also predominate among economic practitioners is the view expressed by the GDR economist, Johann Köhler, that environmental protection measures "don't make us richer in material goods, but rather draw away working forces from the area of production of material goods."[42] In other words, if one must choose between environmental protection and economic growth, citizens and leaders alike would probably opt for the latter. Must one, however, choose between the two goals?

Environmentally conscious economists and legal scholars in the GDR argue that economic growth and environmental protection are mutually reinforcing, not contradictory goals: Neglect of the environment will, in the long term, inhibit economic growth and thus hold back improvements in the standard of living. If the natural resource base of the country is damaged, then nature's "free services" (e.g., readily available pure water, the purification capacity and antierosion effects of forests, natural soil fertility, natural decomposition of waste) must be replaced by expensive man-made processes (e.g., purification facilities, chemical fertilizers and pest control, extra health expenses).[43] The interdependence between economic growth and environmental protection is also acknowledged by political leaders, but with a different emphasis: An efficient economy assures adequate investment funds for environmental protection.[44] Nonetheless, the environmentalist perspective is gaining broader adherence.

At the central level, the Ministry for Environmental Protection and Water Management, established in 1971, works out the main guidelines for environmental planning (especially water management), oversees implementation of laws, and makes proposals to the *Ministerrat* regarding environmental questions. Productive enterprises and combines are required to include environmental protection in their short- and long-term plans. At the level of *Bezirk*, *Kreis*, city, and *Gemeinde*, the local representative bodies and their executive councils (*Räte*) also approve regional measures for environmental protection and, with the help of standing commissions and specialized technical organs

(*Fachorgane*), are responsible for coordinating and verifying the effectiveness of measures undertaken by enterprises in the region.[45] Numerous other organs also play a role in overseeing implementation of state policy: the environmental inspectorate (formed in 1985), the water inspectorate, the hygiene inspectorate, the fish health service, the meteorological service, and others. Financial sanctions also encourage enterprises to make more careful use of natural resources.[46]

Although these complex legal and organizational structures should assure an effective environmental policy, policy often falters at the implementation stage. The fundamental problem is the relatively low priority of environmental protection, compared to the goal of increased material production. Even if local organs are able to convince enterprises to include ambitious environmental projects in their preliminary economic plans, higher planning organs may water down or cut these projects altogether, as scarce supplies of labor, capital, and materials require that choices be made. In practice, this means that local projects that reinforce centrally established priorities (e.g., assurance of safe drinking water supplies, improved collection and utilization of waste) may well survive the complex planning process, while those that break new ground may not. The key question is, Who determines what is actually realizable and what is simply wishful thinking? Ultimately it is the *Ministerrat*, and at this level productive priorities are most often going to prevail. GDR specialists admit that effective environmental protection often depends on the personal initiative of the enterprise manager, as well as on the active engagement of local state officials and citizens in pressing enterprises to respond. The law, so to speak, provides a lever, a countervailing force to balance the predominant pressure in favor of production over protection. If individual commitment is insufficient, it is most likely that environmental projects will be sacrificed to other priorities.

The average citizen may make complaints through petitions (*Eingaben*) to the responsible authorities. These are apparently quite common regarding environmental questions and, by law, must be answered by the appropriate state authority. They produce diverse outcomes. In some cases they alert authorities to unnoticed problems or draw attention to a situation that can be resolved within established priorities. At the local level, siting questions are frequent subjects of *Eingaben*. For example, a storage point for brown coal might be moved to the city's periphery in response to citizen complaints about dust pollution in a residential area. A particular tree might be spared cutting. In other cases, state policy may limit the ability of local officials to respond to *Eingaben*. An instance cited by a local GDR official may illustrate the difficulty: Construction of a heating plant near a residential area initially posed no pollution hazard, since it was to utilize "clean" natural gas as fuel. When the shift to brown coal took place in the early 1980s, the plant was already under construction and could not be moved, but now it was to be a coal-fired plant, producing high pollution levels. Residents complained that the plant was too close to their homes. Little could be done, given the central commitment to brown coal. Ameliorative measures (e.g., a higher smokestack, dust barriers) were the only available options. In cases like this, the response to the *Eingabe* is primarily an explanation of the necessity of the pollution. A petition sent to the *Staatsrat* of the GDR, the *Rat* of the *Bezirk* Rostock, and the *Rat* of the district (*Kreis*) Grevemühlen on June 29, 1986, met a somewhat similar fate. Distributed by organs of the Evangelical Church in Berlin-Brandenburg and Mecklenburg, this petition called for an end to the importation of waste from the West and for full information, particularly in regard to the waste dump Schönberg. The answer assured the petitioners that the Schönberg dump is safe and well regulated and does not accept toxic waste. Petitioners were invited to a meeting at the Ministry for Environmental Protection and Water Management for further explanation.[47]

Despite the constraints on effective citizen pressure, local state organs may be able to call some polluting enterprises to account. Because scientists and specialists on environmental matters may be members of the local standing commissions and technical organs (*Fachorgane*) responsible for environmental issues, these bodies sometimes command the expertise necessary to place effective pressure on enterprise officials. But some of these scientists are also undoubtedly part of a coopted intelligentsia, i.e., they benefit from the existing system through higher salaries, opportunities for foreign travel, greater access to Western publications, and generous housing. Thus they may air their criticisms in private or articulate them in a toned-down form. This is not to say that there are no real "environmentalists" among GDR intellectuals. There are, and they apparently see themselves as a self-conscious pressure group sharing common goals.[48] Nonetheless, GDR leaders have generally been effective in keeping this type of environmentalism within limits that do not endanger either systemic stability or priorities.

The citizen

Popular attitudes toward environmental deterioration are hard to assess, since survey research data is limited and GDR citizens may be reticent in stating their real views to foreign visitors. A West German scholar, Gerhard Würth, cites some interesting East German studies from the early to mid-1970s which involved small-scale opinion surveys of both adults and schoolchildren. Some 90 percent of the 800 persons questioned in Bitterfeld and Schwerin in 1971 believed air pollution to be damaging to the health, and two-thirds of those in Bitterfeld wanted to move away, in large part because of the pollution. Of a group questioned in 1974, 30 percent were bothered by noise pollution.[49]

As the environment has become an ever more salient issue in West Germany, the GDR citizen has also been exposed to more and more information through the Western media, even if only occasionally to reports about the GDR itself. The environmental question has also become an increasingly important theme in GDR fiction.[50] Informal contacts with GDR citizens and growing environmental activism within the GDR Evangelical Church in the 1980s both suggest a rising level of concern and at least a small dent in popular resignation. Even in the 1950s, officially sanctioned societies for conservation of nature, in the narrow sense, served as outlets for interested individuals. Numerous organizations now exist for those with a particular interest: hunting societies; fishing clubs; an organization of small gardeners, homesteaders, and breeders; and numerous branches of the Kulturbund, including ones for ornithology and bird protection, for nature and homeland, and for roses and orchids, among others.[51]

Since passage of the *Landeskulturgesetz* in 1970, the regime has intensified efforts to mobilize popular support for the law. The term "socialist *Landeskultur*" has a broader meaning than *Umweltschultz* (environmental protection) in the West. In addition to pollution control and nature conservation, it also includes such diverse activities as city planning, designation of protected cultural objects, and, in general, an improvement in living and working conditions. It is presented as a constructive process of environmental improvement, not simply the prevention or amelioration of environmental damage. The tone of public education and mobilization campaigns is positive, emphasizing the active involvement of the citizenry in improving the quality of life in the local setting. Professional organizations also encourage members to perform duties at the workplace with proper respect for ecological principles. Such organizations include, for example, the trade unions, the Kammer der Technik (an organization for engineers), the Bund der Architekten (for architects), and the Agrarwissenschaftliche Gesellschaft (for agricultural specialists).[52] In their neighborhoods and at the workplace communal contracts with local state authorities establish citizen duties for environmental improvement (e.g., responsibility for clearing ice in winter, for helping to maintain recreational areas or parks, participation in laying pipelines for drinking water in rural areas). *Mach mit!* (Participate!) campaigns mobilize residents to beautify their cities and residential areas through better upkeep of buildings, planting of trees and scrubs, or cleaning up of waste heaps. Local state organs also designate voluntary *Naturschutzhelfer* (nature protection helpers) to assist in the planning, implementation, and enforcement of environmental policy at the local level under the leadership of volunteer specialists (*Naturschutzbeauftragte*).[53]

This heavy reliance on volunteer activity reflects the scarce material and labor resources available within planning mandates. In 1980, mobilization of popular interest culminated in the formation of a new umbrella organization within the Kulturbund of the GDR—the Society for Nature and the Environment (SNE). Some 60,000 members strong in 1986, the organization incorporated members from existing subgroups of the Kulturbund, but brought a unifying theme and drew in additional members, including specialists (biologists, foresters, experts in water management) and in some cases even entire enterprises whose activities impinge heavily on the environment. For example, in Bezirk Dresden, some twenty-five institutions and enterprises are members of the SNE. Organized on a regional basis (on the Bezirk level), this society also has twelve specialized divisions such as conservation, entomology, ornithology and protection of birds, hiking and tourism, botany, and so forth. Sections may make recommendations to state organs and otherwise organize a wide range of activities. For example, initiatives in Schwerin in 1980 involved care of parks, development of hiking trails, and organization of environmental exhibits. Specialized commissions carry out research projects on topics such as the condition of endangered species. A campaign initiated in the Dresden region (*Gepflegte Landschaft—gepflegte Umwelt*) mobilized 105,676 hours of voluntary work, worth an estimated .5 million marks. Subsequently, similar initiatives have been organized throughout the GDR under the same slogan.[54]

In part, organization of the SNE was intended to direct the energies of concerned citizens into acceptable channels, which would reinforce rather than challenge official priorities. But one should not interpret such organizations exclusively as "transmission belts" for control from the top. They also allow communication of citizen interests to state officials and have allowed realization of some citizen initiatives. While groups like the SNE clearly must operate within the parameters of state policy, control from above is probably much less rigid than one might expect.

Church activism

Thus far we have focused on official environmental groups. Equally important, although much smaller in size, are semiautonomous activities organized within the GDR Evangelical Church. Since the mid–1970s, environmental questions have been of growing concern to many GDR Christians, especially to young people, and as activity has developed inside the church, non-church members have also been drawn to these informal groups. The modus vivendi worked out with the state over the last several years has allowed the church a certain organizational autonomy in exchange for loyalty to the system. Therefore, the church has been able to provide an umbrella for a wide variety of environmental (and peace) activities and for discussions that embrace issues not aired in the official media. Young people find a freer atmosphere, in which they can more openly express their concerns. Church leaders also help them to find ways to work within the system, rather than seeking emigration, becoming resigned, or engaging in unacceptable forms of protest.

These small groups of environmental activists carry out diverse projects, sometimes described as "small steps." While it may be impossible to bring fundamental change, these small steps, taken together, may make a difference; but of equal importance to the participants, they allow the individual to express a personal commitment to an ecological life-style. Thus the ecological question takes on a spiritual and moral dimension. Activists question materialism and consumerism, implicity suggesting an alternative to regime priorities. Young Christians discuss alternative life-styles which seek fulfilment through "being," not "having." Solidarity with the poorer nations of the Third World is presented as a corrective to the prevailing materialism. Church members in less polluted areas of the GDR have taken children from the highly industrialized centers in the south for holidays, to allow them to recover from the excessive pollution.[55] Other small steps are meat-free days, auto-free weekends, reduced use of household chemicals, organic gardening, fasts, and group tree-planting actions.[56] The element of Christian asceticism in some of these actions is fundamentally at odds with the official values in the GDR, and the spiritual foundation contradicts the materialism of Marxism-Leninism. Nonetheless, the spiritual emphasis may also help make existing material shortages in the GDR more palatable, and in this sense Christian environmentalism may not seem so threatening to the political authorities.

Like other GDR citizens, church activists suffer from a lack of information about environmental conditions in the GDR. They emphasize self-education and dissemination of available information through environmental seminars, workshops, and exhibits. Personal contacts with scientists and individuals with special expertise are utilized to gain information. Sometimes various church newsletters, hectographically reproduced, are distributed through the mail to interested individuals; in other cases they are passed from hand to hand to increase exposure.[57] These newsletters, which are available in small numbers due to restricted materials and facilities, represent a semiautonomous source of information subject to "self-censorship" rather than direct state censorship. Since January 1980, the Church Research Facility in Wittenberg (das Kirchliche Forschungsheim Wittenberg) has produced a biannual "Letter for Orientation in the Conflict Man-Nature," numbering twelve issues by October 1985. These include book reviews, information on local activities, reports on environmental damage, and essays on Christianity and the environment. Longer reports have emanated from work groups at Wittenberg and elsewhere in the GDR. Topics have included agriculture and the environment, environmental protection in the household, forest damage, and alternative recipes. Since September 2, 1986, an "environmental library" has been open several evenings a week in the Berlin Zionsgemeinde to increase access to environmental publications. It also serves as a meeting place for informal discussion and as a location for regular lectures relating to environmental and other issues. A police raid on the library in November 1987, involving confiscation of materials and underground publications, as well as the detention of some activists, may mark the beginning of intensified control over such activities.[58]

Since the establishment of the official Society for Nature and the Environment within the Kulturbund of the GDR in 1980, some church activists have also joined that organization. Attempts to cooperate with state organs have met varying fates. One church-organized tree-planting action in 1981 failed when a state organization did not deliver the promised saplings, presumably due to bad weather and insufficient growth of the plantings. Meanwhile the local FDJ organization *was* apparently supplied with trees.[59] In other cases, however, and especially in recent years, state organizations seem more willing to support this type of initiative[60] in order to minimize the alienation of young people and, of course, get the trees planted. State authorities look less favorably on other types of activities. For example, group bicycle tours of polluted areas may meet official resistance; signs are posted to prohibit bicycle traffic on the route and participants are diverted. "Environmental worship services" in villages slated for dismantling due to brown coal strip mining are also viewed unfavorably by the regime. However, in 1985 a representative of the Bezirk council reportedly was available to answer questions after such a service in Potzschau, south of Leipzig.[61] In Erfurt, the SNE now allows church activists to serve as voluntary water protection commissioners (*Wasserschutzbeauftragte*).[62] Apparently the authorities would like to harness the constructive energies of these young environmentalists, rather than simply suppress them. As long as the activities remain clearly under the umbrella of the church, do not "take to the streets" (giving the appearance of a demonstration), and further official goals, they seem to operate with relatively little interference.

The Chernobyl accident inspired new initiatives inside the church. On June 5, 1986, 140 citizens addressed a petition to the Ministerrat containing a fundamental criticism of nuclear power. The petitioners demanded improved information on the dangers of nuclear power, clear data on post-Chernobyl radiation levels, a construction-stop on new plants, a reorientation of energy policy to end reliance on nuclear power by 1990, increased research on alternative energy sources, and improved energy conservation.[63] Later in June, a petition supported by thousands of GDR citizens was delivered to the Volkskammer, this time demanding a referendum on the further development of nuclear power.[64] Church activists have also sought to gather and disseminate available information among themselves. These actions represent a marked contrast to the pre-Chernobyl situation, when antinuclear sentiment was rarely aired.

Although church-related activism involves limited numbers of individuals, the moral commitment of those who do participate gives it a greater social weight than the numbers would suggest. For unlike the larger official organizations, these small semi-independent groups challenge the information monopoly of the state and stimulate creative initiatives; they capture both the energies and imagination of talented young Germans.

Conclusion

The impact of pollution often goes undetected until the damage is done; even scientists with sophisticated research facilities disagree over the long-term effects on health and well-being. Therefore, the GDR citizen, hindered by poor information and surrounded by reassuring messages from the authorities, may find environmental problems less pressing than many others. Housing shortages, difficulty in finding a "thousand small things," worse air and more noise at work than at home, and limited possibilities for foreign travel may all prove more frustrating on a day-to-day basis than the unseen effects of nitrates and heavy metals in food and water, endangered species, or polluted ground water. To be sure, some environmental damage is becoming increasingly obvious: stinky air and dirty laundry, rivers and lakes closed to swimming, damaged forests, and dead fish. But many GDR citizens probably see these as largely unavoidable costs of progress, against which one can do little if anything. Perhaps the state could do better here as elsewhere, but, one might think, the worst problems come from the brown coal, and here economic realities will prevail.

Both the GDR and Western media make it clear that socialism has no monopoly on environmental damage; in capitalist and Third World countries localized environmental catastrophes are now regular affairs. Due to the GDR news blackout, domestic problems go unreported and, unlike in Western countries, the average citizen doesn't learn about a specific toxic waste hazard next door or of measured contamination in food and water. These dangers are theoretical and abstract in the GDR; the shortage of fresh fruits and vegetables is real and visible. Perhaps environmentalism is a luxury of the rich.

The costs of activism may also seem high, perhaps higher than they really are. Work in official organizations is praised, not censured, and one can even participate in some church activities without major consequences. Yet if one oversteps the bounds—tries to organize too independently or learns too much—there are penalties—to career, to education, and in some cases even imprisonment.

The environmental awakening is arriving slowly in the GDR, but it is arriving. The question in the GDR is the same as in the West. Will citizen and regime realize and respond to the dangers before they are irreversible?

Notes

1. Based on information from the office of the Senator für Stadtentwicklung und Umweltschutz, Berlin (West). For regulations governing smog in West Berlin see "Verordnung zur Verminderung schädlicher Umwelteinwirkungen bei austauscharmen Wetterlagen (Smog-Verordnung). Vom 25. Oktober 1985," *Gesetz und Verordnungsblatt für Berlin* 31 (Nov. 13, 1985): 2282–84.

2. Radio interview of Dr. Hellmut Breitenkamp of the Referat Luftreinhaltung of the Berlin Senate, transmitted on RIAS I (Berlin-West), Feb. 8, 1987, 6:35–7:15 a.m. Interview carried out by Martin Irion.

3. Peter Wensierski, *Von oben nach unten wächst gar nichts: Umweltzerstörung und Protest in der DDR* (Frankfurt am Main: Fischer Taschenbuch Verlag, 1986), 23.

4. See, e.g., *epd* (evangelisches pressedienst), Landesdienst Berlin, no. 113, June 18, 1984; and "Mehr kommunizieren als konsumieren," *Die Kirche*, July 14, 1985.

5. *Statistisches Jahrbuch der Deutschen Demokratischen Republik 1986* (Berlin: Staatsverlag der DDR, 1986), 155, 257.

6. "Luftverunreinigung in der DDR: Die Emission von Schwefeldioxid und Stickoxiden," *DIW Wochenbericht* 52, no. 30/85 (July 25, 1985): 342.

7. Interview with Cord Schwartau of the Deutsches Institut für Wirtschaftsforschung

(DIW) in Berlin (West), March 11, 1987. See also "Emissionen von SO_2 aus Braunkohlekraftwerken in der DDR," *DIW Wochenbericht* 54, no. 11/87 (March 12, 1987): 154–57.

8. *DIW Wochenbericht*, no. 30/85, 337.

9. *DIW Wochenbericht*, no. 11/87, 155.

10. Karlwilhelm Horn, "Vorwort," *Wissenschaftliche Zeitschrift der Humboldt Universität Berlin*, Matematisch-naturwissenschaftliche Reihe, no. 5 (1970), 448.

11. Marlies Menge, "Für Filter fehlen die Devisen," *Die Zeit* (Hamburg), March 25, 1983, 21 (Canada edition); and Gerhard Würth, *Umweltschmutz und Umweltzerstörung in der DDR* (Frankfurt am Main: Peter Lang, 1985), 68–72.

12. G. W. Dominok and R. Schweissinger, "Zur Epidemologie der 10 häufigsten Malignome in Bezirk Cottbus," *Das deutsche Gesundheitswesen* 39, no. 30 (1984): 1770–71.

13. "Experte hält 90 Prozent des Waldes der DDR für geschädigt," *Der Tagesspiegel*, February 17, 1987.

14. See *DIW Wochenbericht*, no. 11/87: 155–57.

15. Ibid., 157; and Michael Schmitz, "Der ungeteilte Dreck," *Die Zeit*, March 6, 1987, 42.

16. Speech by Hans Reichelt, "Der Schutz der Umwelt erfordert Entspannung im Geist von Helsinki," *Neues Deutschland*, July 9, 1985, 3.

17. Würth, 41.

18. Manfred Melzer, "Wasserwirtschaft und Umweltschutz in der DDR," in *Umweltschutz in beiden Teilen Deutschlands*, ed. Maria Haendcke-Hoppe (Berlin-West: Duncker und Humblot, 1985) 79; and Würth, 248–51.

19. Erich Honecker, "Bericht des Zentralkomitees der Sozialistischen Einheitspartei Deutschlands an der XI. Parteitag der SED," 17–21 April 1986 (Berlin: Dietz Verlag, 1985), 31; see also "Die Kernenergie der RGW-Länder," *DIW Wochenbericht* 53, no. 25/86 (June 19, 1986), 309–10.

20. See Wensierski, 92.

21. See Joan DeBardeleben, "Esoteric Policy Debate: Nuclear Safety Issues in the Soviet Union and German Democratic Republic," *British Journal of Political Science* 15 (1985): 227–53.

22. For a discussion of the evidence, see Wolfgang Mehringer, "Reaktorsicherheit in der DDR," in *IGW-report über Wissenschaft und Technologie in der DDR und anderen RGW-Ländern*, Heft 1 (Institut für Gesellschaft und Wissenschaft/Universität Erlangen-Nürnberg, 1987), 34–52.

23. See *Neues Deutschland*, April 29, 1986, 5; May 2, 1986, 2; May 3/4, 1986, 1; May 5, 1986, 1; and May 6, 1986, 5.

24. *Neues Deutschland*, May 3/4, 1986, 1.

25. *Der Tagesspiegel* (Berlin-West), Feb. 13, 1987, 2.

26. Ibid.

27. Honecker, *Bericht*, 31.

28. See Andreas Kurjo, "Landwirtschaft und Umwelt in der DDR: Ökologische, rechtliche, und institutionelle Aspekte der sozialistischen Agrarpolitik," in *Umweltprobleme und Umweltbewusstsein in der DDR*, "Deutschland Archiv" (Cologne: Verlag Wissenschaft und Politik, 1985), 60–63.

29. Karl Hohmann, "Die Industrialisierung der Landwirtschaft und ihre Auswirkung auf die Umwelt in der DDR," in Haendcke-Hoppe 65, 61–63.

30. Based on material provided to the author by Peter Wensierski from his forthcoming book (coauthored with Wolfgang Büscher), *Ökologische Probleme und Kritik an der Industriegesellschaft in der DDR heute.*

31. See, e.g., *Berlinger Morgenpost*, March 1, 1987, 1; and Hohmann, 56–57.

32. Kurjo, 66–67.

33. Hohmann, 45–46.

34. "Natur und Landschaftschutz in der DDR," *Presse-Informationen*, Presseamt beim Vorsitzenden der Ministerrats der DDR, no. 146 (Dec. 17, 1986), 6.

35. Würth, 211–14. As Würth points out, little concrete data is available for the last twenty years. See also Melzer, 73–80, 84–85.

36. Eberhard Garbe and Dieter Graichen, *Sekundärrohstoffe: Begriffe, Fakten, Perspektiven* (Berlin: Verlag die Wirtschaft, 1985), 35.

37. Ibid., 77.

38. Ibid., 74, 90, 111, 147; Hans Reichelt, "Die natürliche Umwelt rationell nutzen, gestalten, und schützen," *Einheit* 39 (Nov. 1984): 1013.

39. Ellenor Oehler, ed., *Landeskulturrecht* (Berlin: Staatsverlag der DDR, 1986), 202–4.

40. "Gesetz über die planmässige Gestaltung der sozialistischen Landeskultur in der DDR," *Gesetzblatt der DDR*, Teil I, no. 12 (1970), 67ff.

41. For an overview of environmental law, see Oehler, *Landeskulturrecht*.

42. Johann Köhler, "Zu den Problematik der produktiven und der unproduktiven Arbeit sowie der Dienstleistungen," *Wirtschaftswissenschaft* 22 (June 1974): 886.

43. See, e.g., Ellenor Oehler, et al. *Landeskulturrecht: Lexicon*, s.v. "Gratisdienste der Natur" (Berlin: Staatsverlag der DDR, 1983), 67; and Horst Paucke and Günter Streibel, "Gratisdienste der Natur," *Wirtschaftwissenschaft* 31 (Sept. 1983): 1317–32.

44. See, e.g., "Internationale Konferenz zum Umweltschutz in Helsinki," *Neues Deutschland*, July 9, 1985, 1, and Reichelt, "Die natürliche Umwelt," 1012. For a detailed discussion of the relationship between economics and ecology in the GDR see Joan DeBardeleben, *The Environment and Marxism-Leninism: The Soviet and East German Experience* (Boulder, Colo.: Westview Press, 1985), Chpt. 5–7.

45. Oehler, *Landeskulturrecht*, 51–52.

46. For further discussion of these measures and citations of relevant legislation, see DeBardeleben, *The Environment*, 159, 246; and Ellenor Oehler, ed., *Die staatliche Leitung der Bodennutzung: Rechtsfragen* (Berlin: Staatsverlag der DDR, 1985), 95–96.

47. The response to the *Eingabe* is summarized in a newsletter "Die Umweltbibliothek," put out in October 1986 by an environmental group in the Zionsgemeinde, Berlin.

48. This impression is based on interviews with scientists in the GDR.

49. Würth, 63–67.

50. For an overview see Hubertus Knabe, "'Der Mensch mordet sich selbst,'" *Deutschland Archiv* 16 (1983): 954–73. For a recent example, see Christa Wolf, *Störfall* (Berlin, Weimar: Aufbau Verlag, 1987), also published in the FRG (Darmstadt: Luchterhand, 1987).

51. See Richard Mand et al., eds., *Handbuch gesellschaftlicher Organisationen der DDR*, 43–44, 97–98, 107–110, 160–64, 188.

52. See ibid., 23, 34–36, 98–101.

53. Oehler, *Landeskulturrecht. Lexicon*, 124–25.

54. Peter Wensierski, "Die Gesellschaft für Natur und Umwelt," in *Umweltprobleme und Umweltbewusstsein in der DDR*, 151–68; Manfred Fiedler, "Initiativen für Umwelt und Natur," *Einheit* 39 (Nov. 1984): 1024–27; and *Mitteilungen für die Staatsorgane in Bezirk Dresden*, no. 3 (1986), 13.

55. "Aktion 'Saubere Luft' für Ferienkinder," *Frieden und Freiheit*, June 1985; and Wensierski, *Von oben nach unten*, 44. On the spiritual dimension, see DeBardeleben, *The Environment*, 87–91, 97–98, 189.

56. See Wensierski, *Von oben nach unten*, 161–94; and Detlef Urban, "Die Umweltarbeit der Kirchen," in *Kirchen und Gesellschaft in beiden deutschen Staaten*, ed. Gisela Helwig and Detlef Urban (Cologne: Verlag Wissenschaft und Politik, 1987), 131–36.

57. DeBardeleben, *The Environment*, 79, 87–91; and Detlef Urban, "Kirchen treten

an die Öffentlichkeit," in *Die evangelischen Kirchen in der DDR*, ed. Reinhard Henkys (Munich: Chr. Kaiser Verlag, 1982), 341–49.

58. *New York Times,* November 29, 1987, A24.

59. "Aus einem Interview in einer Jungen Gemeinde," in Urban, "Die Umweltarbeit," 132.

60. "Bericht eines Mitgliedes des Arbeitskreises Umweltschutz-Eisenach," ibid., 133; and "SED würdigte Engagement der Kirchen in Ökologiefragen," *Frankfurter Rundschau*, Sept. 11, 1984.

61. "Mehr kommunizieren als konsumieren," *Die Kirche*, July 14, 1985.

62. Gesine Schmidt, "Bericht über praktische Arbeit von Ökogruppen," in Wensierski, *Von oben nach unten*, 166.

63. Portions of the appeal were published in West Berlin's *Tageszeitung*, June 23, 1986.

64. See "DDR-Bewohner fordern ein Umdenken in der Energie- und Informationspolitik," *Frankfurter Allgemeine Zeitung*, June 24, 1986.

Part V

Culture and Leisure Time

Leisure Time in the GDR

Trends and Prospects

HELMUT HANKE

The GDR is not a leisure-time society and never will be. Indeed, the prospects look rather grim for the "leisure-time society," so zealously proclaimed in bourgeois circles until but a few years ago. We were correct in not allowing ourselves to be further influenced in the seventies by this euphoria. Labor is the deciding factor in socialist societies—the only societies today that guarantee full employment and job security until the age of retirement—and labor is more emphasized than elsewhere. In the balance between work and leisure, real socialism stands fully in the tradition of the culture and way of life of the working class. Of course leisure is a universal need and an important indicator of social progress in a "society of producers" and a "republic of labor" (Marx). According to Marx, a society is richer the less time it uses for the production of its material means of subsistence, and the more time it sets free for other kinds of production, and for the all-round development of the individual, and above all for augmenting leisure time: "A saving of labor time is tantamount to an augmentation of free time, i.e., time for the full development of the individual, which in turn, as the greatest force of production, has a retroactive effect on the productive power of labor."[1]

This is of course especially true in and for socialism, in which production is not a means to an end and so subserves not the creation of surplus value, but rather the production of ever more copious and more developed means and opportunities for the development of the personality of all members of society, and hence the creation of more free time and better means for putting it to use. This includes enabling and preparing human beings to make conscious use of their free time, and to utilize and increase what society makes available.

Leisure as an achievement and a task

The struggle to guarantee a normal working day and a certain measure of free time has been going on since the birth of the organized labor movement. "Eight hours work, eight hours recreation, eight hours sleep!"—that was the slogan of the first universal day of struggle of the international working class on May 1, 1890. The eight-hour day was introduced in Germany as a result of the November Revolution. The annual vacation, today taken for granted as a regular part of the working year, became a reality only after long struggles. In the 1920s it was six days, later on twelve days.

Since 1945 many workers in the GDR have enjoyed an annual vacation of two weeks as well as a 46-hour, 6-day week. A further shortening of work time was not possible in the postwar years and the years of socialist construction. By the midsixties, production had reached such a level that further changes in the balance between work time and leisure time were effected. In 1966 the minimum vacation was increased from 12 to 15 workdays.

The workweek was shortened from 45 to 43¾ hours with the introduction of the five-day week (1966, initially every two weeks, and after 1967 every week). Since then the workday has been 8¾ hours for all persons who work one or two shifts.

More differentiated cuts in work time and an increase in the minimum vacation from 15 to 18 days (1972) have been and are a component part of the social policy program ratified by the 8th Party Congress of the SED. A further three-day lengthening of vacation leave became effective on January 1, 1979, when Saturdays were no longer counted as vacation days. Thus all workers in the GDR enjoy at least three-and-a-half weeks vacation. Women with two and more children, workers who work in a three-shift and continuous shift system, and other persons working under special conditions receive differentiated cuts in work time. All in all, workers in the GDR thus have had a significant measure of free time in the early eighties. Of the 365 calendar days of the normal year, 120–124 days are not working days (Saturdays and Sundays and other free days, legal holidays, vacations). In addition there is the daily free time after work, the well-deserved evening of relaxation.

As shown in Table 1 (in percent of those employed), the work time of the gainfully employed has become more differentiated as a consequence of the cuts in work time.

In 1985, every fifth person (above all, shift workers) in the GDR worked a 40-hour week. Thus in the mideighties, the highest measure yet of leisure time has been reached in the GDR. This too was part of the good balance sheet that the 11th Party Congress of the SED was able to draw up with reference to fulfilment of its principal task.

The reality of leisure time is also evident in daily life. The "working day" ends between 3:00 and 5:00 p.m. depending on when it begins. The inner cities

Table 1

Work Time (in % of employed)

	1970	1980
43.75 hours	92	77
42 hours	8	7
40 hours	0	16

with their shopping centers come to life after working hours, and traffic conges-
tion sets in. Depending on the season and the weather, long lines of autos head in
and out of the cities on the weekend; some seek recreation (and the exertion
associated with it), others the shopping opportunities and the cultural and sports
facilities offered in the cities. The beaches on the Baltic Sea, and the swimming
pools inland teem with people on hot summer days; hikers and tourists are always
under way. In the winter the snowy regions in the midland mountains are favorite
destinations for outings and recreation, and old and young enjoy skiing and
sledding.

On the whole, the working day, the regular ''evening of relaxation,'' the free
weekends, a relatively long summer vacation and a shorter winter vacation define
the yearly pattern and the rhythm of life. This rhythm of our way of life also has
an appreciable effect on cultural behavior, especially in the large cities, where a
good part of public cultural life takes place in the months between October and
June, and there is a ''season'' again, so to speak. The ''cultural summer'' is
important for those who stay in the city as well as for visitors and tourists. Major
public events on weekends, the scheduling of premiere evenings, the opening and
closing times of recreational establishments, the duration of events and their
scheduling are also important. Cultural offerings in vacation and holiday centers
and hotels, vacation resorts and recreational areas, and at campgrounds and
nature reserves, all tailored to need, are very effective. Thus our cultural arrangements and facilities are especially effective where people have time to
pursue their cultural likes and needs and where we make a conscious effort to
adapt the form and content of what is offered to the time available. Thus leisure
time is and remains a preferred space of cultural activity; an important part of
cultural work is encouraging and organizing the leisure-time activities of majorities and minorities.

And so a greater appreciation of time is also necessary with respect to leisure
time, since leisure time is scarce and is perceived, rightfully, as a precious good,
a space for leisure, rest, and creative activity. Indeed, ''work-free time'' is only
partly ''freely disposable time'' able to be organized according to one's own
judgment, through individual choice. The citizens of the GDR have many things
to do, and their time is highly organized. The working day defines how time is

used; most working people spend 10–11 hours "at work" (including pauses and time spent going to and from their jobs). The time of arising is in the early morning hours; most go to bed at 10:00 p.m., unless they are partying or go out (to visit friends and acquaintances, to restaurants and cultural establishments, to dance halls or bars, to sports and entertainment events).

Shopping, the family, the household, the house or apartment, the gardens and plot of land, the car and summer house—all require time. Many people are socially active; majorities and minorities develop personal needs and hobbies which they pursue in their free time. For these people especially, and indeed for many of us, it is not surprising that there is not enough time—especially leisure time—and that the stereotype holds true of people simply having "no time" and being always on the go. For many reasons, objective and subjective, adult working people in the GDR lead a life in which time is scarce. Free time (however one wishes to define it) is in short supply, and is perceived as a precious good. The program of the SED outlines the further path: "The party has set its sights on a further, more differentiated lengthening of the vacation time in relation to the rate of growth of the productivity of labor, as well as a step-by-step transition to the 40-hour week through reducing the working day and retaining the 5-day week. At the same time, the free time of working people is expanded by a rational organization of services and facilities."[2]

Trends in free-time occupations

The socialist way of life develops in work and in leisure time, with work influencing leisure in two ways: first, the amount of free time and the means and opportunities for shaping it depend on the productivity of labor, its result, and its effectiveness. Secondly, leisure pursuits are largely dependent on the work situation and on work time, on the content of labor, and on the physical and mental stress on workers in the labor process. Adults in the GDR are working people with leisure-time pursuits, whose free time essentially is defined by the social character of labor under socialism and by concrete work conditions. Thus the following relation applies to the balance between work time and leisure time: "At a given intensity and productive force of labor, the part of the social working day necessary for material production is shorter, and thus the amount of time made available for free, intellectual and social activities on the part of the individual is greater, the more uniformly labor is distributed among all able-bodied members of society, and the less one social stratum is able to shift the burden of the natural necessity of labor from itself and onto another stratum."[3] With regard to working time (80 percent of working people work 43¾ hours in a five-day week), the duration of vacation (18–23 working days unless arranged especially otherwise), and the amount of free time, there is broad social equality in the GDR. Therefore, a universally valid standard for the pace and rhythm of life and a basic social type of leisure-time behavior has taken shape. This is largely because work, its content, the time spent on the job, and the job situation are the most important determinants of leisure-time pursuits of adult working people, and tendentially of the entire population. Work essentially determines:

—the temporal structure of the life process, the situation and the amount of free time (dynamic changes are taking place in this domain as a consequence of the effects of intensification, i.e., increasing shift work, flexible working time arrangements in services, in commerce, administration, etc., the formation of meaningful leisure pursuits outside the weekend as well, and the accompanying change in demands and habits);

—the content of free time in many respects, insofar as it is time for the reproduction of labor power; the division of labor in production tends to influence the specific features of leisure-time pursuits;

—material and ideal, social and individual opportunities for free time and its use.

The dialectic between the reproduction of labor power and the development of the personality is and remains characteristic of leisure time. As sociological studies have shown, workers (and indeed all those gainfully employed) need their free time, today as well as in the time of Marx, "for growth, development and keeping physically healthy," "to enjoy the open air and sunshine," "for meals," and "for healthy sleep to collect, renew, and refresh life forces." It is for this reason, and in this connection, that free time is "also a time for forming the human being, intellectual development, the fulfilment of social functions, social intercourse, and the free play of physical and intellectual life forces."[4]

Many projects for the development of culture-oriented leisure-time behavior and a number of publications on leisure and recreation take insufficient account of the reproductive functions of leisure time. Physical recreation, sleep, chores in the family, playing with children, etc., are not counted even primarily as free time (according to the time budget statistics of the survey of 1985, adults sleep seven-and-a-half hours on the average on workdays, eight and three-quarter hours on Saturdays, and nine hours on Sundays!). Housework is considered a total loss of life time. Analysis is premised less on real-life processes during leisure time and more on a biased concept of leisure time which accepts only certain life forms and activities as leisure-time behavior. Then, in evaluations, these alone are regarded as more or less obligatory for a socialist way of life. Social activity, education, information, the enjoyment of art, and creative activities—these alone are accepted as "meaningful" leisure time. But even as these socially and culturally important modes of conduct grow, the leisure time of working people also remains a time for recreation and physical equilibration, idleness and rest, sociability and entertainment.

Sociological analyses of real free-time behavior also bring to light this complexity. In the leisure time of the vast majority of the population, necessary, ever-recurrent activities are carried out in a huge and constant volume; here too, a permanent reproduction of the societal and the individual life process takes place.

The time for free, self-chosen activities, on the other hand, seems to be rather too short, and this explains the widespread feeling of a lack of free time. Indeed, free time has a dual nature. On the one hand, it is nothing more than a quantitative concept: leisure time is time that is free of socially regulated, heuristically prescribed, and temporally normed work, i.e., basically the time before and after a job in the life of a working adult. (It seems to me that the concept of leisure time is applicable only to secondary school pupils, apprentices and students, and gainfully employed adults.) With regard to the unity of the individual reproduction process as well, a "broader" concept of leisure time is warranted. *Leisure time can be fully regarded as a contrary concept to work time and be used methodologically in this sense* as well, if of course eating, loving, sleeping, drinking, and unavoidable dressing and undressing are not further reckoned to be part of life and leisure. In everyday consciousness as well, leisure time is an all-inclusive concept, and associated with the daily end-of-the-day relaxation, the work-free weekend, and vacation periods. The current practice of calling this "off-work time" unfortunately does not correspond to the facts, however useful the breakdown of the time budget into work time and off-work time may be for time budget research. Neither "off-work time" nor free time is free of work, as anyone knows. Sound common sense rebels, therefore, not without some justification, against designating everything having to do with time off the job as leisure. The attribute "free" does after all allude to freedom, to doing as you please, being unrestrained, to making one's own choice, and to the absence of constraint. To this extent, in everyday consciousness as well, leisure time or free time is understood to refer to that part of "off-work time" that is free of required activities and ever recurrent obligations, i.e., time that is essentially at an individual's disposal, and also is so perceived by the individual. To this extent leisure time is also essentially individually disposable time outside of work time or temporally structured activities (school, education, studies, military service) that are always bound to necessary obligations. Cultural theory can link leisure time to the individual, and leave "social free time" or "disposable time," following Marx, rather to the economist. However, we should not overuse the concept of leisure time; it is ultimately no more than a kind of quantitative measure. It is unquestionably not a complement to work; recreation and idleness would certainly be better suited for this even if idleness, in the sense of free unrestrained activity and active enjoyment of life, surely does not belong to the educated forms of socialist culture. Research must also keep to a specific catalog of activities in a narrow conception of leisure time; it cannot begin with the concrete individual, and individual values and preferences which after all vary quite considerably, especially with respect to the use of free time. Thus for some, sweaty activities such as mountain climbing, running, or taking a sauna are the true elixirs of life, while for others they are activities to be avoided absolutely. It is basically the same with all leisure-time practical and intellectual activities. Nonetheless sociological research is able to discriminate a number of basic trends in the free-time behavior of working adults in the GDR.

Let us now describe these briefly:

Work time and the expenditures of time associated with it are the critical factors defining the course of the day for working people. The temporal pace of the way of life in the GDR and the other socialist countries essentially is determined by the alternation between work and evening relaxation, the working week and the weekend, the working year and vacation. The various forms of socialization of labor and property (nationally owned factories, cooperative property, private work), but even more so concrete working conditions, have an influence on the scope and content of leisure time. The essential differences between intellectual and physical work, between city and country, and in living standard and cultural level of social classes and strata are also manifested in differences in how leisure time is shaped. Further progressive changes are contingent upon the continuing diminution of social differences in living conditions and on the formation of sophisticated socialist cultural needs for the entire people and of a conscious leisure-time human behavior.

The various forms of reproduction of labor power and the necessary chores in household and family take up the greatest part of free time (e.g., sleep, housework, shopping, preparing and eating meals, and taking care of and raising children).

What Marx called ''free labor in the household, within a moral framework, for the family itself'' and Engels called ''housework'' or ''private housework,'' must be done by people themselves, by all members of society, under socialism.[5] A cultivated way of life is and remains contingent upon the effective and rational fulfilment of these tasks. Essential aspects of the satisfaction of material and cultural needs are related to housework; in this area too, in general there are aspirations toward a higher quality of life and higher level of culture. Good cooking and a comfortable home are absolutely necessary components of a socialist way of life, in any case in our notion of culture and according to our own national traditions.

Many practical leisure-time activities have to do with improving and beautifying individual living conditions, work in the house or in the garden, and involve participation in socially useful work in one's neighborhood and community. A plenitude of active occupations is characteristic of leisure time under socialism. Ours is definitely not a kind of ''passive consumer society.'' On the contrary: there is much active work even in leisure time in our country. There is a tendency for ''leisure-time work'' to increase, especially as a consequence of the higher standard of living and more sophisticated individual needs and demands on life. The main reasons for this are:

—the increase in the establishment and use of gardens and plots, bungalows and cottages, with a tendency toward an essential differentiation in leisure-time behavior between city and country as well as by season; more than 50 percent of all households cultivate and use gardens, usually house gardens and small gardens. According to time budget surveys, time spent in garden work has increased on the average from three to five hours per week per person (blue-collar and white-collar workers). No other items in the time budget have shown such a development.

—secondary jobs of the most varied types, in particular, raising animals and crops on private plots in the countryside, involvement in the VKSK (an association of small gardeners, settlers, and small animal breeders of the GDR), personal hobbies, collecting activities, etc. (More than 20 percent of the GDR households produced eggs, meat, honey, milk, and wool for sale to the state in 1985. Even more supply vegetables and fruits.)

—paid and unpaid "evening work," especially large amounts of time spent in putting up new buildings, modernizing and renovating houses and apartments, as well as villas and bungalows;

—a steady, high proportion of unpaid social activity in leisure time, including participation of large segments of the population in meetings and assemblies of various organizations and administrative boards.

Active forms of recreation and physical exercise outdoors show an increasing trend, including evening strolls, window-shopping, leisure-time sports, garden work, tourism, and hiking. We must assume that these activities will continue to expand with the further intensification of the social reproduction process, growing urbanization and urban forms of living, increasing shift work, etc., and other factors. Another factor is a greater mobility of the population, which is made possible and further facilitated by the growing number of private cars. The urban environment, country landscapes, and recreational areas near cities are being used increasingly for contact with nature and active physical recreation. (At present about 50 percent of all households use their private cars for these purposes as well as for visiting acquaintances, friends, and relatives.)

The time spent on education, social activity, information, enjoyment of art, sports, sociability, and entertainment continues to account for a large part of leisure time. All studies show several major groups of leisure-time activities:

(a) Entertainment, information, enjoyment of art and education through the use of the mass media and individual cultural activity. Daily use of the television, radio, and press is typical of our way of life, and studies have long shown that on the average two hours per day are spent watching television (usually in the evenings) and one-and-a-half hours for the radio (early morning, evening, Saturday and Sunday mornings).

Let the critics of the media note that time budget research shows growing amounts of time spent in active use of the media. Blue-collar and white-collar workers spent nine-and- a-half hours weekly in 1974, and 11.75 hours weekly in 1985 in this manner. There are three factors working together here: the steady improvement in the living situation and the accompanying binding of leisure time to house and home; (2) the equipment of households with color televisions (in 1985 40 percent of all households), stereos, and cassette recorders; (3) the fuller and more varied media offerings and the development of better picture and sound quality.

(b) Socializing and entertainment within the family, in circles of friends and acquaintances, with one's workmates, games and amusements at home, in the garden, or on one's plot of land, in restaurants and taverns, in cultural houses or clubs, organizations, associations, and unions.

(c) Active cultural involvement of the most varied kind (handicrafts, arts, technical, scientific), diverse hobbies and amateur activities, usually individual and for personal purposes, often in the company of others as well, less in strictly organized forms and more in leisure-time associations.

(d) Visits to exhibitions and museums, clubs and cultural houses, cultural events and public festivities, the movies, theaters, exhibitions, and concerts. Major public cultural events in the city and in the countryside, on the streets and on public squares are especially appealing: these include national and local festivals, fairs, processions, music festivals, car and motorcycle races, old-timer rallies, dances, and entertainment in the open air.

(e) Unpaid social activity, political work, continuing education (political, specialized, general) are all leisure-time activities in which millions of GDR citizens regularly take part.[6]

Leisure time, the "time for higher activities" and "idleness," is restricted for working adults by the plenitude of social demands and individual duties. In particular, working women and mothers, managerial personnel in all areas and at all levels, and socially very active citizens with rich cultural needs have too little time, even "time to live" in conformity with the social opportunities and individual needs. Haste, rushing about, and the pressures of time burden life's course and do not necessarily promote productivity and creativity in work. Without leisure and rest, culture cannot fully thrive and become a permanent part of people's habits and life-style. All these things considered, it is necessary to give greater consideration to the relationship between work and leisure time, between intensification and culture, in theory and in politics. Therefore, a leisure time that promotes productivity and is individually gratifying, together with practical and intellectual, productive and reproductive, cultural and athletic activities is an important area for social efforts and individual contributions. Intensification of production cannot be answered by a further expansion of earlier leisure-time activities. Leisure time must definitely be a complement to work, but it must also be an alternative to the work world. Freedom must reign more forcefully here alongside necessity: freedom of choice of the time and of the place for an activity, change of job, and freedom to do as one pleases. A more productive world of work makes for a richer world of leisure time, but it also implies a more active, more modern, more tolerant concept of leisure time: as an offering and a project.[7]

We also need a more aggressive stance in all forms of cultural work with regard to the antipodes to a meaningful free time: i.e., immoderate alcoholism, the benumbing and stupefaction of the senses by endless musical gushings, an unselective and uncritical use of the media, emulation of Western fashions and cultural trends, and primitiveness, crudeness, and brutality, wherever they occur.

Leisure time and intensification

The dialectic between work and leisure time which is typical for our lives is intensified under the conditions of general transition to intensively expanded reproduction in all branches of the economy. Theoretical considerations and cultural policy concepts of leisure time must without fail take into account that intensification has placed numerous additional demands and new forms of stress on whole groups of the working population.

Work around the clock will be called for in broader areas of the reproduction process, and is economically necessary as well for making use of the full capacity of high technology and information processing technology. Overtime is often still a condition for plan fulfilment, not only in the service sector and in transport, but also in heavy industry and agriculture. Shift work will also be further increased. Managerial personnel at all levels and in all areas are permanently under more time stress than the majority of their colleagues. The good economic performance and the generally stable and successful development of the GDR over the past few years are in part very much the product of the very high personal effort of many managerial personnel in collectivities, job spheres, factories, and combinates. This applies as well to party and state functionaries and officials of mass organizations and fraternal parties. These persons especially often lack the necessary free time for rest, recreation, and self-cultivation. They do not find time to keep informed and enjoy art and entertainment. Even where individual needs are cultivated appropriately, some sacrifice of active recreation and cultural activity must be made for reasons of time; professional work, social activity, meetings, conferences, and travel all demand time.

Scientists and engineers in Jena explained in informal talks that they spend a good deal of their free time working at their jobs as well, but that there are a few things that they cannot do without: namely, listening to good music in a quiet, peaceful atmosphere, and movement in the open air. It is certainly necessary to consider more effective means of active physical exercise for these social groups especially, and to study more attentively the international experience with fitness training for managerial personnel and scientific and technical personnel. Indeed, individuals are responsible for their health and performance, but the social prerequisite for needed improvements in efficiency cannot be created individually. Universal, lasting changes in the content and organization of labor are part of the process of intensification of the mode of production and of our way of life. Cultural establishments would also do well to adapt to these trends. Technical interests develop actively alongside artistic needs; computers also occupy free time. The body also, as well as the mind, needs movement; not only are bowling and tenpins very popular, but apprentices and young workers enjoy testing their strength and build their muscles through muscle training, while body building, karate, and other martial arts are becoming more popular. Strength is always useful, not only in work, but also in love, and a well-built muscular young man has more chances with the female sex than a pale weakling. It is even better when an alert mind moves and animates a beautiful body.

On the whole labor is becoming more intensive on all sides; modern technology is penetrating increasingly into the preparatory stages of production, administration, organization, and management. The number of jobs requiring the continuous presence of a person and unabating attention is increasing. International experience tells the same story: in general work is made easier by the use of modern technology, but at the same time it becomes more psychologically demanding. The decline in physically heavy one-sided work is accompanied by the trend toward a growing poverty in movement, even in material production. Jobs requiring sitting and standing continue to grow in number, and stimulating activities encouraging movement are in demand, and perhaps not only in leisure time, as international examples in highly productive firms show. To prevent precipitate hopes: about 70 percent of industrial workers in the GDR still do predominantly physical work, and their supportive joint and muscular apparatus is placed under exaggerated stress in production, which could explain why some industrial workers participate only reluctantly in traditional or new athletic and cultural offerings in their leisure time (internationally as well, it is mostly those whose jobs involve primarily intellectual work and who are under considerable nervous stress who jog in their leisure time). But the division of labor continues to grow in the productive branches as well, and activities that are even more one-sided are created as the traditional division of labor is abolished. All these things make the problem of creating intellectually stimulating activities encouraging active body movements in leisure time a condition of intensive expanded reproduction under socialism. We will not give up our ideal of an all-round developed individual; indeed, individuals themselves would like to work effectively, live in a cultivated way, and keep healthy. Of course many can do a lot more for this on their own initiative, but they also need the help of society, and stimulating and fascinating activities for active participation and a convivial social life. New communal cultural facilities as well as impressive mass athletics events (such as the peace relay or the big hiking days) are indications of growing possibilities.

New kinds of stresses and different ways of structuring time are closely connected with the increase in shift work. At the end of 1984, 23.9 percent of all industrial workers were working three shifts, 12.3 percent were working two shifts, and 69.7 percent were working normal shifts. Shift work, flexible working hours with several consecutive free days, has become typical for many people working in the service sector, the health sector, in retail trade, and in transportation. This applies also to "leisure-time workers" in the recreation sector and in sports, in culture, in entertainment, and the other arts. Shift work is becoming increasingly a part of processes preparatory to production, as well as in information-processing branches. It remains to be seen whether shift work is tending to become the norm, but it is certain that in the 1990s at least one-third of all working people will be doing shift work, and living with flexible work schedules. A consequence of this is free time stretching over several days, often a week long. But intensive, temporarily longer-lasting work periods with short alternations are a consequence as well. This work pace gives rise to another way of organizing time; on the one hand the demands of short-term reproduction of labor power dominate absolutely, while on the other there is more time available for more intensive engagement with personal hobbies and amateur pursuits. Leisure time will also be more mobile, and not confined to the weekends. In any case, we think that specific sports and cultural work for and with "shift workers" is more urgent than ever. The communal infrastructure, physical training and sports, the cultural sphere, and even the media, have so far been slow in reacting. Shift workers appear on GDR television criticizing that not enough relaxing entertainment is offered after the late shift, e.g., programs and series, journalistic sessions and films, which help an individual wind down from work and relax. Television is seen as a practical sleep therapy—a thoroughly correct demand made of the medium. All experience shows that traditional needs are changed by intensification, and new temporal structures emerge in which recreation, information, physical exercise, culture and art, as well as entertainment, are sought. Thus we think intensification will alter our overall way of life on the job and leisure time. The 27th Party Congress of the CPSU called attention to this: "As experience shows, the development of the scientific and technical revolution has resulted in a perfection of social relations, a rethinking, the emergence of a new psychology, and the implementation of dynamism as a way of life and a norm of existence."[8]

Major consequences of intensification are already discernible in leisure time in the GDR:

—Changes are occurring in the time patterns of our way of life through increasing shift work and flexible work schedules. Uninterrupted periods of leisure time are growing longer for larger segments of the population. The "normality" of our way of life is being broken; the infrastructure, the media, local cultural life, recreation and sports will have to promote this process through more flexible time scheduled for what they offer;

—New and higher demands are being placed on the occupational performance of the working class, the collective farmers, and the intelligentsia; in particular, a revolution is taking place in the leisure time of the scientific and technical intelligentsia;

—The professional, spatial, and temporal mobility of the workforce is increasing, with people working and living in different places and changing jobs and firms several times during their working life (this is a fact today, e.g., in the Berlin construction program, work on the railroad, all forms of assembly work, maritime occupations, and mobile branches of production);

—Other new possibilities for joint and individual use of leisure time are being created by all the new media and all the leisure-time facilities of industry, retail trade, communal cultural work, physical training, and sports.

Of course all these things assume sophisticated personal needs and cultivated individual abilities for actively and consciously shaping one's own life in leisure time. Public organization and cultural incentives are still needed for this insofar as other leisure-time ideas and concepts are constantly being fed into GDR homes through the bourgeois media. In any case we academics should do more to see that all who are responsible for the work and lives of the population, as well as those who produce for leisure time and work in the recreational sector, acquire a better understanding of a socialist concept of leisure time.

Although the individual is responsible for his or her leisure time, that individual cannot alone create the societal preconditions for a brisker economy and developed culture in leisure time.

Leisure time as a value

People's consciousness of time is growing, insight into the limitedness and unrepeatability of an individual's life is common in a society such as ours with its materialist outlook and the higher demands that the general population make on life. Leisure time cannot yet be the decisive yardstick of production and of wealth; necessities still dominate our actions: of these, the necessity of ensuring peace and the survival of mankind is number one. In the system of personal values, leisure time still understandably lags behind money, consumption, and housing, to name only three basic "material" life demands of many. Nonetheless, leisure time is gaining in worth, especially among the politically engaged and culturally more sensitive part of the population, the youth. The international debate on the value of life and culture in an atomic age has certainly contributed to this; the ardent desire to survive for another and better life has had its effect. The worldwide criticism of human alienation, consumerism, and suppression of time makes its mark just as much as do the penetrating questions of art into the meaning and purpose of human existence in today's world. Romantic hopes and nostalgic melancholy glimmer, yearning for the "good old days" surges up anew: on the whole progressive ideas and progressive demands on life are at work here. For this reason as well a Marxist awareness of time and the world is extremely fitting; all tendencies that face up to the times and understand leisure time as a value must be vigorously promoted. The following analytic and hypothetical points may be made for our country:

(1) A higher claim on life involves a creative awareness of the uniqueness and unrepeatability of an individual life. Even in the face of the continued threat to human existence by the nuclear danger, and the sharpening of global problems, the need to live actively and consciously, to make as good use of present time as possible, to master and enjoy life as well and as effectively as possible, is growing. The greater self-awareness of individuals is reflected in a greater

sensitivity to time, in the perception of the right to one's own free time, and in the need for leisure and rest, individual development, and self-determined activity in leisure time.

(2) The economy of time more often determines individual leisure-time behavior. Necessary, recurrent activities in leisure time should be carried out as effectively and as rationally as possible. The loss of free time due to long periods spent waiting, delays in transportation, the considerable time wasted in shopping, and for taking care of personal matters, etc., are being viewed increasingly critically. Individuals will react each in their own way to intensification: if work is to be better and faster everywhere, the effectiveness and rationality of all life processes must be increased. Of course citizens must also do their part for this: boring, stodgy people bring nothing to the economy or to culture.

(3) Leisure time should above all mean recreation and relaxation after work, and should at least in part be an alternative world to work. Entertainment and sociability, fun and games, media culture and art should enrich everyday life just as much as recreation and physical activities, excursions, and travel. Free time should be stimulating and interesting, boredom is taboo, wasting time on indifferent and fruitless activities is increasingly rejected.

(4) Leisure time should be useful, for oneself, for one's family, for others, and for society. Leisure-time work is regarded as compensatory, but also essentially as useful activity. It should serve health and at the same time help to make life better and more beautiful: this is especially evident in work in the home and the garden. Second jobs are also increasing: society has an extreme interest in the important services of the small plot producer of farm products, in crafts work, and in the additional personal incomes of individuals. Leisure time should be of use in a broader sense as well: namely, it should serve physical and moral well-being, the cultivation of contacts and human relations, and the maintenance and improvement of health and joy in living.

(5) Leisure time is an issue of international dispute. Capital wants to invest the leisure-time culture of the masses with its values, and permanently bind the working classes to the capital valorization process through consumption, media culture, and entertainment. The ideology of acquisitiveness and possession must also determine leisure time, and here too individual needs are supposed to triumph over social interests. The superiority of the wealthy and strong is celebrated and the masses should "voluntarily" abandon the higher aspirations of life and individual development. The labor movement and the socialist countries must counterpose to all this a concept of leisure time that is oriented to the development of the personality of all and the flourishing of a communal spirit.

(6) Free time remains a high priority as a "space for human development" (Marx) and a part of the production process. The needs and possibilities for individual, many-sided activity in leisure time are growing, since intensification means the production of more means and more time for a way of life rich in needs and full of enjoyment. On the other hand, leisure time remains a time for

reproduction of labor power and a time for the reproduction of a standard of living that is rising for the individual as well, and this in turn means spending even more time and energy, especially on more sophisticated needs.

These things constitute a claim of society as well as an individual demand: a person is himself of course primarily responsible for what he does in his free time, with what, and with whom, and how he attends to his duties on the job, the enjoyment of life, and the values of culture.

On the whole, an active and conscious use of free time is an important precondition for the development of the society's forces of production and of its individuals: "An economy whose strength relies increasingly on the ability of man to control the latest technologies, requires a creative climate throughout the whole of social life if it is to thrive."[9] And we might add in leisure time especially.

Notes

1. Karl Marx, *Grundrisse der Kritik der politischen Ökonomie* (Berlin: Dietz, 1953), 599.
2. *Programm der Sozialistischen Einheitspartei Deutschlands* (Berlin: Dietz, 1976), 26.
3. Karl Marx, *Das Kapital*, vol. 1 in Marx/Engels, *Werke*, vol. 23 (Berlin: Dietz, 1972), 552.
4. *Ibid.*, 280.
5. Karl Marx, *Das Kapital*, vol. 1 in Marx/Engels, *Werke*, vol. 23, 216 and 417; and Friedrich Engels, *Ursprung der Familie, des Privateigentums und des Staates*, ibid., vol. 21, 158.
6. Similar trends have been described by objective observers of real life in the GDR in this area as well. Compare: Brigitte Deja-Lölhöffel, *Freizeit in der DDR* (Berlin [W]: Verlag Gebrüder Holzapfel, 1986).
7. See, on time budgets and the amount of available leisure time: *Lebensniveau im Sozialismus* (Berlin: Die Wirtschaft 1983), 205–26 and *Sozialpolitik* (Berlin: Die Wirtschaft, 1985), 187f.
8. *Politischer Bericht des Zentralkomitees der KPdSU an den XXVII. Parteitag der Kommunistischen Partei der Sowjetunion*. Speaker: M. S. Gorbachev (Berlin: Dietz, 1986), 13.
9. *Bericht des Zentralkomitees der Sozialistischen Einheitspartei Deutschlands an den XI. Parteitag der Kommunistischen Partei der SED*. Speaker: Erich Honecker (Berlin: Dietz, 1986), 54.

Translated by Michel Vale

Media Use in Free Time by the GDR Population

Comments from a Culture Sociology Perspective

LOTHAR BISKY

The daily cultural life of the working masses is marked increasingly by the use of the mass media in the free-time culture of the 20th century. The system of cultural mass communication which has grown up and taken root in the last two decades is being restructured by the use of new media. A knowledge of the stable structures and changeable aspects of current media use is therefore especially relevant to the changes to be expected in how leisure time is structured. The most important trends in the use of the media by the GDR population in the mideighties emerge from an assessment of the results of cultural sociological studies.

Manifold and diverse use of the media has become a full-fledged part of the cultural behavior of the masses of the population in the seventies in the GDR. Even in the sixties, TV viewing, radio listening, reading the press, and listening to records and cassettes were characteristic, along with the then more frequent moviegoing. During the seventies, and especially since the beginning of the eighties, new dimensions of media use have come into being as the number of receivers, records, etc. in the home has grown, so that now an absolute majority of households have a basic stock of electronic entertainment equipment which make it possible to listen to the radio, watch television, or listen to records and cassettes at any time, while enjoyment of cultural offerings of the media in the home and outside of it (on portable radios) can be more diversified. With respect to media use and its role in daily cultural life, not only has there been a quantitative growth, but also a qualitatively new situation with the following distinctive characteristics has been created:

(1) Media use more in accordance with needs and expectations (due not in the last instance to the possibility of choosing among radio, television, listening to music, reading, visiting the movies, etc.);

(2) Being able to choose from among a multifaceted range of media possibilities in conformity with the individual situation and the individual's mental disposition;

(3) An increase in the relative lack of independence of media use on location (portable equipment) and time (program variety, stocks of phonograph records and cassettes in households). Two and three televisions, several radios in the household, televisions and radios in the garden house and summer, car radios, etc., are today a mass phenomenon;

(4) For the majority of citizens currently living in the GDR, media use is no longer a novelty (as was for example television in the early sixties), and today the generations occupying crucial positions in society are increasingly those for whom a varied use of the media had been characteristic since childhood. Thus a vast range of experience in the use of the media is already at hand, and experiences with media use are determining media behavior in qualitatively new ways.

Mass everyday use of the media as a social and cultural reality

Before we go into the scope and content of media use, we should call attention to a point that is of fundamental significance for assessing it: namely, the absorption of culture acquires qualitatively new dimensions as a consequence of the ease of accessibility of the media or their multifaceted cultural services, which today are a permanent part of the everyday cultural life of millions of people (e.g., daily access to political information, listening to music early, watching television in the evening, to mention only a few). This varied and rich use of the media often results in comparisons being made between the amount of media use and other cultural modes of behavior, and in a certain sense attention (of research as well) is directed toward these new quantities. As a consequence, this not infrequently conceals from view three essential starting points which are important in connection with the use of media:

(1) It is overlooked that the use of the media cannot be evaluated culturally if it is not placed in relationship to the totality of cultural activities, and if—and this is especially important in this context—the use of the media is isolated from the overall context of cultural communication. Usually this leads to erroneous assessments and one-sided evaluations.

(2) The differentiation in media use, and peculiarities in media reception such as its assimilation by, and inseparable connection with other social activities and cultural modes of behavior are not taken sufficiently into account. It can thus happen that precisely the specific functions of the mass media with regard to

cultural progress under socialism are overlooked.

(3) Comparisons of media reception with other cultural activities, and especially with the reception of the "traditional" arts are often emphasized. Usually this results in a contrast, and sometimes even an opposition, that is not only fruitless, but also misses the specificity of the cultural functions of the media. Whereas on the one hand it is certainly not customary to compare classical ballet with reading literature, television entertainment is often assessed applying the criteria of the theater and not infrequently comes out the loser. And so occasionally qualitative criteria, unjustified at such a general level, creep into statements about, say, television behavior. There is today unanimity in cultural sociology that these contrasts and oppositions are inappropriate and in many respects even contradict the results of research.

These preliminary comments have not been intended to diminish the outstanding role of media use in everyday cultural life; however, they will hopefully help to situate media use properly in the cultural communications process (in accordance with our theoretical conceptions), show it in its context, and contribute to a clearer picture of the specific functions of the media. Therefore, in presenting findings regarding trends in media use, it should always be taken into account that these are an inseparable part of a multitude of other cultural communications processes.

Any analysis of cultural communication must take into account the interrelationships between production and reception. No communication takes place without reception or without the use of what is produced and supplied. This question is of crucial significance, especially for the realization of the communicative functions of the mass media. To fulfil their communicative functions properly, it is necessary ". . . to ascertain clearly and distinctly in every question, and at every point the moods of the masses, their true needs, aspirations, and thoughts without a trace of false idealization."[1]

The general trends in media use in the seventies stabilized in the early eighties. They may be characterized as follows:

(1) The manifold use of the mass media is becoming a dominant cultural mass process. Thus 70 percent of the population watch television roughly two hours daily and listen to the radio about two hours daily, usually in conjunction with other activities. In practically every household, at least one daily newspaper, and usually several newspapers and magazines are read. All sociological studies indicate growing needs for communication (exchange of opinion, discussion).

(2) One of the effects of a unified socialist education system has been a distinct rise in the general and specialized education of the bulk of the population, and this is especially true of the level of education and skills of the younger generation. This has meant higher standards with regard to how the mass media function.

(3) Needs develop in a manifold way, and in some areas (e.g., reading) they can only be satisfied with the greatest effort (of publishers and news media).

(Therefore the question today under socialism can no longer be posed in the one-sided form of, namely, how the media must take into account the present cultural level of the bulk of the population in their activities; but rather it must also be asked how they can do justice to the existing level!).

(4) A closer collaboration between mass communication and other processes of communication in society is becoming characteristic. What the mass media offer is more effective when there exists a collective consensus about the values of socialism and the socialist way of life. In numerous communication processes—among the workforce, in culture and clubhouses, in the family and in leisure-time groups, on trains and in restaurants, there occurs a mass exchange of opinions on books, films, television programs, etc., and media offerings are compared with people's own social experiences and discussed on that basis.

(5) In contrast to predictions put forth in other quarters, the use of the mass media has not forced other cultural activities into the background; only adult moviegoing has diminished somewhat as television viewing has increased.

(6) In the seventies, tendencies toward differentiation of media use were discernible alongside these general trends (which are characteristic for all classes and strata).

These tendencies may be attributed to:

—a differentiation of needs in correspondence with social structure. This not only applies to differences between classes and social strata; a qualitative differentiation process also is to be observed within classes and strata. The relation between physical and intellectual work has had a particularly great impact here.

—differences in objective living and working conditions. Remuneration according to performance also means a differentiation in the income from labor, which is also reflected in possessions, the number of records and cassettes owned, etc.

—a territorial differentiation of cultural life. Although major differences between the city and the countryside have been reduced, the possibilities of cultural activity are still different in city and countryside, or in large cities and small cities respectively.

—individual differentiation of media use in accordance with individual variations in life-style, or special needs, interests, and demands.

Media use does not have a general leveling out effect on needs, taste, and demands. Rather, both uniform tendencies of media use in all the principal social groups as well as differentiation individually, within all principal social groups, are characteristic. Sociological studies confirm that the content and nature of work, the level of social relations, and active social involvement have an influence on media use. As working and living conditions progress, members of all classes and social strata participate more actively in shaping the life of society under socialism, and as the level of culture and education continues to rise, we may expect a mass process of change in media use which will also of course depend on the level of media offerings.

If we focus on social differentiation in media use, the difference between youth and adults is in some cases clearer than the difference between classes and social strata. This applies to the type of music preferred, the entertainment programs on the television, to the fact that young people account for more than 70 percent of all moviegoers, and to the lesser importance of television for youth who are unmarried and have no children to care for. In addition, a frequent preference for collective forms of reception (music, movies) is striking among youth. Audiences at television programs and rock music arrangements are also clearly the younger members of the population.

Ernst Schumacher presented the following calculations to a seminar at the Academy of Arts on February 29, 1984. "Statistically seen, a GDR citizen spends 20–25 minutes annually attending a concert, 30–40 minutes visiting a museum, 2 hours attending a theater, 7.5 hours going to the movies, 120 hours reading (in which fine literature accounts for the smallest portion) and 750 hours watching television. . . ."[2]

The significance of such figures should not be exaggerated. However, it would be more problematic to disregard them, especially as they will not change fundamentally over the next few years, and could even grow with the introduction of video recorders, etc. Popular music, radio and TV entertainment, and films are the principal types of media used. These tendencies are taken into consideration by the mass media in planning their programs. Entertainment productions are most popular. We will now examine a few trends in more detail.

All analyses of the recent years indicate a growing need for entertainment, and at the same a clear differentiation in these needs. It is to that extent quite important to determine more exactly what these growing needs for entertainment imply concretely. Studies carried out in 1984 among industrial workers in large Berlin factories show that the needs for entertainment fall into four categories:

—First, the entertainment arts in the narrow sense, of which relaxation, distraction, and entertainment in the course of other activities is expected.

—Second, entertainment through movie films and TV, as well as television plays and films.

—Third, entertainment productions that are perceived as special cultural experiences (visits to the Friedrich Urban Palace, the Palace of the Republic, etc.).

—Fourth, needs for entertainment in the narrow sense of the word; social gatherings, in which questions small and large are discussed casually and satisfyingly with colleagues, friends, and acquaintances.

Let us now look into the needs for entertaining films, television series, and television films and plays. Industrial workers usually welcome our taking these needs more thoroughly into consideration in our television programs. But these needs in themselves indicate that the mere ascertainment that entertainment is the primary expectation tells us nothing about demands and expectations with regard to the content and esthetic qualities of this entertainment. Conversations show that more than "mere distraction" is desired from films and television plays and series.

Industrial workers distinguish very clearly here between "dull, superficial" entertainment and "discriminating" entertainment. They expect these offerings to have a content that says something to them, and has or could have some personal relevance. They want everyday problems to be taken up in an entertaining and relaxing manner. In their conversation, the workers did not distinguish between entertainment and art. Expectations were with regard to entertaining programs that take up or touch upon their own social experiences, spur reflection and encourage, and take the viewer seriously as a partner. One formulation by an industrial worker expresses this expectation excellently: "A really entertaining story has parallels to our own lives, makes you laugh once in a while, and gives you the strength to keep going the next day." High standards are placed on artistic quality and craftsmanship in this respect, and not in the last instance as the result of "internationalized viewing experience." It may be inferred at least hypothetically that the expectation that programs should take up everyday questions, and perhaps be relevant to one's own social experience, reflects the need for a social and cultural identity as a citizen of the GDR, and the expectation of being a part of the process of shaping a consensus on the values of socialism and its way of life.

To interpret such needs it is important to understand that a functional differentiation of social use of what is offered by the cultural media has entrenched itself as a determining tendency. For film this means that there is an increasing tendency for the same spectators to see films labeled "entertainment" or "high standard," respectively, depending on the situation, on the film, etc. The social categorization of the public in terms of differing standards has been largely superseded, which does not mean, of course, that differences no longer exist. But these differences are of another kind today than some years ago. The level of education and culture, as well as viewer experience, have left their mark. In general it may be said that needs are ahead of the actual product. In the mid-eighties, the question is no longer the one-sided one of how the cultural level of viewers can be taken into consideration in entertainment (i.e., adjusting it to their level), but more of how one can do justice to this cultural level. It cannot be clearer that mediocrity in production cannot justly appeal to the needs of the masses for entertainment. The functional differentiation of film viewing habits occasionally leads to misunderstandings which have consequences for interpreting the level of need. Such misunderstandings derive primarily from the fact that the cultural aspects of general media habits are not yet sufficiently entrenched in consciousness. Through the media, entertainment in the context of everyday life activities, as a parallel activity, etc., has perhaps become representative of a mass trend in music and style which indeed the media also need as a "background and a condition for their quite unique mass appeal."[3]

Media use in the context of everyday life activities, and especially medium entertainment, has become characteristic. This coincidence of habits often gives the media a certain casual quality insofar as other activities and/or social relations are going on at the same time. Media use as a "secondary activity," as a parallel activity, has now become a mass phenomenon. Media use while doing housework hardly even merits comment. As regards television, most people are usually informed beforehand, and programs are preselected. However, not infrequently the different channels are scanned or the television is sometimes turned off. In switching through the various channels, the program opted for is the one that seems to correspond to the expectations of the moment. This also tends to give a certain casual quality to television viewing. Listeners and viewers are faced with the problem of finding that which corresponds to their need, their momentary situation, the expectations of family members, etc. The casualness of viewing has to do with the degree of attention given to a program. If attention must be divided between two or more activities, it is no longer exclusively focused on the program.

A fluctuation in attention is also very frequent even if no other activity is going on alongside of listening or viewing. Casualness alternates with concentration depending on the programs offered. Thus it is not a consistent mode of behavior; frequent variations in the intensity of attention are characteristic. But this casualness is not the only conspicuous change in reception behavior, which is also becoming increasingly more conscious and selective. In particular, in the case of entertainment programs, the entire program is not always absorbed with the same concentration; sometimes only parts of it or individual bits are picked up. Conversations, sometimes even reading, are interspersed. Media reception is becoming more demanding. Expectations with regard to content and the external attractiveness of entertainment programs have clearly become greater. Most people have many years of viewing and listening experience. People know what the medium can do; they have standards for comparison. A consciousness of the division of labor has set and this consciousness also expects effective and qualitatively good products from the media. Reception has to that extent become more critical. If it is not casual, reception usually is an active process of taking in, a critical and productive give and take. Thus reception behavior must not be regarded as a proportional distribution of certain behavioral modes among the listeners and viewers. When reception is casual, it is not always possible to draw conclusions about the overall reception behavior of the individuals concerned. Occasionally the casualness of reception must be regarded as a kind of behavior with which the recipients shun the low standards of the offering. Another determining factor is the endeavor to utilize time effectively, and to structure monotonous activities more ''tolerably.'' Reception behavior alternates as a function of the situation of the recipients and of what is being offered. But the greatest caution must be exercised with regard to generalizations. Reception behavior is variable and flexible. It has also changed owing to the extent of reception: quite a bit has already been seen or heard before. A person's own viewing and listening experiences are becoming increasingly important for selection and for evaluating what is taken in. Manifold media use has become a part of everyday cultural life. Habits have been formed and stabilized in association with life's daily rhythm, the alternation between work and leisure time, and the social life cycle. It must never be forgotten that it is working human beings who make use of the media. The old model of art reception, which visualized private people gathered together publicly in the bourgeois salons of the past century (concentrated reception followed by communication through discussion) is not a valid description of how the working masses receive media entertainment. Entertainment reception must be investigated in the context of the everyday working and living conditions of the working masses.

It is important for the cultural process that the media, with its cultural services, has pervaded everyday life, and is used in manifold ways in a variety of social situations and in the most diverse places. Participation in cultural communication processes has expanded considerably as a consequence. From this perspective alone, it is clear that it is idle to measure media use with the same yardstick as concentration in the concert hall. It is much more important to understand the singularity of this mode of cultural behavior, which is utterly new in respect of its mass nature, and to see it as a qualitatively new phenomenon in cultural life in no sense competitive with other cultural behavior. Instead it must be seen as a significant expansion of cultural communication which is especially significant in the process of intensification. Although media entertainment represents the bulk of this process in quantitative terms, it should not be overlooked that the entire media program is caught up in it: informative and educational programs are also listened to and viewed. In view of the limited free time available for culture in daily life this must be regarded as an important cultural service of the media. The specifically cultural role of the media also first becomes clear in this context, in the unity of information, education, the enjoyment of art, and entertainment. Quantitative statistics are simply not the primary factors in assessing what is offered, or in its use. What is culturally significant in the media is precisely the fact that they offer a continuous supply of information, education, art, and entertainment, and thus raise the level of knowledge, of education, and of culture.

One of the peculiarities of the cultural output of the media is the tendency toward rationalization, the increasing use of technology, and standardization.

> The law of serial programs, as an expression of standardization, defines output in the form of family series, criminal series, ongoing stories, pocketbook series, or also in the form of fixed program times for certain programs. At the same time, everything is fundamentally reproducible, and can be retrieved on a mass scale; spatial and temporal distance have been overcome for the consumers of the mass media.[4]

These tendencies correspond to the habits of media use, which show a very high degree of constancy.

Various levels are operative in media reception. Let us illustrate this with the example of films.

At a *first* level, a film is interpreted, and so experienced, solely on the basis of what is seen and heard, without social and esthetic experiences and knowledge bearing on the content of the film (e.g., political, economical, cultural, and historical) being drawn upon for interpreting and appraising the film. The film is seen as a sequence of diverse actions and events. The Soviet art scholar Mejlakh speaks of an "elementary" reception in this regard. Various empirical studies have shown that this type of reception is frequently very pronounced in children.

A *second* level is distinguished from the former by the fact that the film is interpreted as the bearer of various political, moral, cultural "messages"; reception is "conceptual or systemic."[5]

At this level, what is seen and heard in films is placed in a larger social context whereby the recipients apply their own experiences, knowledge, and value orientations to what they experience in the film.

Finally, a *third* level is reached when a film is interpreted as the product of a specific political, moral, cultural, or even philosophical tradition, direction, or current; when it can be placed within a broader design.

Quite broad experience, knowledge, and value orientations that extend far beyond the immediate meaning of a film must be accessible and must be brought into relation with the film by the recipients. They will then be able, for example, to abstract sufficiently from their direct film experience to enable them to recognize and interpret the film's message as a model of a specific social state of affairs, a sociocultural tradition, or a philosophical current.

The three levels of reception often overlap. In casual reception, it is usually the first level that is operative. The Samurai films or Westerns can be seen and enjoyed at the level of action, without any grasp of the cultural codings, cultural meanings, and messages contained in these films.

The tendency toward a functional differentiation in use habits shows that there is a mass basis for a "higher" level of reception as a fundamental process, without the "first steps" of reception being discarded. Taking all tendencies together, one may infer at least hypothetically that a functional differentiation of habit is more and more becoming a determining factor in reception behavior. The contradictoriness of these phenomena must always be borne in mind. Of course there is also onesidedness and banality. Media reception on all its levels has a special quality and singularity, lending it its special status. It is not just studies of the uses of rock music that show how people are able to come to terms with our life values and our way of life through major hits. Numerous empirical studies of film reception in the movie theaters also have shown what productive imagination is brought by spectators to films that are interesting and challenging. The persistent judgment that watching television is a "passive mode of behavior" and fruitlessly contrasting it to "creative" behavior overlooks this aspect of the productive assimilation and confrontation, the creative interpretation and richness of thought which are at work in the reception of some television programs (although of course not of all). These elements of productive and creative assimilation must not be overlooked, especially in the case of the young generation, which has grown up with the media.

Finally, the intensive influence of a comprehensive media experience is felt in all forms of cultural communication, and this brings us to the problem of the cultural efficacy of the media.

It must be assumed that the consequences of media use are contradictory, they cannot be reduced to one simple schema, are by no means the same for all groups and all individuals, and occasionally are also contradictory for members of the same group. However, this contradictory effect cannot be explained in terms of the media product, since it is the same. To explain it, the recipient must be taken into account.

If we start out from actual media habits clearly oversimplified one-sided models must be abandoned. For example, a person who at present watches television one hour daily watches 365 hours per year, and 3,650 hours in ten years. The notion that every single program must fundamentally influence the personality of the viewer contradicts common sense. It is therefore important to look into the long-term consequences of media use. In special situations, in which vital questions are touched upon or many highly interesting events take place, the media will of course be much more effectual than in normal situations, in "everyday media life." Let us take a look at the long-term consequences of media use. First there is the rhythm adopted by everyday life, which is in part conditioned by media use. For example, certain mass habits are formed that are quite conspicuous: e.g., water consumption, electricity consumption, relatively fixed family habits of watching television at certain times, listening to music at certain times, etc. This rhythm of daily life, eating meals at times that fit in with television programs, concentration of family members at specific times in front of the "box-shaped family member in the living room corner,"[6] changes in family communication and other things, bear evidence that the media have become a component part of everyday cultural life.

In any event, use of the media—even if at times only in the accompaniment of another activity—during the many pauses which everyday life offers, belongs to one of the specific cultural effects of the media. There has also been a massive increase in parallel activities, i.e., combined activities during leisure time.

Over the long term, the media clearly augment political intelligence, knowledge, general education, and cultural experience. Nearly all GDR citizens have access to television in the Federal Republic. Viewing and listening experience has increased considerably, and has also been internationalized by the media. For example, citizens who are especially interested in films accumulate a film experience (in part through television) that comprises domestic output, imported products from socialist and capitalist countries, a familiarity with several works of specific directors and actors, trends in the art of film making, certain genres, etc. Similar trends are discernible in popular music and the entertainment arts. To this extent the experience of art has not only become more comprehensive, it has also become more intensive in many respects under the influence of the media, which has justly been called a source of secondary experience. One of the cultural effects of the media is the notable broadening of secondary experience to influence, complement, and enrich primary experience. The audiovisual media especially influence the way people look at the world, and are in this sense at work at an elementary level to shape people's philosophical outlook. Their influence on people's views of the world, and of other people and countries, and their long-term influence on people's understanding of history can no longer be disregarded. For this very reason it is important to recognize and utilize the vast possibilities of the media in developing value orientations and views of the world.

To sum up these aspects of the cultural efficacy of the media, we can agree with Tapio Varis's[7] thesis that the media not only reflect society, but also create a reality: a reality in consciousness. From this standpoint, the interrelationship between the mass media, primary social experience, and manifold interpersonal communication is of particular importance.

The numerous discussions about television programs and films, popular music, and sport programs show very clearly that the media have effects beyond their immediate reception. Thus the media influence everyday communication in manifold ways. Not only do they provide food for conversation, but a better understanding of the values of our life and of a socialist way of life is achieved on a mass basis in the discussion of media events. The influence of the media on cultural needs and expectations is especially great. This applies as much to the reproduction of existing needs as to the development of new needs from domestic or international offerings.

What Walter Benjamin called reception in amusement has also increased under the influence of the media.

> Reception in amusement, which is becoming more and more conspicuous in all areas of art, and which is a symptom of deep-going changes in apperception, has its true exercise in film. The film appeals to this form of reception in its shock effects. Film suppresses the cult value not only by putting the public in the position of examiner, but also by the fact that in the movie theater this position also envelops the attention. The public is an examiner, but an amused one.[8]

This reception in amusement has been made a mode of cultural behavior by the media, and the multifaceted use of music has indeed also contributed to this. But it also means that news, surprising forms, etc., are registered very attentively by the public, and that new trends and even fashions of mass cultural communication are registered with attention. Youth in particular react swiftly to such innovations. Both research results and experience have shown that reception in amusement, as a mass form of reception, does not, despite all its contradictoriness, suppress concentrated reception, but rather exists side by side with it.

The long-term effects of the media on the social mind, which both is reflected in mass cultural output, and has a feedback effect on them, are of special importance. Hopes and yearnings, moods, and even social fantasies are influenced quite distinctly over the long term by media cultural offerings, and indeed everyday consciousness, and value orientations in everyday behavior can hardly expect to escape that influence as well.

Taking all the views on the cultural efficacy of the media together, it seems clear that they exercise a decisive role in intellectual and cultural life and are of great importance in the development of socialist culture. When media use in free time by the GDR population is analyzed, it is important not to overlook the various tendencies sketched out above in their interaction and interrelations. The amount of time spent in media use, and its content, tell us little if the type and the manner of reception are not also taken into account or the cultural effects of the media are not kept in view. Media research in the context of the sociology of culture therefore has specific questions to ask. How these questions can be brought into a productive relation with leisure time research from the standpoint of other disciplines is a question whose answer is becoming increasingly important.

Notes

1. W. L. Lenin, *Werke*, supplementary vol. (Berlin: Dietz Verlag, 1917–23), 399.
2. Quoted from a work protocol of the Arts Academy; see also E. Schumacher, "Problema der Wechselwirkungen der Darstellenden Künste," in *Weimarer Beiträge*, no. 7 (1984): 1133ff.
3. P. Wicke, *Populäre Musik und Sozialistische Kultur. Beilage zur Zeitschrift Unterhaltungskunst*, no. 6 (1984): 2.
4. Autorenkollektiv under the direction of Erwin Pracht, *Ästhetik heute* (Berlin: Dietz Verlag, 1978): 409.
5. See B. Mejlach, *Künstlerisches Schaffen und Rezeptionsprocess* (Berlin, Weimar: Henschek Verlag Kunst und Gesellschaft, 1977).
6. C. Eurich and G. Würzberg, *30 Jahre Fernsehalltag* (Reinbek, Hamburg: Rowohlt, 1983), 55.
7. T. Varis, "Information und Kommunikation über Abrüstung," in *Wiss. Beiträge der Karl Marx Universität Leipzig 1983*, 51.
8. W. Benjamin, *Lesezeichen* (Leipzig: Reclam, 1970), 400.

Translated by Michel Vale

Colleague Frankenstein and the Pale Light of Progress

Life Conditions, Life Activities, and Technological Impacts on the GDR Way of Life

VOLKER GRANSOW

I

"Is there a Special German Road to Socialism?" This was the headline of a widely noted article published by the East German theoretical journal *Einheit* (Unity) in February 1946.[1] If one reads *Einheit* today, nearly forty years later, the question is somewhat different: "What is Software?"[2] The Eleventh Party Congress of the SED in April 1986 confirmed high technology as top priority. Soviet General Secretary Mikhail Gorbachev chose this congress as a platform for his call to answer the challenges of technological change, probably because the GDR seems to be a model of technological and economic efficiency, at least by Soviet standards, and unlike stagnating Czechoslovakia, tumultuous Poland, and westernizing Hungary. At the Party congress, the SED leadership did its best to promote this image. Gorbachev's reform proposals seemed to have been carried out in the GDR as early as 1971, when Party General Secretary Erich Honecker came to power. Generally speaking, it was a Party congress of continuity, harmony, and absence of conflict.

What is the relationship between technological change and society? In order to explore the impacts of technical changes on everyday life in the GDR it is necessary to give an outline of the characteristic life conditions and life activities. But, first of all, the frame of reference shall be sketched.

The discussion about a socialist way of life started in the GDR during the seventies under the influence of Soviet scholars like J. Kapustin and A. P. Butenko.[3] Their main questions were whether the way of life is a form or an element of human life activity, whether the way of life is determined by socioeconomic or nonsocioeconomic factors, and—last but not least—whether there is a difference between the *socialist way of life* as an addition of virtues or a model for the future and the *"way of life in socialism."*[4] Jürgen Kuczynski adopted the latter position and stated bluntly that the way of life in the countries of real socialism is a product of the mixture of various social formations: "socialist, capitalist, religious-feudal."[5] This position is the only one that is useful for empirical research.

Nevertheless there is apparently a need for more differentiation—especially if one wants to proceed from the empirical analysis of the way of life to an evaluation of the quality of life. Luckily there is already a developed contribution to cultural theory, namely the differentiation between objective and subjective culture. Culture is described as a dialectical process of appropriation of the objective culture to the subjective culture.[6] This position is linked to an understanding of the way of life "in socialism" by stressing that culture develops in the dialectical relationship between life *conditions* and life *activities*.[7] It is also underlined that a certain way of life is common to all industrial societies "of our time."[8]

But this notion restricts the measurement of cultural change in order to reconcile individuals to given conditions. Therefore, it must be combined with a more differentiated approach. A dialectical and critical approach provides the framework for such an analysis because it avoids both the pitfalls of behaviorism and a narrow basis-superstructure model. Following Bauer, Gramsci, and Williams,[9] the cultural process can be understood as a "complexity of hegemony." This means that social struggles become an integral component of culture.

Given this frame of reference, it is possible to sketch an outline of such life conditions as natural environment, work, consumption, social differentiations according to sex, age and profession (II). The next problem is how people are reconciled to these conditions. The relationship between life conditions and life activities shall be examined (III). This will provide the background for the discussion of the introduction of new technologies and technology policy (IV). Further, the consequences of new technologies for everyday life will be analyzed. The debate about biotechnology may serve as an example for splits among the scientific-technical and artistic intelligentsia (V). Finally, some conclusions shall be drawn about whether there is a special relationship between the steady emergence of intellectual talents and society, what life conditions mean for life activities, in which direction political culture is going, and—last but not least—what the impacts of new technologies will be for all these phenomena (VI).

II

An important precondition for the "shaping" of life is *natural environment*. This means for a majority of GDR citizens not only a restriction of recreation to the area between the Baltic Sea and the Harz Mountains, but also getting used to an average temperature between 6 degrees Celsius (42 degrees Fahrenheit) in Meiningen and 9.5 degrees Celsius (nearly 50 degrees Fahrenheit) in Berlin.[10] This fact explains to a certain extent why leisure activities during the week are mostly indoors. The situation is further complicated by environmental constraints. There are high emissions of sulphur dioxide, which in turn cause the acid rain responsible for air and water pollution and for damage to the forests. This is due to the fact that the GDR is one of the world's leaders in the production of lignite, but also adheres to a practical priority of "economy" to "ecology."[11] Another serious constraint of the environment is the ever increasing number of private cars. In 1986, roughly every second household owned a private car.[12] Thus it is not very surprising that the "Society for Nature and Environment" has today more than 50,000 members, although it was founded as late as 1980. This organization also has the function of a "bridge" between party-state and society, including the more radical and autonomous ecology groups operating in the "shelter" of the Protestant church.[13]

Similarly important are the conditions of *work*. They determine the use of time outside the workplace. In a trade union brochure, for instance, it was stated that it is "nonsense" to sign a contract between a factory and an opera house, if the majority of workers are injured by noise.[14] Empirical investigations in key sectors of the economy indicate serious problems in the area of work content. The unity of social, technical, and economic criteria has not been attained. Machine operators are frequently reduced to the role of machine minders and residual functions from the previous activity are usually simple and repetitive and may lead to monotony. Job enrichment and job enlargement measures have been minimal.[15] On the other hand, more than two-thirds of all work is still predominantly physical labor. But one should not underestimate the "coziness of the collective"—an underdeveloped sense of competition and a high grade of support for each other—which is, at times, responsible for the relatively low productivity of labor.[16] Labor also serves as a starting point for overcoming the differences between work and leisure by the development of cultural schemes in the work collectives. In 1984, about 50 percent of the workforce was using cultural schemes.[17] This cultural mass-work has a perspective of its own, as is reported both by statistics and subjective observations. It means frequent entertainment, having parties, and even opportunities for shorter or longer love relationships.[18] Furthermore, cultural mass-work is partly responsible for the dramatic changes in the structure of qualifications, the decrease of unskilled workers to 20 percent, and the increase of skilled workers to 60 percent.[19]

The equipment of households with consumer durables shows the GDR citizens quite ready for *consumption*. The rate of equipment with consumer durables per 100 households is 137.5 percent for refrigerators, 99.3 percent for washing machines, 117.6 percent for TV sets.[20] Data for eating and drinking indicate ever increasing figures for per-capita consumption. The consumption of meat increased from 1975 to 1985 from 77 to 98 kg, the consumption of butter rose from 14.7 to 15.7 kg, the increase in cigarette consumption was from 1.451 pieces per head to 1.833 in 1985. The consumption of alcoholic beverages rose from 8.0 liters to 10.3 (liquor from 8.6 to 15.2, beer from 119.7 to 141.6).[21] Without being an ascetic, one might ask whether this amount of alcohol, tobacco, and fat consumption is indicative only of the joy of life, especially if one considers that according to the Protestant church 10 percent of all adults are regular drinkers.[22] And one has to take into account the increases in cardiac infarctions, diseases of the circulation and of lung and liver.[23]

Besides nature, work, housing, and consumption, other factors affect life activities. An important factor is *social differentiation*. Especially striking is the differentiation according to *sex*. On the average, women do twice as much housework as men; the time used for housework, shopping, and taking care of children is, for women of every age, higher than for men, the time for watching TV, reading, etc. is always lower.[24]

Evidence for changes in female behavior is supplied by Jutta Gysi. She reports that the percentage of children born to unmarried mothers rose from 17.3 percent in 1978 to 32 percent in 1983![25] Jutta Gysi observes, on the one hand, traditional behavior even among younger women; on the other hand, she sees a dramatic increase in "incomplete families," especially among the younger generation. A similar paradox is mentioned by Marilyn Rueschemeyer. In her study on professional work and marriage in the U.S., the Soviet Union, and the GDR, she remarks:

> Generally, the institutional and ideological supports given to women, especially in the German Democratic Republic, facilitate their independence. The professional women I spoke to did not take for granted that they had to marry. . . . If the woman chooses to divorce or not to marry, she is not isolated. She has her work, she has her colleague group. She has access to *cribbes* for her child; she has the right to an apartment. The stability of the marriage, then, is not based on the economic dependence of the woman. That women are no longer economically dependent on their husbands, however, does not mean they all have an interest in abandoning their families. On the contrary, both in the Soviet Union and the German Democratic Republic, there was a great commitment among many of the men and women I spoke with to retaining the family and participating in a common shared life.[26]

This result seems to be somewhat enigmatic and demands explanation. Marilyn Rueschemeyer tries to find a solution:

There are pressures and constraints of daily life unrelated to work which can have similar effects on personal relations outside of work as competitive work pressures and ambitions. Some of these seem more prevalent in the German Democratic Republic and the Soviet Union than in the United States. They include the lack of good and easily available housing accommodation for at least some of the professionals, the time and effort required for obtaining a variety of desirable consumer goods and—for some at least—the strains of the political atmosphere. These and similar factors can counterbalance the effects of reduced competition and alienation as well as of the structural supports for working women as far as the quality of the marital relationship is concerned.[27]

Other social differentiations in the East German society can be observed according to age, qualification, and profession. There are big gaps between the generations, which are probably reinforced by demographic transformations.[28] As far as the social structure in general is concerned, it has been pointed out that processes that have shaped today's GDR have come to a halt:[29]

—the quantitative growth of the working class;
—the integration of women into work;
—the quantitative growth of the intelligentsia;
—the decreasing numbers of small artisans and craftsmen;
—the growth of the city population;
—the change in the structure of qualifications.

This halt is connected with the transformation from extensively to intensively extended reproduction. Ingrid and Manfred Lötsch argue that intensively extended reproduction is connected with structural changes and completely new demands for disposability. If this process is not realized properly, they see the danger of "dysfunctional structures."[30]

Their main concern, however, is the relative autonomy of the intelligentsia. Lötsch and Lötsch are in favor of social differences if they do not imply inequality in general.

In his lucid history of the GDR Dietrich Staritz is somewhat skeptical about the points raised by Lötsch and others. He stresses the gap between those thoughts and the traditional ideal of equality. Nevertheless Staritz notes a new orientation for a neutral form of the notion of elite, for a stronger differentiation of the income of the intelligentsia, and even for a policy of privileges. Conversely, he observes a growing deficit in a utopian scheme providing identity.[31]

Henry Krisch is more outspoken than Dietrich Staritz and stresses that, although the GDR has built a society of broad access to opportunities, it has not become egalitarian in its rewards. There are already—not only in the future— great discrepancies that continue to exist. He concludes that

> although the continuing political dominance of the SED as a ruling party and the omnipresence of the security forces in GDR life are beyond dispute, there are

indications (at least in theoretical discussions) that the party and state leaderships are aware that social differentiation will be a fact of GDR life for the middle-range future, if not longer. Both effective economic growth and implementation of social policy will require a more differentiated administrative and political approach to social groups. In the differentiated treatment of particular groups (materially as well as otherwise) lies the opportunity to harness the energies of those groups for the regime's purposes.[32]

Further conditions for differences in the development of creative abilities and in the satisfaction of cultural needs are given through the relationship between city and countryside, the membership in political and social organizations (including the important protestant church) and, last but not least, by scarcity.

Scarcity is one of the main issues in everyday life in the GDR. It concerns nearly everything, from time itself to services and supply. One of the big taboos in GDR public life is the scarcity of travel possibilities, another phenomenon is the scarcity of public life itself.[33] In 1976 there were complaints that it would be hard to get some types of furniture, some technical goods of consumption, the thousand little things, etc.[34] In 1986, Egon Krenz, member of the SED's politbureau, stressed the lack of shoe repairs and demanded the production of a thousand little things. Erich Honecker stressed the need for toothbrushes and water buckets even in the age of high technology.[35] Nevertheless, one should not forget that the GDR is a country of scarcity, but not of poverty. The average monthly income per household was 1746 marks in 1985[36], the average rent is significantly below 100 marks; records are sold from 10 marks, lyric poetry from 90 pfennigs, theater tickets from 2 marks upward. But in a way these prices further scarcity, because they are one reason why some goods are sold out quickly.

III

As far as one can rely on East German time-budget analysis, there exists the following hierarchy of average leisure activities:[37] (1) watching TV; (2) meeting friends; (3) reading; (4) visiting cultural institutions; (5) social activities. One must take into account that these are old figures and that they are concerned with the average activities without differentiation between weekend leisure and the workweek. Furthermore, one must consider the fact that these figures are based on a narrow concept of leisure, which means that 3.7 hours of leisure are supplemented by roughly 15 average hours of housework, children, and "physiological needs"—whatever that may be. Nevertheless it is indicated by all studies—even the newer and more differentiated ones—that watching TV is a predominant activity. And, in fact, the number of theatre and cinema visitors has decreased dramatically—from 309 million in 1955 to 70 million in 1985. The primary need to be satisfied in watching TV is that of "entertainment" (stated by more than 50 percent vs 1.1 percent who favor cultural policy).[38] If one asks for the contents of the media in actual consumption, one learns that this is a field where "not a few" people have the impression that the dynamics of development come from the Western world.[39]

The fact that the "Dallas" series is widely watched on West German TV is even acknowledged in the leading party journal *Einheit*.[40] Although no serious numbers are published about the percentage of East Germans watching Western TV, one can assume that the big desire for entertainment is all too often satisfied by Western stations. Communist observers noted the real danger of the division of life into a "socialist" life at the workplace and a "capitalist" life in private.[41] Others are critical of a superficial reception of TV, especially among younger audiences.[42] The smaller acceptance of political topics may have its reason in the political contents as well as in the artistic form. TV news is smooth, superficial, or boring, in a way reminiscent of autogenous training.[43]

Radio seems to be much more effective as an instrument of political leadership. This is not fully appreciated by time-budget researchers, because listening to radio is a so-called "second activity." But one can assume that radio is used, on workdays, by about 70 percent of the population. The need for information and politics plays a much higher role in the use of radio than in watching TV.[44] Nevertheless, there are complaints that broadcasts with a high proportion of words have strong losses of efficiency.[45]

While radio and television are used by all strata of the population, cinema is a domain of the youth. There the basic need is entertainment as well. But evidently the young people in the GDR like to watch GDR films, if they deal with contradictions and problems of present-day life. This is indicated both by polls as well as by successes like "Solo Sunny" or "Island of Swans."[46] In the age of electronic entertainment, music is of special relevance. In this area, there is quite a visible schism between the ages. While young people prefer rock music, it is explicitly disliked by many grownups.[47] This is of greater interest, considering that Helmut Hanke calls it an "open secret," that "we" (whoever that may be) "found recognition among the young working people almost only with GDR rock music."[48] One of the cultural aims of the Honecker administration was support for the "Singebewegung" among the young people of the GDR. The members of the singing movement organized leisure collectively. They sang Western protest songs, workers' songs, folk songs, but mostly more or less critical songs about the GDR. During the seventies, however, its membership decreased from 63,796 to 43,600.[49] This decrease was probably a result of the crisis of cultural policy, which came into being because of the destabilizing effects of Eurocommunism, the human rights campaign, and the Western economic crisis, and found its main expression in the expatriation of Wolf Biermann in 1976. On the other hand, the decline of the singing movement could serve as a cause for reflection about tendencies toward apolitical behavior, which is in a way underlined by the findings of the great importance of entertainment needs in reading[50] and the vast increase in museum visitors.[51]

But there are tendencies toward value change, too. As early as 1978 there was a debate in the students' journal, *Forum,* in which Jürgen Kuczynski challenged the position that worktime is the measure of social progress. He argued that free time would be the measure of social progress, and that relations within socialist production were relatively meaningless.[52] His position was supported in part by the readers, until the discussion was brought to a close—as was the journal itself a few years later.

But the shift in values had already left the sphere of academic discussion. In the late seventies and during the eighties "new social movements" have arisen in the GDR. Although they are basically concerned with ecological issues and the organization of an autonomous peace movement, they represent not only social and political movements, but a whole alternative culture. Their issues go far beyond peace and armament and include such topics as the liberation of women and gays. These movements challenge the amalgam of values that are characteristic for the dominant political culture.[53] It is hard to count them, but in the authoritarian GDR society it is highly spectacular if somebody leaves the niche. Thus, the 6000 people attending an autonomous peace rally or a blues mass may be expressing the feelings of many more.[54]

The rejection of army service by a number of young people and the harsh reactions of the leadership have further contributed to a rethinking of alternative issues, which by now are more "oppositional" and encompass all central questions of societal self-understanding:[55]

—a critique of the destruction of the environment;
—a critique of consumerism;
—a critique of the ideology of work;
—a critique of too few opportunities to participate in political life.

There are three main conclusions to be drawn from this discussion of life conditions and selected life activities. First, the structure of qualifications and the efforts of cultural mass-work have certainly contributed to creativity and thoughtfulness. This may be one reason for the steady emergence of new talents in spite of the continuous brain drain to the West.

Second, life conditions form overall restrictions for life activities. Leisure time is mainly time for reproduction, used for the consumption of media entertainment. More specific activities are highly determined by social differentiation according to work, education, sex, and age.

Third, in terms of (political) culture, communist culture is weakened, whereas industrialist, traditionalist,[56] and alternative cultures are getting stronger and stronger.

IV

During the last decade there was a growing concern in Western societies about the computerization of nearly all aspects of public life. In spite of these concerns, the

SED called in 1976 for the rapid introduction of microelectronics as an essential part of its economic strategy.[57] At the Party Congress in 1986, microelectronics were considered to be key technologies, as well as biotechnology and nuclear power (this was shortly before the Chernobyl catastrophe). The public was informed that the GDR was on the way to produce 1-megabyte chips and even 4-megabyte chips.[58] This sounds very ambitious and reminds one of the trust in scientific-technological progress displayed by the late Walter Ulbricht, Erich Honecker's predecessor.[59] But the East German technical accomplishments are remarkable only as far as hardware is concerned. There are many difficulties in the field of software. And technology assessment seems to be the weak link. Hütter and Jobst, for instance, present a lengthy explanation of microelectronics as an important part of the scientific-technological revolution. Not till then do they start to deal with the problems that the new technologies create for the personality of the engineer.[60] Marschall and Steinitz's book concentrates on the "efficiency" of microelectronics—the notion of "rationalization" is reserved for capitalism.[61]

The domination of a naive-instrumentalist understanding of technology is remarkable. The productive powers appear to be the subjects of sociocultural changes. Both Hütter and Jobst and Marschall and Steinitz argue that there is no such thing as capitalist or socialist microelectronics. They prefer to talk about the different "applications" of new technologies.[62] Comprehensive criticism of industrialism is qualified as the "confusion potential."[63] Nevertheless there seem to be some problems even in "socialist application." They assume that the demand for laborers will decrease and that a flexible education will be necessary—which is definitely not the case today. Hütter and Jobst put it even more concretely: They talk about the loss of social positions, the high rates of fluctuation, and the reduction of communicative relationships.[64] Alice Kahl and her coauthors analyze the relationship between collectives and the way of life after the introduction of new technologies. They find striking similarities to the results of Western industrial sociology, especially the formation of informal social substructures (work groups). Unlike Western sociologists, however, they consider the main problem to be the nonexistence of these collectives for governmental leadership.[65]

There is extensive literature from East Germany which stresses that there are a lot of cleavages at the workplace due to the introduction of new technologies. Skilled workers may seek to maintain traditional boundaries between jobs in order to resist an erosion of their status and skills. Furthermore, new technologies and new forms of work organization may be viewed as a part of a strategy to increase work intensity rather than to improve the quality of working life.[66] The explanation for this planned introduction of an ever-increasing number of robots into East German industry seems to be simple: more labor is not available, over three-fourths of the working age population, including about 80 percent of working-age women, are employed.[67] The GDR is just sharing problems: it is highly developed, has few raw materials, and is dependent on the world market.[68]

Therefore there seems to be no chance—at least with the present leadership—for a turnabout in technology policy[69] (with the exception of nuclear power[70]). Taking this for granted, the question is what the consequences for the GDR way of life are likely to be.

V

The official stress on the introduction of new technologies at the workplace does not mean that there are no consequences for everyday life outside work. On the contrary, computerized bank tellers have been introduced.[71] Electronic calculators are used now in many East German schools.[72] The "Verlag Neues Leben," a publishing house of the Free German Youth, has already printed two editions of a best-selling brochure called "Computer on the March?"[73]

Computer games are highly accepted among teenagers.[74] But one should not forget that this technological revolution is taking place under the conditions of political surveillance and economic scarcity. There are no personal computers for personal use. The relatively small number of personal computers made in the GDR are mostly sold to schools.[75] Although there is a GDR production of rock videos, these small films are only broadcast by TV, because videocassette recorders are only sold at "intershops," which means for convertible currency or its equivalent. But this may change in the foreseeable future.[76]

For the most important life conditions, there seem to be consequences that protract existing problems:

—In the area of nature/environment there is talk about the consequences of production. It is admitted that the important users (combines, factories, etc.) appropriate nature according to their "individual" criteria of efficiency,[77] rather than taking environmental concerns into consideration.

—Since the days of the *Forum* debate[78] there has been no attempt to rethink the official position about the relationship between work time and disposable time. Even the introduction of microelectronics allows only hints that the extension of shift work would be the necessary condition for a step-by-step reduction of worktime.[79]

—As for social structure, it can be assumed that the demands of an increasing computerization will lead to further social differentiation, thus putting the goal of a classless society at an even farther distance.[80]

—Consequences for education are restricted to science and technology. A new subject "fundamentals of automatization" has been introduced into vocational training since September 1, 1986.[81] Experiments with computer education (learning BASIC, etc.) are conducted at various schools. In vocational training with "Abitur," informatics has become compulsory.[82] But there is absolutely no evidence for a critical technology assessment in language or social studies.

—In entertainment it is stressed that the increasing introduction of rock videos has its political advantages.[83] A new radio station devoted to a younger audience has been founded.[84] There is special concern about an upgrading of entertainment and overcoming the division between "light" and "serious" arts.[85]

But this does not mean that there are no critical voices. It was said in a discussion among cultural scientists that "not only" SDI and nuclear armament are responsible for a pale light of progress, and that there should be a dialogue between the scholarly examination of culture and the criticism of technology put forward by artists.[86] And this criticism—or critique— is considerably intense. It has even been argued that there is an increasingly evident conflict between the scientific-technical intelligentsia and the artistic intelligentsia, who are no longer equally fascinated by the anticipated blessings of technology.[87] The recent debate about biotechnology may be a good example of this assumed split between scientific-technical intelligentsia and artistic intelligentsia.

The debate started as early as 1981, when the prominent GDR molecular biologist Erhard Geissler asked for more trust among scientists and cultural activists, after Jurij Brezan—among others—had called genetic manipulation a "crime."[88] In 1984, Geissler took the performance of Kipphardt's play "Brother Eichmann" to talk about "Brother Frankenstein" in order to defend genetic research and technology as an example for modern natural science against the hostility toward science displayed by Christa Wolf and others.[89] Geissler considered the artistic intelligentsia to be absolutely uninformed. The dangers depicted by writers and other artists would not at all legitimize "holding back bioscientific advances or giving up scientific-technological progress as such."[90] The debate following Geissler's article in *Sinn und Form* showed a widespread mistrust in progress. One gets the idea that the discussants were talking about a dissolution of the relationship between the growth of productive powers and the advance of science on the one hand, and cultural progress as the elaboration of human possibilities on the other hand.[91] The debate was also joined by Benno Müller-Hill, a genetic scientist from West Germany, who was talking about "Colleague Mengele." He pointed to the historic experience with genetic experiments during national socialism. He argued that the "scientification" (Verwissenschaftlichung) of politics was the terrible new experience of fascism.[92] In his rejoinder, Geissler seemed to be unconvinced. He brought the debate to a close by attacking "scientific pessimism" and arguing for a social framework that prevented the misuse of scientific research results.[93]

The key words of this debate are far from being isolated in the intellectual community of the GDR (and they have a practical dimension proven by the increasing membership of the environment protection league). Eckart Förtsch has shown that in the works of GDR writers and especially in the works of Hanns Cibulka the following issues are raised:[94]

—the dangers of a "peaceful" use of nuclear power;
—the diseases caused by pollution;

—the poisoning of nature by chemical industry;
—the mechanisms of psychic repression ("Verdrängung").

VI

In conclusion, four points can be made:

First, the steady emergence of both new artistic and intellectual critical talents in the GDR may well be due to the structure of qualifications and the efforts of cultural mass-work. This cannot be belittled by the continuous brain drain to the West.

Second, conditions in the GDR form overall restrictions for life activities. Leisure time—at least during weekdays—is on the average mainly time for reproduction, used for the consumption of media entertainment. More specific activities are highly determined by social differentiation.

Third, in terms of (political) culture, communist goal culture is weakened, whereas industrialist, traditionalist, and alternative cultures are getting stronger and stronger. By now the alternative culture displays elements of the oppositional culture.

Fourth, all these tendencies will probably become even more visible due to the impacts of the planned rapid introduction of new technologies. In spite of the official technological optimism, there is widespread concern among the artistic intelligentsia and in the alternative culture about the future of progress. The rapid destruction of the environment, the experiences with the "peaceful" use of nuclear power, and the danger of extermination through overarming have given rise to fundamental doubts about unlimited progress.

Notes

1. See Anton Ackermann, "Gibt es einen besonderen deutschen Weg zum Sozialismus?" *Einheit*, no. 1 (1946).
2. See Eberhard Prager and Evelyn Richter, "Was ist Software?" *Einheit*, no. 2 (1985). See also "Das Thema—Schlüsseltechnologien," *Einheit*, no. 7 (1986).
3. See the reference given by Venohr and Langhof: Klaus-Dieter Venohr, "Sozialistische Lebensweise," *Weimarer Beiträge*, no. 7 (1977); Michael Langhof, "Sozialistische Lebensweise—ideologischer Kampfbegriff oder sozialökonomische Planungskategorie?" *Deutschland Archiv*, special issue (1980).
4. See Bettina Gransow and Volker Gransow, "Jahrbuch für Soziologie und Sozialpolitik 1981/1982" (review), *Soziologische Revue*, no. 1 (1984).
5. Jürgen Kuczynski, "Zur Soziologie des Alltags," *Jahrbuch für Soziologie und Sozialpolitik* (1982), 120.
6. See Dietrich Mühlberg, *Woher wir wissen, was Kultur ist* (Berlin: VEB Deutscher Verlag der Wissenschaften, 1983).
7. See Hans Koch, ed., *Zur Theorie der sozialistischen Kultur* (Berlin: Dietz, 1982), 233–331.
8. Ibid., 243 (a quotation from G. Ch. Shaknazarov).

9. See Raymond Williams, *Problems in Materialism and Culture* (London: Verso, 1980).

10. *Statistisches Taschenbuch der DDR* (Berlin: Staatsverlag, 1986), 158.

11. See Werner Gruhn et al., *Umweltprobleme und Umweltbewusstsein in der DDR* (Cologne: Wissenschaft und Politik, 1985).

12. *Statistisches Taschenbuch*, 117.

13. See Gruhn, 151–68.

14. Isolde Dietrich, *Kulturvoll leben* (Berlin: Tribüne, 1975), 117.

15. Michael Dennis, "The Red Robots Are Here," *GDR Monitor*, no. 12 (1984–85).

16. See Irene Böhme, *Die da drüben* (Berlin: Rotbuch, 1982).

17. *Statistisches Taschenbuch*, 40.

18. See Peter Spahn, *Unterhaltung im Sozialismus* (Berlin: Dietz, 1980).

19. Eva-Maria Langen, *Technisierungsgrad der Arbeit und Qualifikation der Produktionsarbeiter* (Berlin: Dietz, 1979), 48–49. The figures are realistic projections for 1990.

20. *Statistisches Taschenbuch*, 117.

21. Ibid., 115.

22. See Brigitte Deja-Lölhöffel, *Freizeit in der DDR* (Berlin: Holzapfel, 1986), 66.

23. See Rose Bischof, "Kommentar," *DDR-Report*, no. 5–6 (1986): 292.

24. See Deja-Lölhöffel, 24–27. This position is widely held among researchers of GDR leisure behavior in East and West (see the literature quoted by Bettina Gransow and Volker Gransow, "Disponible Zeit und Lebensweise," *Deutschland Archiv*, no. 7 [1983]: 748–49). Of course, there are different evaluations. The only person with a dissenting position is Jutta Gysi. She states that women would have the same leisure time as men if longer work time, etc. were taken into account. See Jutta Gysi, "Soziale Reproduktion in der Familie," in *Soziale Triebkräfte ökonomischen Wachstums*, ed. Wissenschaftlicher Rat für Soziologische Forschung in der DDR (Berlin: Dietz, 1986).

25. Jutta Gysi, "Frauen- und Familienenwicklung als Gegenstand sozialistischer Politik," in *Jahrbuch für Soziologie und Sozialpolitik* (Berlin: Akademie, 1984), 105.

26. Marilyn Rueschemeyer, *Professional Work and Marriage. An East-West Comparison* (New York: St. Martin's Press, 1981), 175–76.

27. Ibid., 176–77. See also Christiane Lemke, "Women and Politics in East Germany," in *Socialist Review*, no. 81 (1985); Ulrike Enders, "Kinder, Kueche, Kombinat," in *Aus Politik und Zeitgeschichte*, no. 6–7 (1986).

28. See Wulfram Speigner, Theoretische Ausgangsposition der Einflussnahme auf die Veränderung des Reproduktionstyps der Bevölkerung, in *Jahrbuch für Soziologie und Sozialpolitik* (Berlin: Akademie, 1984).

29. See *Soziale Triebkräfte*, 18–19.

30. Ingrid Lötsch and Manfred Lötsch, "Soziale Strukturen und Triebkräfte in *Jahrbuch für Soziologie und Sozialpolitik* (Berlin: Akademie, 1985), 169.

31. Dietrich Staritz, *Geschichte der DDR 1949–1985* (Frankfurt: Suhrkamp, 1985), 226–28.

32. Henry Krisch, *The German Democratic Republic. The Search for Identity* (Boulder: Westview, 1985), 120.

33. Arbeitsgruppe, "Fortschritt als Frage," in *Weimarer Beiträge*, no. 8 (1986): 1297: "Der Mangel an Öffentlichkeit wird von mehreren Schriftstellern . . . beklagt."

34. Renate Müller and Lothar Neumann, *Zeitfaktor und Hauptaufgabe* (Berlin: Tribüne, 1976), 34.

35. See *Neue Zürcher Zeitung*, November 5, 1986; *Neues Deutschland*, October 25, 1986.

36. *Statistisches Taschenbuch*, 117.

37. According to Günter Manz, ed., *Lebensniveau im Sozialismus* (Berlin: Die Wirtschaft, 1983), 216.

38. UNESCO, ed., *Cultural Needs and Aspirations* (Paris: UNESCO, n.d.), 125–26.

39. Hans Koch, ed., *Zur Theorie des sozialistischen Realismus* (Berlin: Dietz, 1974), 234.

40. Hans Koch, "Die Künste bei der Ausprägung der Werte des Sozialismus," *Einheit*, no. 1 (1984): 69.

41. Joachim Streisand, *Kultur in der DDR* (Berlin: Deutscher Verlag der Wissenschaften, 1981), 164.

42. See Peter Voss, ed., *Die Freizeit der Jugend* (Berlin: Dietz, 1981), 137.

43. See Stefan Heym, *Wege und Umwege* (Munich: Bertelsmann, 1980), 346.

44. See UNESCO, 127.

45. Monika Bloss, Kolloquium "Massenkultur—populäre Künste—Unterhaltung," *Weimarer Beiträge*, no. 9 (1986): 1543.

46. See Lothar Bisky amd Dieter Wiedemann, *Der Spielfilm—Rezeption und Wirkung* (Berlin: Henschel, 1985).

47. See Gisela Helwig, *Jugend und Familie in der DDR* (Cologne: Wissenschaft und Politik, 1984).

48. Helmut Hanke, "Entwicklungstendenzen musikalischer Bedürfnisse," *Musik und Gesellschaft*, no. 11 (1981): 649. For a different view, see Bloss, 1542.

49. See *Junge Leute—hier und heute* (Berlin: Panorama, 1977), 62.

50. See UNESCO, 127–30.

51. See *Statistisches Taschenbuch*, 130.

52. See *Forum*, nos. 8, 11, 13 (1978).

53. See Henry Krisch, "Changing Political Culture and Political Stability in the German Democratic Republic," *Studies in Comparative Communism*, no. 1 (1986).

54. See Wolfgang Büscher and Peter Wensierski, *Null Bock auf DDR. Aussteigerjugend im anderen Deutschland* (Hamburg: Rowohlt, 1984).

55. See Antonia Grunenberg, "Jugend in der DDR: Zwischen Resignation und Aussteigertum," in *Aus Politik und Zeitgeschichte*, no. B 27 (1986), 17; "Die Eingabe einer DDR-Freidensgruppe an Erich Honecker und die SED," in *Frankfurter Rundschau*, May 13, 1986.

56. Because I was only dealing with selected activities, I have neglected the increase in traditionalist culture. But this increase is very evident. It started during the seventies as a response to increasing industrialism and the "national vacuum" after the proclamation of the socialist German nation in the GDR. It is a movement from above and below. From above, because the leadership's demand for legitimacy leads it to an upgrading of German history (Prussia, Saxony, Frederick II, Bismarck, Luther). From below, because the demand for identity is expressed by a vast increase in the numbers of museum and exhibition visitors. See Johannes Gurks, *Museumsbesuch* (Berlin: Tribüne, 1980); Horst Haase, ed., *Die SED und das kulturelle Erbe* (Berlin: Dietz, 1986).

57. See Rüdiger Inhetveen, "Röhren und Roboter. Mikroelektronik in der DDR," in *Wechselwirkung*, no. 25 (1985): 21.

58. See Erich Honecker, *Bericht des Zentralkomitees der Sozialistischen Einheitspartei Deutschlands an den XI. Parteitag der SED* (Berlin: Dietz, 1986), 49.

59. See Hartmut Zimmermann, "Politische Aspekte in der Herausbildung, dem Wandel und der Verwendung des Konzepts 'wissenschaftlich-technische Revolution' in der DDR," in *Deutschland Archiv*, special issue, 1976.

60. Manfred Hütter et al., *Mikroelektronik und Gesellschaft* (Berlin: Akademie, 1984).

61. Wolfgang Marschall and Klaus Steinitz, eds., *Schlüsseltechnologie Mikroelektronik* (Berlin: Dietz, 1985), 136.

62. See Hütter et al., 5; Marschall and Steinitz, 27.

63. See Hütter et al., 50.

64. Ibid., 108.

65. Alice Kahl et al., *Kollektivbeziehungen und Lebensweise* (Berlin: Dietz, 1984), 69.

66. See the references and arguments given by Mike Dennis, "Degradation or Humanization? Work and Scientific-Technical Progress in the GDR," in *Studies in GDR Culture and Society*, vol. 6 (1986), 59–80; see also Fred Klinger, "Soziale Auswirkungen und lebensweltliche Zusammenhänge der sozialistischen Rationalisierung," in *Informationsabende DDR*, ed. Evangelische Akademie Berlin (West), no. 41 (1984): 63–92; Katharina Belwe, *Wechselwirkungen zwischen produktionsstrukturellen Veränderungen und sozialstrukturellen Entwicklungen in der DDR* (Manuscript; Bonn: Gesamtdeutsches Institut, 1985).

67. See Krisch, *The German Democratic Republic*, 90–119.

68. Staritz, 229.

69. See Raymond Bentley, *Technological Change in the German Democratic Republic* (Boulder: Westview, 1984).

70. "Ich bin der Meinung, dass die Kernkraft nicht das letzte Wort ist." From Interview of Erich Honecker for "Dagens Nyheter," in *Neues Deutschland*, June 25, 1986.

71. See *Der Spiegel*, no. 20 (1986): 81.

72. Michael Mara, "Jugend in der DDR entdeckt den Computer," in *Der Tagesspiegel*, April 8, 1986.

73. See Hannes Gutzer and Hans-Dieter Pauer, *Computer im Vormarsch?* 2d ed. (Berlin: Neues Leben, 1985).

74. See Mara.

75. See *Der Spiegel*.

76. See Arbeitsgruppe, 1310.

77. See Günther Bohring and Helmar Hegewald, "Umweltbewusstes Handeln in der sozialistischen Gesellschaft," *Deutsche Zeitschrift für Philosophie*, no. 10 (1986): 899.

78. See note 52.

79. Reinhard Göttner and Nina Seydewitz, *Roboter heute und morgen* (Leipzig: Urania, 1985), 98–99.

80. See Albrecht Kretzschmar, *Soziale Unterschiede—unterschiedliche Persönlichkeiten* (Berlin: Dietz, 1985).

81. See Wolfgang Rudolph, "Berufsbildung—wichtiger Faktor der umfassenden Intensivierung," in *Berufsbildung*, no. 6 (1986).

82. Ibid.

83. See Bloss, 1544.

84. See "Jugendradio DT 64. Gespräch mit Petra Schwarz," in *Sonntag*, no. 13 (1986).

85. See Robert Weimann, "Funktion und Niveau der Unterhaltung in den Künsten," in *Sinn und Form*, no. 2 (1986).

86. See Arbeitsgruppe.

87. See Gert-Joachim Glaessner, *Technical Intelligentsia and Politics* (Manuscript; Berlin/Conway, 1986), 3.

88. See Erhard Geissler, "Zu einigen Aspekten des Verhältnisses von Molekularbiologie und Kunst," in *Weimarer Beitrage*, no. 10 (1981), 134, 140.

89. See Erhard Geissler, "Bruder Frankenstein oder—Pflegefälle aus der Retorte?" in *Sinn und Form*, no. 6 (1984); Christa Wolf, "Aus den 'Frankfurter Vorlesungen,'" in *Sinn und Form*, no. 1 (1983).

90. Geissler, "Bruder Frankenstein," 1302.

91. See Werner Creutziger, "Brief an Erhard Geissler"; Manfred Wolter, "Entwarnung?" in *Sinn und Form*, no. 2 (1985).

92. See Benno Müller-Hill, "Kollege Mengele—nicht Bruder Eichmann," in *Sinn und Form*, no. 3 (1985).

93. See Erhard Geissler, "Frankensteins Tod—Bemerkungen zu einer Diskussion," in *Sinn und Form*, no. 1 (1986).

94. See Eckart Förtsch, "Fragen 'menschheitsgeschichtlichen Ausmasses.' Wissenschaft, Technik, Umwelt," in *Die DDR-Gesellschaft im Spiegel ihrer Literatur*, ed. Gisela Helwig (Cologne: Wissenschaft und Politik, 1986).

Church and Society in the GDR

Historical Legacies and "Mature Socialism"

ROBERT F. GOECKEL

In recent years both scholars and policymakers have devoted considerable attention to the churches in the GDR. Responsible for much of this new interest have been the novel rise of an independent peace movement closely associated with the churches and the summit meetings between the church and the SED in 1978 and 1985, both of which were developments conducive to Western media coverage. However improbable these developments may seem given the problematic nature of political change in the GDR and the Warsaw Pact states, they become more understandable against the backdrop of the role of the churches in GDR society. This essay hopes to provide insight into this role, in particular that of the Evangelical/Lutheran churches.

Three major themes unify the following analysis of the role of the Evangelical/ Lutheran church. First, the church retains a quite considerable independent presence in GDR society, despite the toll that secularization and ideological pressure have exacted on formal statistics of church adherents or religious identifiers. Indeed the church's presence is growing, often in ways that are difficult to measure by formal statistics. Second, the relationship between the church and society represents an admixture of historical inheritance and socialist overlay. Though not subject to SED discipline like mass organizations, the church and its agenda have not remained unaffected by socialism. At certain times the historical inheritance and socialist overlay conflict with each other; at others they reinforce each other. Finally, despite the earlier conflict with the state and the present dominance of the state over society in general, the church-state relationship currently contains elements of interdependence. Areas of conflict remain between them, but both sides try to limit the effects of such conflicts.

1. The historical background to the current church-state relationship

The state's policy toward the church has not always reflected a recognition of this interdependence and indeed has evolved quite considerably over time.[1] In the early postwar period (1945–1949), the state pursued a relatively mild policy toward the church, reflecting mutual wartime opposition to Hitler and Stalin's relative flexibility on the German question. In the period from the formation of the GDR in 1949 until 1958, the drive for socialist transformation led the state to seek to curtail the church's social presence, as reflected in the elimination of the state-collected church tax and religious instruction in the schools and heightened emphasis on scientific atheism in the activities of the official youth organization, the FDJ. Externally, the state retained a relatively mild policy, attempting to use the churches' all-German ties to hinder the rearmament of the FRG.

After 1958, the state, defeated on the inter-German issues, focused on the consolidation of socialism in the GDR and sought to break most links with the FRG, including those of the still all-German church. The state prevented all-German meetings of lay congresses and church leadership organs, although it continued to "tolerate" the considerable hard-currency subsidies from the Western church to the East German church. Internally the period 1958–1971 saw an ambiguous policy by the state. Rhetorically, SED chief Walter Ulbricht sought to mobilize Christian support for his "socialist human community," arguing that "Christianity and Marxism do not represent a contradiction." In practice, however, pressure on the churches and Christians continued, particularly by the bloc party, the Christian Democratic Union (East).

Since 1971 under Erich Honecker, the regime's policy, both externally and internally, has become milder. As a result of the division of the German church along East-West lines in 1969 and Honecker's accommodation to the Soviet policy of detente, the GDR has tolerated the East German church's continuing informal ties with the West German church and has fostered its participation in international church bodies such as the World Council of Churches. Domestically, the state began to grant certain institutional perquisites to the church (e.g., new church construction), although discrimination against individual Christians continued unabated. This trend has been reinforced since the unprecedented summit meeting between Honecker and the church leadership in March 1978. Increased institutional benefits have accrued to the churches, as demonstrated by greater access to official media, state support for lay congresses, and tolerance of church work in new areas such as prisons and alcohol rehabilitation. The lot of individual Christians has improved slightly, although discrimination in education and career persists.

The state's shift does not represent fundamental ideological change, but rather pragmatism on its part. It is true that indoctrination in scientific atheism in GDR society is quite mild, compared with the 1950s and other socialist countries. However, despite the rhetoric implying that religion and the churches will be taken into "mature communism," the tenet of atheism remains intact and indeed the heightened attention to scientific atheism in the party's political-educational program attests to its sensitivity to this question. Nonetheless, researchers of scientific atheism have recently conceded that "depending on the level of development of socialism, even in this society there exist objective roots of religion, ideological, psychological, moral sources for religion."[2] They have noted the particular adaptability of Protestantism under conditions of socialism. This corresponds to a recognition by scholars of the increasing role of religion in the world. Thus, despite the success of its earlier attempts to curtail the church's attraction, the state now realizes that short of draconian measures, religion and the church are not likely to disappear soon in the GDR. Moreover, the state realizes that some dimensions of the church's roles are useful to the state, making a pragmatic interdependence with the church attractive.

2. The role of the church in contemporary GDR society

The church's position in contemporary GDR society can be usefully analyzed in terms of a taxonomy of six roles: the church is at once an organization of Christians, an advocate for peripheral non-Christian groups, a provider of social welfare, a carrier of national traditions and identity, a bridge between East and West Germany, and a force for peace. These can be viewed as concentric circles, ranging from the more narrowly defined role as an organization of Christians to the truly global role as a force for peace.

The church as an organization of Christians

The church's primary role in society is that of providing an organizational basis for the practice of religious rites and collective expression of religious values. This is also the most narrowly defined role of the church—it entails fulfilling the needs of individual Christians and is essentially inward-directed. Thus the church exhibits many of the same characteristics and pursues many of the same goals as other large social organizations. Questions of organizational structure and maintenance, beliefs, representation of members vis-à-vis the environment—all flow from this role as an organization of Christians.

It should be noted that with the formal separation of church and state and the end to universal church membership this role has taken on added importance. The church can no longer claim to speak for all of society and sometimes cannot even claim to speak for its own followers. As a result it must now devote greater attention to winning and retaining the loyalty of members as well as meeting its institutional needs. The end to universal church membership, or what is referred to as the *Volkskirche* (church of the people), is demonstrated in Table 1.

Table 1

Church Membership, by Confession

	% Evangelical	% Catholic
1939	85.7	7.2
1946	81.9	11.9
1950	80.5	11.0
1964	59.4	8.1
1978	47.2	7.2

Source: Wolfgang Buescher, "Unterwegs zur Minderheit" in Henkys, 423; *DDR Handbuch* 1985, 715, 213.

Table 2

Church Adherence in Two Regional Churches

Berlin-Brandenburg			Mecklenburg		
	1961	1971		1955	1969
Baptisms	21,112	8,231	Baptisms	11,377	2,790
Marriages	7,791	3,143	Marriages	4,247	798
Religious Instruction	80,415	66,957	Confirmations	11,139	3,642
Burials	28,345	25,614	Burials	app. 6,000	app. 6,000

Source: "Ostberlin," Broschure der Landeszentrale fur Politische Bildungsarbeit zur Thema "Kirche in der DDR."

Source: "Zahl der Kirchlichen Trauungen in der DDR zuruck-gegangen," *Der Tagesspiegel*, 10 February 1971.

Table 2 reveals that this decline in support for the church has affected all other measures of church adherence, with obvious exception of burials. Among those who are nominal members of the church, barely one percent attend church regularly. Clearly a large number are members in name only, kept on the churches' records in order to retain at least some point of contact with them.

The decline of the *Volkskirche* is hardly unique to the GDR—the process of secularization is causing similar phenomena in numerous European societies. However, the drive for socialist transformation in the GDR certainly accelerated the process. The atheism campaigns of the 1950s and 1960s, as well as the administrative pressures exerted, took their toll on church membership. The state measures had much less effect on the Catholic church, in part due to the greater coherence of the Catholic church generally and its historically conditioned ghetto mentality rooted in its minority status in Germany. The decline in church adherence seems to have slowed in recent years—the number formally leaving the church has dropped off and indeed the number of adult baptisms shows a modest increase. This latter phenomenon reflects increasing interest in the church and religion particularly among unbaptized youth. Nonetheless, the church has reluctantly begun to come to terms with reduced numbers and resources, with existence in "ideological diaspora."[3]

The erosion of the *Volkskirche* has entailed not only an absolute decline in numbers, but also a change in social composition.[4] Not surprisingly, the decline has been most drastic in large urban areas, with church strength relatively more intact in rural areas. In addition, church adherence among men has fallen disproportionately, resulting in an overrepresentation of women in the church. The age composition of the church has also been affected, with middle-age cohorts impacted more than those of an older age. Finally, in terms of the class composition of the churches, the erosion of strength in the working class, long underway, accelerated; consequently, farmers, as well as those in the remaining private sector, have become overrepresented. Certainly these trends, evident by the 1960s, contributed to the state's confidence regarding the long-term decline of the church in socialism.

The structure of the church also reflects the effect of the GDR system on the historical institution.[5] The Evangelical Lutheran churches in the GDR inherited an extremely fragmented and decentralized structure, based on the *Landeskirchen* (provincial churches) characteristic of Germany before unification. During the Weimar period efforts to achieve greater unity met with limited success. Moreover, the internal structure of the *Landeskirchen* was quite bureaucratic and hierarchical, particularly in the areas earlier under Prussian control. However, the centralization of political power, the decline of the *Volkskirche*, and the increased geographical mobility in the GDR have all had the effect of stimulating greater efforts at unity. To date, this has resulted only in the formation of an umbrella organization of *Landeskirchen*, the Federation of Evangelical Churches in the GDR. Moves toward greater unity have faltered on questions of continued inter-German ties.[6] In addition, the decline in church institutional strength has led to greater reliance on the laity in the church, thus partially mitigating the bureaucratic tradition.

The theology of the church has also been altered by socialism, as well as by the experience with the Third Reich.[7] The latter shook the Lutheran theological tradition of subordination to the state, often referred to as the "two kingdoms doctrine." Although the tendency toward political abstinence remains, the church is now more willing to speak critically of state policy. By the same token the socialist ideology of the state has challenged the church to address social-political issues, even legitimizing such attention. This is reflected in heightened church advocacy on issues of human rights, social justice, and peace. Thus socialism has shifted the churches' theological agenda. The Catholic church has been less affected by this change, remaining relatively abstinent politically until recently.[8]

As an organization of Christians, the church also acts much as as interest group would, advocating the interests of its individual members in their dealings with the state. These matters usually involve questions of conscience or discrimination against Christians.[9] For example, in 1953 the church sought to defend its members from the assault on the Youth Parishes, eventually reaching an agreement with the state. The church was less successful in its fight against the state's youth consecration ceremony, the *Jugendweihe*, introduced in 1955 to woo youth from the church confirmation ceremony. More recently, the church has defended individuals encountering discrimination in admission to the college-track high schools or experiencing career problems due to their refusal to serve in armed military units. Like many interest groups in the West, the leadership of the church is caught between the demands of its membership, expressed in democratically based church synods, and those of the state. Thus like these groups, the church not only seeks to protect its members vis-à-vis a hostile environment, it also seeks to minimize members' disappointment with the results of its efforts by exhorting them to sacrifice.

The institutional needs of the church organization also reveal a great deal of interdependence with the state. Theology departments at six state universities have long been responsible for training approximately one-half of all new clergy since World War II.[10] The state provides compensation to faculty and stipends to students. Although the church has sought to guarantee its supply of clergy by founding three of its own theological schools, which have graduated the remainder of new clergy, it is clearly dependent on the state's cooperation, which the latter continues to provide in order to influence the education of future clergy. More recently, under Honecker the state has permitted the construction of new churches, incorporated church personnel into the official retirement system, and now allows the church to broadcast several television programs per year, in addition to weekly radio broadcasts of church services. These examples illustrate institutional needs of the church which have become acute as a result of declining church adherence and which have served as the basis for limited cooperation between the state and church.[11]

Thus, as an organization of Christians, the church's role in the GDR society has diminished as a result of the declining church adherence. The historical inheritance of decentralized bureaucratic structures and tradition of political abstinence have been partially modified by its socialist environment. Despite the apparent trends in church adherence, the state and church exhibit considerable interdependence, as the state attempts to mobilize the support of churches and Christians and the church seeks to meet the needs of its members and the institution.

The church as advocate for socially peripheral groups

Although the church naturally acts primarily on behalf of its narrow interests, both institutional and individual, the absence of other social organizations independent of the state has left the church with a larger role in the GDR than in the West. The church attracts those who, for whatever reason, find themselves at odds with official policy or seek alternative outlets of expression.[12] Unlike in Poland, where the Catholic church still embodies society, major social groups such as the working class and intellectuals have long been alienated from the church and have not seen it as a viable alternative to participation in official organizations. Until recently this alienation also affected the attitude of youth toward the church.

Three factors have worked against this alienation and ghettoization. First, the church is the only organization in society that is not a transmission belt of the SED, subject to the discipline of democratic centralism. Although the church now concedes to the SED the leading role in society, it remains grass-roots oriented internally. This carries the disadvantage of being somewhat cut off from the mainstream of society, a situation that sometimes leads to feelings of isolation among the clergy. On the other hand, this position outside the official system makes the church attractive to new groups which offer the possibility of reinvigorating the church and giving it a new sense of purpose.

Second, social changes associated with modern industrial society have resulted in new problems and values in the GDR. For example, the GDR has been plagued by problems of worker productivity and corruption at the workplace. Alcoholism and alcohol consumption have increased alarmingly, as in other socialist countries, with concomitant negative economic and health effects.[13] Among the youth, dissatisfaction with the quality of life ranges from opposition to regimentation of free time and limited access to Western culture to concern with new issues which are taboo for the state, e.g., ecology and environmental protection, consumerism, increased aid to less-developed countries, treatment of homosexuals, and militarization of society.[14] For the church, these new problems and values provide opportunities.

Finally, the churches are themselves now more willing to serve as advocate for those on the periphery. The experience of the Third Reich and postwar theological emphasis on a "church for others" has led the church to be more receptive to the concerns of non-Christians. Of course, the church also sees this as a form of outreach to attract new members in an era of declining church adherence.

In recent times, the state has responded to the church's advocacy with greater tolerance. For many years, it sought to limit the church to cultic ritual and impeded nontraditional outreach efforts, particularly those directed at youth.[15] Lately, however, the state has tacitly accepted a widening of church activity. For example, church work with alcoholics and problem youth has met with grudging state approval. Blues masses and church conventions have found increasing resonance among youth, due to the opportunities for spontaneous expression. The church often provides a forum for writers who are officially taboo, such as Stefan Heym, and employment for those who have lost their jobs as a result of applying for exit visas.

Church activities often reach the limit of tolerance of the state and sometimes of the traditional church members too. The state has sometimes intervened to prevent dissident writers from appearing in churches. The state has been prompted to crack down by popular symbolic protests, such as the wearing of church arm patches depicting the "swords into plowshares" motif in 1982, or the ringing of church bells for peace, planned for November 1981.[16] Likewise, actions by individuals may cross into the zone of the impermissible—for example the arrest of some churchmen working with peripheral peace and environmental groups.[17] Often older or less political church members are also skeptical about the church's advocacy for peripheral groups. Indeed, some of the social upheavals producing these opportunities for the church also cause internal problems, for example the increase of divorce and cohabitation among clergy. The church has reacted at times by attempting to domesticate the peripheral groups, at other times by distancing itself from them.[18]

In its work with peripheral groups the church has demonstrated an increasing presence in GDR society. Its role derives from historical mission and the changing needs in socialist society. For its part the state finds itself more tolerant of such church activity because the latter institution can ameliorate problems that are ideologically uncomfortable to the state.

The church as provider of social welfare

The church plays a not insignificant role in the health and welfare system of the GDR, again a historical tradition of the church which has been modified greatly by the socialist transformation.

Of course, the church's role in the educational system saw the greatest change. Under the rubric of separation of church and state, in the 1940s and 1950s the state truncated the church's presence, eliminating religious instruction in the school curriculum and eventually limiting it to the church premises.[19] Both Catholic and Evangelical Lutheran churches were allowed to retain a limited number of independent secondary and postsecondary schools solely for the training of clergy. The church's kindergartens came under state pressure throughout the 1960s but the church has been permitted to retain roughly 326.[20]

In the area of health care, the church has been more fortunate; it has retained 47 hospitals, containing 6700 beds, as well as 226 homes for the aged, with 10,215 places. The church thus provides roughly 4 percent of all hospital beds and 8 percent of places for the aged in the GDR and constitutes a significant factor in the provision of health care.[21]

The church's facilities do not operate entirely independently of the state, however.[22] They depend on reimbursement from the state's mandatory insurance funds for the services provided to individual patients. But all capital improvements must be financed from the church's own sources and usually entail Western financial help and technology, as well as fundraising by the church. The church hospitals are integrated into the state planning process, for example in terms of specialization and allocation of physicians. That the church's presence is recognized by the broader society is demonstrated by the popular preference for church hospitals and homes, reflected in waiting lists, and by the strong support in the annual street collection for church diaconal institutions.

The church's work in this area is not without problems, however.[23] With a decline in religious orders, the diaconal institutions have been forced to rely increasingly on lay workers and even non-church members for personnel. This has necessitated paying workers in these institutions higher salaries than other church workers, in order to remain competitive with those in comparable positions in the state sector. However, these are internal problems; the state recognizes and praises the church work in the area of social welfare. It has cooperated in the expansion and construction of church hospitals and homes and the signing of a nurse training agreement in 1975 anchors the church role in health education. Even leading SED members are rumored to seek treatment in church facilities!

The church's diaconal institutions contribute to a presence in GDR society disproportionate to the size of its membership. The church's traditional diaconal activity was truncated earlier, but has now been stabilized and consolidated. The state and church enjoy mutual benefit from cooperating in this area.

The church as carrier of national traditions and identity

Many observers have noted a certain "rehistoricization process" underway in the GDR in recent times.[24] Figures from Prussian history who were long dismissed by GDR historians and leaders as conservative or counterrevolutionary— for example, Bismarck, Frederick the Great, General Scharnhorst—have been "rehabilitated" in the sense of being included in the "socialist heritage of the GDR." Portions of this "inheritance" are being appropriated into "socialist tradition," in other words viewed not merely as "objectively" progressive in history, but as part of a revolutionary class-based tradition.[25] Of course, beneath the ideological verbiage lies the true motivation—seeking to establish links to a past which 40 years of social-political transformation have been unable to eliminate or revise, hoping to turn this past from a burden into a basis for greater domestic legitimacy.

Of course, the GDR has long feted certain historical figures as part of its cultural heritage. Bach and Handel have long enjoyed official favor, in part because of foreign interest and because they are relatively harmless politically. Even groups and individuals performing religious music of these composers, for example the St. Thomas Choirboys of Leipzig, have long benefited from privileged status. The activities surrounding the 300th anniversary of the birth of Bach and Handel in 1985 confirm this.

A more recent, and surprising, addition to the pantheon is Luther.[26] Although earlier vilified as "betrayer of the German nation," the celebration of the 500th anniversary of Luther's birth in 1983 found Honecker hailing him as "one of the greatest sons of the German people," a key "progressive" figure due to his role in the "early bourgeois revolution." The official attention devoted to Luther in 1983 was considerable, ranging from biographies and scholarly research to official ceremonies, and GDR historians are increasingly interested in his theology as a legitimate motive for his behavior. Although the renaissance enjoyed by Luther clearly appeals particularly to the intelligentsia who are concerned about the integrity of German history, this necessarily entails greater legitimacy to the church as interpreter and heir of Luther.

In addition to the church's role in cultural heritage, it also embodies certain values identified with traditional German society. For example, the church remains a strong defender of the work ethic, in a socialist society in which commitment to the work ethic appears on the decline. Despite modernization within the church, it continues to be infused with a Prussian-like atmosphere of order and responsibility. The church, in particular the elements with bourgeois roots, places a high value on learning and education. Finally, of course, there is the traditional Lutheran deference to authority, which though shaken by the Third Reich, remains strong.

These rather conservative values and cultural roots are obviously appealing to a state attempting to conserve the social fabric and build greater political support for the GDR. Although the Evangelical Lutheran church in the GDR cannot claim to embody and speak for the nation (as can the Catholic church in Poland), it has acquired heightened social prestige as the carrier of many of these national traditions and values. Sometimes this is not entirely a welcome development to the churches, given the conservative overtones such legacies acquire in the socialist context.[27] However, both church and state evidently benefit from this renaissance of cultural traditions and identity.

The church as a bridge between East and West Germany

The church also plays the role of a bridge between the two Germanys, a role that has taken on added importance in recent years with the chill in relations between the superpowers. The church represents the only independent societal organization in the GDR that claims historical and current ties to a Western organization. In the early postwar period the GDR *Landeskirchen* were members of the all-German Evangelical Church in Germany (EKD), the umbrella organization designed to promote greater church unity. Indeed, these all-German ties, including meetings of leadership bodies and synods, were allowed to continue relatively unhindered until the building of the Berlin Wall in 1961. However, polemical attacks on the FRG church intensified after the signing of the Military Chaplaincy Agreement between the EKD and the Federal Republic in 1958. These were accompanied by administrative measures against all-German church activities, which after 1967 made conducting church business on an all-German basis virtually impossible. Finally in 1969, under the influence of these measures and a new constitution which dictated that "state borders shall be the limits of the churches' organizational possibilities," the GDR *Landeskirchen* seceded from the EKD and formed their own organization, the Federation of Evangelical Churches in the GDR.[28]

However, the division was less than total. The Berlin-Brandenburg *Landeskirche* and the Evangelical Church of the Union, the latter a union of confessionally similar churches, remained nominally all-German. Moreover, in its constitution the Federation retained a commitment to "special relations" with the West German church, a clause that has sometimes caused consternation in state circles.[29] These "special relations" have long entailed considerable Western financial assistance to the GDR churches, on the order of 100 million DM per year for the current account, plus special contributions for capital expenditures such as restoration of the Berlin Cathedral and construction of new churches. In addition, after initial caution by the GDR church, the churches have engaged in increasing consultation and exchanges, which have resulted in cooperation in nonsensitive areas, such as theology, particularly since the state dropped its earlier goal of a "GDR-specific theology." In recent years this inter-German cooperation has extended to even more politically sensitive areas, on occasion taking the form of joint statements by the EKD and the Federation, for example regarding peace on the 40th anniversaries of the beginning and end of World War II. The churches' statements carry particular weight in the context of the affirmation by Kohl and Honecker of a "special German responsibility for peace"; however, the church does not hesitate to criticize official GDR policies which it perceives as inhibiting the inter-German relationship, for example the raising of the minimum exchange for Western visitors in 1980 and the constraints on Western journalists' reporting of church activities since 1980.

Despite these continuing ties, the GDR church has become more assertive and divergences from the EKD have increased.[30] Soon after 1969 the Federation gained prominence by supporting the World Council of Churches' Anti-Racism Program, while the EKD was reluctant to support the African liberation movements supported by the funds. When talking with GDR church leaders, one detects a sense of pride in this position, as well as in the fact that they have come to terms with the end of the *Volkskirche* sooner than the EKD. In recent times this divergence has widened over the issue of nuclear weapons: the GDR church has strongly condemned all nuclear weapons and nuclear deterrence; the West German church has not issued such a total rejection. Spokesmen in the GDR church were critical of the EKD's unwillingness to oppose NATO's INF deployment. The source of these differences seems to lie in the new generation of church leaders, who lack the shared experiences of the previous generation.

It is ironic, then, that as the churches have grown increasingly independent in their stances, the two German states and their populaces should show increasing interest in the "special relations" between the two churches. To the public the church is a symbol of all-German ties, maintaining polemic-free communication to the West. For some who focus on the privileges that Western funds can buy, the church also represents the "golden West." The GDR has come to realize that the church's all-German character and credibility may help strengthen detente in a time when a new cold war looms. To the FRG leaders, the church has long represented a symbol and facilitator of all-German ties. In maintaining a close relationship to the GDR with the goal of peace and stability in Europe and perhaps eventual reunification, various FRG leaders have maintained ties to the GDR church. For example, Herbert Wehner and Johannes Rau, both SPD, and President Richard von Weizsaecher, CDU, have enjoyed warm relations with the GDR church.

In inter-German affairs the church has acquired a social presence disproportionate to its size. These ties have been attenuated by the division of Germany and affected substantively by socialism. However, despite the state's political differences with the West and the danger that the church's ties to the West bring, the state has not attempted to break those ties entirely. Nor has the church sought total autonomy from the West, despite the increasingly different development of the two churches and the demands of some in the church for greater modesty and independence in the church finances. Both church and state are linked by a mutual interest in a continued special relationship to the FRG, though they may define this relationship differently.

The church as an independent force for peace

Finally the church plays a significant role as a force for peace.[31] Obviously this role is tangential to all the roles previously discussed—from the core of believers to peripheral groups to society-at-large. Beyond this, however, the church seeks to make an impact far beyond the borders of the GDR. The basis of the church's commitment to peace is doctrinal and resists being limited to the individual's private peace with God which some Protestant denominations emphasize. However, the church's role in peace is also, in part, a dialectical function of the activities of peripheral groups and the mood of society-at-large. The church's peace work is affected, to a lesser extent, by the peace activities of the state. Of course, all state organizations loudly proclaim that peace is a goal of socialism. The official sponsorship of the Peace Council of the GDR and the privileged status of the Prague-based Christian Peace Conference give organizational manifestation to this goal. Although the church has increasingly participated in events of these organizations, it has not officially joined them, unlike churches in other Soviet bloc countries. The church guards its independence from state direction in matters of peace. In particular the church is challenged to independent action for peace by two factors—the actions of the state, in particular the militarization of society, and developments in the international environment, notably the chilling of East-West relations.

The rearmament of Germany after World War II led to considerable Protestant church opposition. In the GDR the opposition to this process has tended to be channeled into support for alternatives to military service. For example, the introduction of conscription in the GDR in 1962 caused considerable resistance, particularly by clergy and theology students, leading in 1964 to the creation of unarmed construction units (*Bausoldaten*)[32] attached to the military. This did not end the controversy, however, since *Bausoldaten* were often employed on military projects and suffered discrimination in career chances. Church criticism continued through the early 1970s until 1975, when an agreement was reached with the state limiting the *Bausoldaten* to nonmilitary objects. However, the scope of the debate regarding alternative service widened in the late 1970s and early 1980s. Increasing numbers of nonclergy opted for *Bausoldat* status (roughly 1000/year currently). Many youth petitioned in 1981 for a positive alternative to military service, a "social peace service" similar to that in the FRG, entailing service in hospitals and other social welfare institutions. The church has backed this proposal, but the state has rejected it as unrealistic. Nonetheless, the church has long given moral support to total conscientious objectors and some segments seem to be moving in the direction of supporting pacifism as "the clearer signal of peace service," as opposed to the EKD's continued equivocal stance supporting "peace service, with or without weapons."[33]

The other factor that has often crystallized church peace efforts has been the international environment, particularly the actions of the superpowers. A number of events and decisions coincided in the early 1980s (for example, the NATO Euromissile decision, and events in Afghanistan, Iran, and Poland), triggering in the German populace fears of a new cold war and leading to the formation of peace movements in Western Europe. The polemical attacks on the USSR by President Reagan and the leadership instability in the Kremlin heightened the anxiety. In general, the church is supportive of detente and trust-building between East and West. It opposes anything that might appear to destabilize the GDR or cast doubt on its international legitimacy, even though the church's special relationship with the EKD is predicated upon such doubt.[34] In 1980 the church specifically criticized the missile deployments of both East and West and by 1983 attacked the NATO missiles in particular. In 1982, in a precursor to a similar decision by the World Council of Churches in 1983, it rejected the spirit and logic of nuclear deterrence, coming close to making it a matter of confessional doctrine.[35] Perhaps the most sustained concrete activity of the church has been its annual "peace decade" which began in 1980 and entails ten days of activities throughout the GDR devoted to peace. Other actions have included lobbying West German (especially SPD) leaders, joint consultations and declarations with the EKD, and the platform offered to independent peace groups. At times the church's peace activities have led to conflict with the state—which responded harshly to the church's muted criticism of the handling of the Polish crisis in 1980, and the use of the symbol "swords into plowshares" in 1982.[36] However, the state's desire to remain credible to Western peace movements and avoid open conflict with the church constrained its actions and gave the church wider room for maneuver.

The deployment of the NATO missiles and the successful negotiation of an INF treaty have taken the wind from the sails of the peace movement in Europe. In the GDR this development was accelerated by the state's decision to permit massive emigration to the West in the spring of 1984, resulting in the departure of many peace activists. Yet the church continues its peace efforts. For example, the church, as well as the populace, voiced strong support for Honecker's visit to West Germany, planned for September 1984 but eventually postponed under Soviet pressure. The church leadership has supported the "peace policy of the GDR." Although the church grass roots recently rejected the leadership's characterization of the church-state relationship as based on "fundamental trust," both leadership and grass roots agree that "all unresolved questions [between church and state] should be subordinated to the task of maintaining peace." Bishop Hempel, then head of the Church Federation, reaffirmed this view in his summit with Honecker in February 1985 indicating again the importance that the church attaches to the issue of peace.[37]

Thus the issue of peace again demonstrates the significant social presence enjoyed by the church. Its activities on the issue derive from its theology and the historical German legacy of World War II, but are influenced by socialism, in particular in its views of the role of the military-industrial complex and "structural violence" in the Third World. The state finds itself interdependent with the church on the issue, since the church's very independence works to the advantage of the state in fostering greater credibility for its own peace efforts in the West.

3. The church's changing conception of its role

In the final analysis, the church's role in GDR society is a product not only of the state's policy and the church's past social roles and historical legacy, but also of the church's own vision for GDR society and its role in that society. In the 1950s, and probably through much of the 1960s, many in the church could probably be called oppositional. They hoped for reunification of Germany along West German lines and rejected socialism. The church saw its role as that of a *Wachteramt* (guardian office), charged with the task of criticizing the state for the absence of democratic freedoms and rule of law. This oppositional stance was perhaps best embodied in Bishop Dibelius of Berlin, who came to the point of denying the legitimacy of even the GDR's traffic laws. By the late 1950s however, divergent views surfaced: some favored "respecting the development of socialism"; others took the rather traditional Lutheran position that the "atheistic ideological state could only be accepted and endured, but not approved and promoted."[38] Still others moved in the direction of acclaiming socialism. Some in this latter group, such as Bishop Mitzenheim of Thuringia, hoped thereby to save the *Volkskirche*; others, such as those in the Weissensee Study Circle, applauded its demise. Some, such as the Union churches, tried to work against the Lutheran tendency to acclaim socialism or suffer it, and warned against both the extreme of "feeling abandoned by God in the given conditions and thus doubting," and the opposite extreme of "interpreting historical and social circumstances as direct manifestations of the will of God and thus accepting them without questions."[39]

The separation from the EKD in 1969 led to considerable soul-searching in the church regarding its vision.[40] For the most part, the church now accepts socialism as its socioeconomic environment. The 1971 formula of then-Bishop Schoenherr of Berlin—"we wish to be not a church against socialism, nor a church alongside socialism, but rather a church in socialism"—still describes its basic orientation today. However since 1968 the church sees its task as "bringing about socialism as a form of more just life together," thereby implying that it can be improved. Therein lies the rub: some, such as leading theologian Heino Falcke (Erfurt) in 1972, have argued for a "critical solidarity" by the church as part of a vision of an "improved socialism." The state rejected this immanent criticism, claiming that the SED alone was capable of improving socialism. Schoenherr's statement that "the question of power has been settled" reflects the sober realism of the church regarding any overt role in the improvement of "mature socialism." Nor does the Hungarian Lutheran model of an acclamatory "theology of service" hold much attraction to the GDR church. The church today accepts socialism, but sees its own role in more limited terms. It seeks to defend the interests of its members, rather like an interest group, as well as to be a "church for others," interceding for peripheral groups and occasionally society-at-large. Some would argue that the church no longer has a vision for GDR society and is merely reacting to the social and political change going on around it. However, perhaps without couching its goals in terms of a politically sensitive vision for GDR society, the church is nonetheless effecting change. Certainly its various roles in GDR society today and the relationship of interdependence with the state offer it the potential to do so.

Notes

1. For a brief overview of the church-state relationship in the GDR, see Hartmut Zimmerman, et al., eds., *DDR Handbuch* (Cologne: Verlag Wissenschaft und Politik, 1985), 720–26. A more extensive history is offered by Horst Daehn, *Konfrontation oder Kooperation? Das Verhältnis von Staat und Kirche in der SBZ/DDR 1945–1980* (Opladen: Westdeutscher Verlag, 1982). For analyses of the church-state relationship in the GDR, see

the author's "The Kirchenpolitik of the German Democratic Republic and the Evangelical Churches, 1968–1978," in *Studies in the GDR Culture and Society*, ed. Margy Gerber (Washington, D.C.: University Press of America, 1981) and "Domestic Dissent in the GDR: The Role of the Evangelical Church," in *East Germany, West Germany, and the Soviet Union: The Changing Relationship*, ed. Thomas A. Baylis, Western Societies Occasional Paper No. 18 (Ithaca, N.Y.: Cornell University Press, 1986). For a comparison of the GDR case with other Lutheran churches in the Soviet bloc, see the author's "Is the GDR the Future of Hungary and the Baltics? Dissent and the Lutheran Church in Eastern Europe," in *The GDR in Comparative Perspective*, ed. Thomas Baylis (London: Croom Helm, forthcoming). Two recent analyses in English, from a more religious perspective, are provided by Stephen P. Hoffman, "East Germany," in *Three Worlds of Christian-Marxist Encounters*, ed. Nicholas Piediscalzi and Robert G. Thobaben (Philadelphia: Fortress Press, 1985), 99–115 and Trevor Beeson, *Discretion and Valour. Religious Conditions and Eastern Europe*, 2d ed. (Philadelphia: Fortress Press, 1982), 193–218.

2. Noted researcher in scientific atheism, Olof Klohr, quoted in Almut Engelien, "Die theoretische Auseinandersetzung der SED mit der Religion," in *Die Evangelischen Kirchen in der DDR*, ed. Reinhard Henkys (Munich: Chr. Kaiser Verlag, 1982), 134–37.

3. Wolfgang Buescher, "Unterwegs zur Minderheit," in Henkys, *Evangelischen Kirchen*, 431. The concept of ideological diaspora is identified particularly with former Bishop Werner Krusche. See his address, "Die Gemeinde Jesu Christi auf dem Wege in die Diaspora," of November 17, 1973, resumed in *Kirche im Sozialismus*, no. 1 (1974): 11–15.

4. For a statistical description of the variations by social group in the overall decline, see Wolfgang Buescher, "Unterwegs zur Minderheit," in Henkys, *Evangelischen Kirchen*, 425–32.

5. Reinhard Henkys, "Volkskirche im Ubergang," in Henkys, *Evangelischen Kirchen*, 451–62.

6. Fearing the formal division it might mean for the Berlin-Brandenburg church, the Eastern synod of Berlin-Brandenburg appears to have laid to rest the project of a unified church in 1984. Its decisions are recorded in *Evangelische Pressedienst Dokumentation* (hereafter, *epd Dokumentation*), no. 21/84 (30 April 1984): 54–59.

7. Reinhard Stawinski, "Theologie in der DDR—DDR-Theologie?" in Henkys, *Evangelischen Kirchen*, 87–95.

8. Klemens Richter, "Veränderte Haltung der DDR-Katholiken," *Deutschland Archiv*, no. 5 (May 1983): 454–59.

9. Regarding the 1953 conflict over youth work and recent problems in the area of education, see Peter Wensierski, "Evangelische Jugendarbeit in der DDR," in Henkys, *Evangelischen Kirchen*, 276–82, and Horst Daehn, "Wissenschaftlicher Atheismus und Erziehungssystem," in ibid., 149–54.

10. Stephen Brown, "Am Rande der Hochschulen," *Kirche im Sozialismus* 10, no. 6 (December 1984): 9–23.

11. For a discussion of the extension of church-state rapprochement to church institutional needs, see Robert F. Goeckel, "Zehn Jahre Kirchenpolitik unter Honecker," *Deutschland Archiv*, no. 9 (September 1981): 942–46.

12. Henry Krisch notes the church's role as an "organized haven for the development of an alternative culture," in his "Politische Kultur in der DDR," in *Lebensbedingungen in der DDR* (Cologne: Verlag Wissenschaft und Politik, 1984), 10–12. For a discussion of recent disaffection and dissent in the GDR, see Michael J. Sodaro, "Limits to Dissent in the GDR: Fragmentation, Cooptation, and Repression," in *Dissent in Eastern Europe*, ed. Jane Leftwich Curry (N.Y.: Praeger, 1983), 82–116, and Pedro Ramet, "Dissaffec-

tion and Dissent in East Germany," *World Politics* 27, no. 1 (October 1984): 85–111.

13. Zimmermann, et al., 38.

14. Christiane Lemke analyzes trends in the use of leisure time by youth, noting in particular the increased significance of nonorganized groupings in such leisure time. See Christiane Lemke, "Jugendliche in der DDR," *Deutschland Archiv* 17, no. 2 (February 1984): 166–82. The church's activities regarding ecology are discussed in Peter Wensierski, "Nach Alternativen wird gefragt. Kirchliches Umwelt-Engagement in der DDR," *Kirche im Sozialismus*, nos. 5–6 (December 1980), 29–44. Opportunities and problems with the church's "open youth work" are discussed in Wensierski, "Evangelische Jugendarbeit," 268–76.

15. See the discussion of the Events Ordinance, long used by the state in its attempts to limit church activities to cultic ritual, in Reinhard Henkys, "Kirche—Staat—Gesellschaft," in Henkys, *Evangelischen Kirchen*, 40–42.

16. Regarding the state's proscription of church bells during a planned minute for peace, see Wolfgang Beuscher, et al., eds., *Friedensbewegung in der DDR. Texte 1978–1982* (Hattingen: Scandica Verlag, 1982), 122–23. On other cases of church-state conflict, for example the "Swords into Plowshares" affair, see Theo Mechtenberg, "Die Friedensverantwortung der Evangelischen Kirchen in der DDR," in Henkys, *Evangelischen Kirchen*, 389–94; Ronald D. Asmus, "Is There a Peace Movement in the GDR?" *Orbis* 27, no. 2 (Summer 1983): 316–17, 323–25; and Joyce Marie Mushaben, "Swords to Plowshares: The Church, the State, and the East German Peace Movement," *Studies in Comparative Communism* 17, no. 2 (Summer 1984): 129.

17. For example, the wave of arrests of peace activists in the so-called "Jena scene" in 1983, documented in *epd Dokumentation*, no. 10a (7 March 1983): 1–6. After NATO deployment, arrests of peace/environmental activists did increase somewhat, along with mass emigration to the West. See *epd Zentralausgabe*, nos. 133, 144 (12 July and 27 July 1984): 7 and 2–3.

18. For a discussion of the church's various responses to peripheral groups—domesticating, disciplining, and distancing—see Goeckel, "Domestic Dissent."

19. Horst Daehn, *Konfrontation*, 29–33.

20. Eckart Schwerin et al., "Kein Einheitliches Bild. Aspekte kirchlicher Kinder- und Jugendarbeit," *Kirche im Sozialismus* 9, no. 6 (December 1983): 29–31; Zimmerman, 307; Reuer, "Diakonie," 238.

21. Reuer, ibid., 221; Zimmerman, 562.

22. Reuer, "Diakonie," 224–27.

23. Reuer, ibid., 227–28, 213–14. For example, Honecker's praise of the church's role in the health and welfare system at the 1978 summit meeting, as noted in Zimmerman, 307.

24. Ulrich Neuhaeusser-Wespy, "Von der Urgesellschaft bis zur SED," *Deutschland Archiv* 16, no. 2 (February 1983): 145–52; Johannes Kuppe, "Die Geschichtsschreibung der SED im Umbruch," *Deutschland Archiv* 18, no. 3 (March 1985): 278–94.

25. See Theologische Studienabteilung, Bund der evangelischen Kirchen in der DDR, "Marxistische Erberezeption" (Berlin/GDR, April 1981, mimeograph).

26. Robert F. Goeckel, "The Luther Anniversary in East Germany," *World Politics* 37, no. 1 (October 1984): 112–33. See the new official biography of Luther by Gerhard Brendler, *Martin Luther. Theologie und Revolution* (Berlin/GDR: VEB Deutscher Verlag der Wissenschaften, 1983), and Ronald D. Asmus, "The GDR and Martin Luther," *Survey* 28 (Autumn 1984): 124–56.

27. The state's emphasis on Luther's conservative political views (e.g., the value of *Stände*, or positions within society; support for military defense, the importance of work, etc.) in its 1983 celebration led the church to counteract this with a more "critical" Luther.

28. Henkys, "Kirche—Staat—Gesellschaft," 29–37; Horst Daehn, *Konfrontation*;

Reinhard Henkys, *Bund der Evangelischen Kirchen in der DDR. Dokumente zu seiner Entstehung* (Witten und Berlin: Eckart Verlag, 1970).

29. Reinhard Henkys, "Die DDR-Kirchen als ökumenische Partner," in Henkys, *Evangelischen Kirchen*, 181–96.

30. Reinhard Henkys, "Dialog—Gemeinschaft. Chancen und Probleme in den Beziehungen der evangelischen Kirchen in beiden deutschen Staaten," *Kirche im Sozialismus* no. 5 (1984): 11–20.

31. The reader is referred to several analyses of the church's role in the peace movement in the GDR. Ronald D. Asmus, "Is There a Peace Movement in the GDR?" *Orbis* 27, no. 2 (Summer 1983): 301–41; Joyce Marie Mushaben, "Swords to Plowshares: The Church, the State and the East German Peace Movement," *Studies in Comparative Communism* 17, no. 2 (Summer 1984): 123–35. For an excellent post-deployment analysis, see Norman Naimark, "Militarism, Pacifism, and the GDR's Peace Policy" (Paper presented at Hamilton College conference "A New Germany?" April 26–28, 1985).

32. Regarding the *Bausoldaten*, see Bernd Eisenfeld, *Kriegsdienstverweigerung in der DDR—ein Friedensdienst?* (Frankfurt/Main: Verlag Haag and Herchen, 1978) and Zimmerman, 151–52.

33. Henkys, "Dialog—Gemeinschaft." The Church Province of Saxony (Magdeburg) has shifted largely to this pacifistic stance. See its resolutions in 1983 in "Synode: Beschluss," *epd Dokumentation*, no. 53 (12 December 1983): 1–12.

34. See the address by Manfred Stolpe, leading spokesman for the Federation on political-international issues, "Modell für deutsch-deutschen Dialog," *Kirche im Sozialismus* 10, no. 2 (June 1984): 15–24.

35. The church's general support for détente and political negotiations as opposed to military actions is clearly set forth in its "Erklärung zur weltpolitischen Situation vom 22. Januar 1980," Buescher et al., 111–15. The church's opposition to deterrence is found in "Beschluss der Synode . . . ," *epd Dokumentation*, no. 47 (11 October 1982): 30–33; its opposition to NATO missiles can be found in "Erklärung zur Stationierung von atomaren Mittelstreckenwaffen in Europa," *epd Dokumentation*, no. 43 (10 October 1983): 66.

36. Theo Mechtenberg, "Die Friedensverantwortung der Evangelischen Kirchen in der DDR," in Henkys, *Evangelischen Kirchen*, esp. 373–74, 387–94.

37. "Beschluss der Synode," *epd Dokumentation*, no. 43 (8 October 1984): 34–35; "Antworten auf Fragen in der Aussprache zum Bericht," *epd Dokumentation*, no. 43 (8 October 1984): 28–33; *Neues Deutschland* (12 February 1985).

38. "Kommunique von 21. Juli 1958," and "Handreichung der VELKD vom 1960," discussed in Hans-Juergen Roeder, "Kirche im Sozialismus," in Henkys, *Evangelischen Kirchen*, 67.

39. "Zehn Artikel von Freiheit und Dienst der Kirche, von 1963," cited in ibid., 68.

40. The following fundamental positions are discussed in ibid., 69–78. Falcke repeated his appeal to work for "improved socialism" in the context of the wave of exit applications in 1984; however, the rush of applications and the social malaise seemed to leave Falcke a voice in the wilderness. See Heino Falcke, "Brief an die Pfarrer . . . ," February 1984, *epd Dokumentation*, no. 21 (30 April 1984): 1–4.

Conclusion

The Transformation of a
State Socialist Society

MARILYN RUESCHEMEYER AND CHRISTIANE LEMKE

The essays collected in this book reflect the complexity and differentiation of GDR society today. Contrary to a widespread image of state-socialist societies as nonpluralist and monolithic, they indicate that the GDR is a highly complex, advanced industrial society sharing some of the problems that trouble Western industrial societies. Differentiation as well as the accompanying partial autonomy of different social groups and institutions are real features of this society even if the consequences of differentiation are also contained by a strong state and a nonpluralistic party system under the leadership of the communist party, the SED.

The growing differentiation of GDR society is the result of far-reaching economic and social change. The changes in the social structure are dramatically apparent when one compares the present situation with the initial phase of transforming society according to the Marxist-Leninist goal culture in the late forties and fifties. The bourgeois intelligentsia has been converted by changed recruiting and training mechanisms into a socialist intelligentsia.[1] Parts of the traditional middle class have disappeared, while a growing number of public servants are employed in health, education, state and social services. At the same time, the new educated strata represent an increasing diversity of concerns and interests. In agriculture, peasants have become cooperative farmers or workers in a state-controlled agricultural system. The working class as a whole emerges as a highly differentiated social stratum, in which training and qualification, income, and position within the work process give rise to changing interest configurations and new values, attitudes, and behavior.

Most significantly, the role of women has changed completely. The number of women working outside the home in industry, in trade and services, and in the large public state sector has increased steadily, and women make up half of the workforce in the GDR. Even if they are still underrepresented at the higher levels of state and political organizations and in leadership positions of the economic sector, they are now fully involved in the labor force and—at least with regard to the middle and younger generation—as well qualified as men. As a consequence, female-male relations have been structurally transformed in the occupational system, and this represents a potential for more far-reaching changes in all aspects of gender relations. As several of the authors in this book argue, there is a significant relation between the place of social groups in society, in particular their role in the work process, and attitudes and behavior outside the workplace—in family relations, socialization, leisure time activities, cultural patterns, and life-styles.

Since the early 1970s the population in the GDR has enjoyed a considerably increased standard of living. The permanent competition with West Germany and the conviction that the viability of the sociopolitical system ultimately depends on finding solutions to economic problems and achieving a high standard of living were the basis for the pragmatically oriented policy since Honecker came to power in 1971. The "unity of economic and social policy" (Einheit von Wirtschafts- und Sozialpolitik), a term introduced by Honecker, envisions a fostering of economic growth mainly by introducing new technologies on a larger scale in combination with a comprehensive social policy and a consumer-oriented economic policy.

As a consequence of increasing social differentiation, a higher standard of living, and more complex needs and expectations of the population, a greater divergence of values and interests has developed. This point is made in the chapters by Helmut Hanke and Lothar Bisky for the areas of culture, media, and leisure time activities, but it also holds true for other social groups, such as women, as Irene Dölling points out in her chapter. Culture and the use of free time have become areas in which the growing diversity manifests itself. It is precisely in these areas that the people evaluate the quality of life apart from their workday routine, even though as Hanke states, the GDR is far from being a leisure time society. Volker Gransow stresses that the introduction of new technologies will generate further differences in life-styles and he discusses the changes and challenges in the society against the background of this technology policy, which was again confirmed at the last, Eleventh SED-Party Congress in April 1986. These transformations will be of the greatest importance for the future of GDR society and the question of how the quality of life is experienced and evaluated by different groups.

The different developments discussed so far have also changed the relation between state and society and the character of state policy.[2] During the initial postwar phase of shaping the economic, social, and political system, state activity was primarily concentrated on the tasks of power accumulation and the destruction of the traditional property relationships and social structures. As time progressed, the task of developing an efficient production and distribution system, which would be able to meet the needs and demands of the population and increase the legitimacy of the political systems, has moved to the fore. Commitment to technical and scientific progress, support of a consumer-oriented policy, slow but irreversible acceptance of the only large autonomous organization in GDR society, the church, and a cautious tolerance of some public discussion in art and literature mark the present relationship between state, party, and society.

As Bradley Scharf argues in his chapter, social policy has become a centerpiece of state policy in the 1970s and 1980s. It is a major instrument of the state, which guides social change and attempts to correct the social conflicts and strains resulting from forced economic modernization. Since the Eighth Party Congress in 1971, this social policy has been regarded as part of the "main task" and as part of the general line to be pursued by the SED, along with a growth-oriented economic policy. It has become the major political activity of the state, and as Scharf shows, there has been an extraordinarily broad range of active social policy programs corresponding to the established broad conception of social policy. This emphasis on social policy required some modifications of Marxist-Leninist theory; its introduction and development certainly also drew upon traditions that had been vital in Germany since the Bismarck era.

An example of one of the central pieces of social policy and its implications for the population is the examination of the new towns of Rostock. Housing policy had a high priority among the social policy programs. As a response to complaints about lack of housing and about the miserable conditions of the existing housing stock these new towns, which now exist in almost every city in the GDR, have become part of everyday life. Thus traditional patterns and life-styles and the differences between those who live in the cities and those who live in the countryside have been changed to more complex patterns, while those people living in the new towns have developed a number of new social patterns and attitudes that were not previously anticipated by planners and architects.

Another crucial point of state policy is critically evaluated in Joan de Bardeleben's chapter on environmental policy. She explains the aims and arguments underlying that policy as well as the limits set by political and economic constraints. The comprehensive environmental protection policy, codified in several legal regulations and controlled by state institutions, most clearly documents the need to limit and control damages caused by fostered economic growth. Economic growth and environmental protection are seen by economists and state officials as mutually reinforcing, not contradictory goals. However, the population is partially aware of numerous kinds of pollution in water, air, and soil, and of lasting environmental damages. While discussion of these matters and relevant information is limited within the GDR, nearly everyone has access to West German television and many are aware of the extensive debate on environmental issues in the industrial societies of the West. To what extent the growing environmental awakening of the population will be met is yet unclear.

The current state policy, which is geared toward economic growth and scientific-technical progress, affects all areas of life, a fact that is reflected in almost every chapter in this volume. It clearly affects the goals and structures of socialization in society, the family, and gender relations as well as the workplace, structures of qualification, leisure, and culture. However, it would be mistaken only to follow a top-down model of analysis, which sees society as totally shaped by the state. Our volume has attempted to do justice to the impact of state policy on everyday life; but again and again we sought to take a grass-roots perspective on the same issues. It was shown that socialization in the state-socialist society, for example, not only takes place in the officially assigned institutions of learning. Rather it is the result of a complex process, which takes place in the micromilieu of family life, school experience, peer-group culture, and informal networks. With the differentiation of society, a divergence of values and attitudes has emerged, which gains significance for shaping social and political values and attitudes.

Gender relations play a significant role in contemporary GDR society in the process of socialization and the forming of life-styles and cultural patterns. The massive labor-force participation of women and the equally broad-based upgrading of their occupational qualifications have given women a vastly increased leverage vis-à-vis their male partners, vis-à-vis the enterprises in which they work, and perhaps also vis-à-vis the state. This increased autonomy of women is differentiated by generation as well as level of education, with the younger and more qualified women having gained the most. In these latter groups in particular, we also see subtle but profound changes in marriage and friendship relations that may foreshadow important future developments in industrial societies.[3]

However, the remaining problems are not unimportant. Irene Dölling argues that present gender differences, which form cultural patterns of everyday life, are characteristic for a certain "stage" of socioeconomic development. In her chapter, she adopts a Marxist-feminist perspective and emphasizes that it is only through the integration of women in the labor force that their emancipation will take place. For the GDR, she insists that patterns of inequality and even discrimination be tackled more consciously. While women in the GDR today have achieved a high level of education as evident in the impressive figures on the increased standard of qualification, their traditional role in the family and the care of children often persists. As Hildegard M. Nickel shows, based on empirical research conducted in the GDR, these patterns are reinforced by gender-specific patterns of socialization within the family and even in schools. She critically considers possible impacts on the chances of women to cope with the changes due to the scientific-technical revolution and calls for a greater awareness and sensitivity, which is, despite the official claim of an equality of the sexes, not sufficiently developed.

The importance accorded to economic growth and scientific-technical progress, which several authors elaborate on in their contributions, has significant effects on important areas of everyday life in GDR society. Most visible is the impact of the ambitious economic growth program in the areas of workplace and qualification. For example, with the importance assigned to using new technologies, increasing productivity, and reducing costs of production, shiftwork has been increased significantly in recent years. As Mike Dennis illustrates in his article on the social aspects of shiftwork, the expansion of shiftwork, especially where it involves nights and weekends, often is disliked by workers. Negative effects on health and quality of life of individual workers and groups have thus to be considered when examining GDR society today.

Related to the scientific-technical revolution are changes in the system of qualification and education. Originally, the educational system was designed first and foremost to raise the general standard of education for all citizens, with special attention given to those social groups that had been underprivileged before, such as women, manual workers, and peasants, and to inculcate a particular view of the world along with the development of the "socialist personality." As Gert-Joachim Glaessner explains in his chapter on educational policy, the emphasis is now shifting toward an education that furthers flexibility, mobility, and the capability for innovation. Due to changes in the structure of job qualification required for economic growth, rapid changes in skills, employment below level, or double qualification are some of the problems troubling educational planners as well as certain social groups of workers and employers.

These problems, however, must not obscure the fact that large-scale upgrading in education and occupational qualification has transformed the life chances of many women and men. A higher occupational skill level earns respect and strengthens self-respect. It has also been shown in many GDR studies to be related to social participation. Furthermore, the more skilled a person is the greater the chances to make demands, if need be, to change jobs; and turnover rates are closely watched in the GDR. Higher skill levels, then, expand the space of personal autonomy for both women and men.

Another, nearly opposite pattern of enlarging one's space for personal autonomy is also related to economic growth and a higher standard of living. Quite a few young people feel that they can afford not to be very ambitious and yet enjoy a comfortable life. That means that they gain more personal independence from the demands made by society and the state than their cohorts who strive for a more respectable or even brilliant career. Such a choice often has a complex motivational background. Many women make it because they are burdened with housework or because they opt for a better balance between occupational and personal interests. Yet the result of an enlarged space for personal autonomy remains.

While in all areas discussed above there is a close interrelation between state policy and the party on the one hand, and the partial autonomy of individuals and social groups on the other, the church enjoys a particular *institutional* autonomy. As in most other state-socialist societies throughout Eastern Europe, the church represents a significant autonomous organization, which is not only important with respect to state-church relations, but also with respect to the role it plays for society and individual citizens in these countries. Historically it often represents the remainder of what used to be the organized civil society of these countries. Politically it is a powerful counterpoint to the state and its Marxist-Leninist ideology. As Robert Goeckel points out, Protestantism is the dominant religion in the GDR—in contrast to other countries in Eastern Europe; thus he mainly discusses the role of the Protestant church. Its role in society is manifold. It provides an organizational basis for the practice of religious rites and collective expression of religious values and it is a carrier of national traditions and identity. Moreover, a fact which is often neglected, the churches provide a whole network of social welfare, especially for the handicapped, the old, and the sick. Traditionally they advocate the socially peripheral groups and take a strong position for peace. Thus, especially in recent years, the church has become an independent force for peace and an umbrella for a number of new, independent groups, which form an alternative political culture in the GDR.

The partial autonomy of different groups that is a result of the transforming of GDR society and the particular institutional autonomy of the church must, however, be seen in the broader context. They are contained by a strong state and the leadership role of the SED. After all state and party action request priority in shaping civil society in state-socialist systems, and state and party do have a pervasive impact on society, though one must not overestimate the possibilities of purposeful planning in this respect. Aside from this profound impact on the structure of society and the decision-making process, there are strict limitations to an open discussion, even though room has been given for some critical discussions in social science and in the cultural field; spontaneous action is virtually impossible and ad-hoc organizations are bound to exist as informal, near-invisible structures. Despite the official claims that the GDR's political system allows for citizens' participation, it is not clear what the forms and the content of such participation are to be under current conditions. There is a tendency to assimilate political participation into a general concept of social participation in society. On the other hand, some critical GDR-scholars publishing on "socialist democracy," such as Uwe-Jens Heuer, acknowledge the fact that increased individual participation may generate conflicts between individual and society, and they assert that the reality of divergent interests in society as a consequence of structural differentiation demand a different, more conscious and active behavior of the citizen toward the state, a task that has not yet been resolved.[4]

In contrast to the differentiation and complexity of GDR society today, then, political institutions have changed much less. Here containment prevails over adjustment and flexibility. The contributions collected in this volume suggest, however, that the GDR is facing a number a problems that constitute major challenges for future development. The primary internal challenges certainly derive from the fostered process of modernization and economic growth. Here we think of problems within the workplace which are linked to the introduction of new technologies on a large scale, environmental damages, the need for the educational system to adapt to the desired innovations, or the possible stagnation in the advance toward a real equality in male-female relations. The fostered economic growth and the introduction of new technologies also lead to a number of political and philosophical questions. Important examples are environmental issues, the use of nuclear power, and genetics. The social costs of economic growth, and the larger issue of the ambivalence of progress are currently concerns which trouble critical scholars and some nonstate autonomous groups.[5]

Among the most important externally caused challenges—which we could not cover in this volume—are the changes due to the opening in German-German relations and the possible impact of *glasnost* in the Soviet Union. Detente with the West has been a mixed experience for the GDR, but it has profited from it in domestic as well as in foreign policy. While the orientation toward West Germany had always been strong among the population, it was not until recently that a cautious opening on the political level was initiated by the party leadership. Honecker's visit to West Germany in the fall of 1987, contacts and conferences of the SED and the West German Social Democratic Party or *Städtepartnerschaften* which have recently been established generate hopes and expectations for more political and cultural freedom, for example the freedom of travel, cultural transfer, or access to information and exchange. In response to changes in the Soviet Union under Gorbachev, the GDR leadership has so far not initiated reforms of its own but rather pointed to the successful record of economic and social policy in the GDR which seems to make reforms unnecessary. Within the population, however, and especially among intellectuals, writers, artists, and many young people, there is a strong sympathy for Gorbachev's proposals for reform and a hope for a more open society.

These major challenges viewed together suggest that GDR society is at a turning point at which both internal and external challenges will shape the future of this society. As in all state-socialist societies, much will depend on the role of the party and the state and the question of "socialist democracy," which would allow different social groups and individuals more autonomy and self-determination. The developments analyzed in this book fall short of the hopes generated by recent political developments in the Soviet Union. Yet the differentiation and growing complexity of GDR society and the related emergence of diverse forms of social autonomy that is evident in people's everyday life have nevertheless transformed the quality of life in the GDR. Whatever the future it is important to understand these developments.

Notes

1. For the current discussion about social differences and the social structure in the GDR see Gunnar Winkler, ed., *Lexikon der Sozialpolitik* (Berlin [GDR]: Akademie Verlag, 1987), 355–58.

2. The role of the state and the mass organizations are critically discussed in Hartmut Zimmermann, "Power Distribution and Opportunities for Participation: Aspects of the Socio-political System of the GDR," in *Policymaking in the German Democratic Republic*, ed. Klaus von Beyme and Hartmut Zimmermann (New York: St. Martin's Press, 1984), 1–108.

3. Marilyn Rueschemeyer, "New Family Forms in a State Socialist Society: the German Democratic Republic," *Journal of Family Issues*, forthcoming.

4. See for example Uwe-Jens Heuer, "Zur Geschichte des marxistisch-leninistischen Demokratiebegriffs," in *Politische Theorie und sozialer Fortschritt*, ed. Karl-Heinz Röder (Berlin [GDR]: Staatsverlag der DDR, 1986), 182–206.

5. For more details see Christiane Lemke, "New Issues in the Politics of the German Democratic Republic: A Question of Political Culture?" *The Journal of Communist Studies* 2, no. 4 (1986): 341–58.

Selected Bibliography

Asmus, Ronald D. "Is There a Peace Movement in the GDR?" *Orbis* 27, no. 2 (Summer 1984): 301–41.

Autorenkollektiv. *Arbeitsökonomie. Lehrbuch*. Berlin: Die Wirtschaft, 1982.

Baylis, Thomas A. *The Technical Intelligentsia and the East German Elite*. Berkeley: University of California Press, 1974.

Bentley, Raymond. *Technological Change in the German Democratic Republic*. Boulder: Westview, 1984.

Bisky, Lothar and Wiedemann, Dieter. *Der Spielfilm—Rezeption und Wirkung*. Berlin: Henschel, 1985.

Böhme, Irene. *Die da druben*. Berlin: Rotbuch,1982.

Borrmann, Rolf and Schille, Hans-Joachim. *Vorbereitung der Jugend auf Liebe, Ehe und Familie*. Berlin: VEB Deutscher Verlag der Wissenschaften, 1980.

Bruhm-Schlegel, Ute and Kabat vel Job, Otmar. *Junge Frauen heute. Wie sie sind—was sie wollen*. Leipzig: Verlag für die Frau, 1981.

Das Bildungswesen der Deutschen Demokratischen Republik. Berlin/DDR: Volk und Wissen, 1979.

DeBardeleben, Joan. "Esoteric Policy Debate: Nuclear Safety Issues in the Soviet Union and German Democratic Republic." *British Journal of Political Science* 15 (1985): 227–53.

————. *The Environment and Marxism-Leninism: The Soviet and East German Experience*. Boulder, Colo.: Westview Press, 1985.

Dennis, Mike. "Degradation or Humanization? Work and Scientific-Technical Progress in the GDR." In *Studies in GDR Culture and Society*, vol. 6, 59–80. Lanham, Md.: University Press of America, 1986.

Dölling, Irene. *Individuum und Kultur*. Berlin: Dietz Verlag, 1986.

Edwards, Gwyen E. *GDR Society and Social Institutions*. New York: St. Martin's Press, 1985.

Gerber, Margy et al., eds. *Studies in GDR Culture and Society*. 7 vols. Lanham, Md.: University Press of America, 1981–87.

Goeckel, Robert F. "Domestic Dissent in the GDR: The Role of the Evangelical Church." In *East Germany, West Germany, and the Soviet Union: Perspectives on a Changing Relationship*, ed. Thomas Baylis, 13–20. Center for International Studies, Cornell University, Western Societies Program Occasional Paper No. 18.

Grandke, Anita. *Familienförderung als gesellschaftliche Aufgabe*. Berlin: Staatsverlag der Deutschen Demokratischen Republik, 1986.

Gransow, Bettina and Gransow, Volker. "Disponible Zeit und Lebensweise." *Deutschland Archiv* 16, no. 7 (1983): 748–49.

Gysi, Jutta. "Frauen- und Familienentwicklung als Gegenstand sozialistischer Politik." In *Jahrbuch für Soziologie und Sozialpolitik 1984*, 95–109. Berlin: Akademie Verlag, 1984.

Handbuch Deutsche Demokratische Republik. Leipzig: VEB Bibliographisches Institut, 1984.

Handhardt, Arthur. "East Germany: From Goals to Realities." In *Political Socialization in Eastern Europe. A Comparative Framework*, ed. Ivan Volgyes, 66–91. New York: Praeger, 1975.

Henkys, Reinhard, ed. *Die Evangelischen Kirchen in der DDR.* München: Chr. Kaiser Verlag, 1982.

Hütter, Manfred; Jobst, Eberhard, et al. *Mikroelektronik und Gesellschaft.* Berlin: Akademie, 1984.

Informationen des wissenschaftlichen Beirats "Die Frau in der sozialistischen Gesellschaft." Series ed. by the Academy of Sciences in the GDR.

Kabat vel Job, Otmar and Pinther, Arnold. *Jugend und Familie. Familiäre Faktoren der Persönlichkeitsentwicklung Jugendlicher.* Berlin: VEB Deutscher Verlag der Wissenschaften, 1981.

Kahl, Alice and Riedel, Steffi. "Wohnverhältnisse, Wohnweise und Wohnverhalten in der sozialistischen Grossstadt." *Jahrbuch für Soziologie und Sozialpolitik 1985*, 136–52. Berlin: Akademie Verlag, 1984.

Kahl, Alice; Wilsdorf, Steffen H.; and Wolf, Herbert F. *Kollektivbeziehungen und Lebensweise.* Berlin: Dietz Verlag, 1984.

Koch, Hans, ed. *Zur Theorie der sozialistischen Kultur.* Berlin, Dietz Verlag, 1982.

Kretzschmar, Albrecht. *Soziale Unterschiede—unterschiedliche Persönlichkeiten? Zum Einfluss der Sozialstruktur auf die Persönlichkeitsentwicklung.* Berlin: Dietz Verlag, 1985.

Krisch, Henry. *The German Democratic Republic. The Search for Identity.* Boulder: Westview, 1985.

Langen, Eva-Maria. *Technisierungsgrad der Arbeit und Qualifikation der Produktionsarbeiter.* Berlin: Dietz Verlag, 1979.

Lemke, Christiane. *Persönlichkeit und Gesellschaft. Zur Theorie der Persönlichkeit in der DDR.* Opladen: Westdeutscher Verlag, 1980.

———. "Women and Politics in East Germany." *Socialist Review*, no. 81 (1985): 121–34.

———. "New Issues in the Politics of the German Democratic Republic: A Question of Political Culture?" *Journal of Communist Studies* 2, no. 4 (1986): 341–58.

———. "Jugendliche in der DDR." *Deutschland Archiv* 17, no. 2 (1984): 166–82.

Leptin, Gerd and Melzer, Manfred. *Economic Reform in East German Industry.* Oxford: Oxford University Press, 1978.

Ludz, Peter C. *The German Democratic Republic from the Sixties to the Seventies.* Cambridge, Mass.: Harvard University Press, 1970, 1984.

Marschall, Wolfgang and Steinitz, Klaus, eds. *Schlüsseltechnologie Mikroelektronik.* Berlin: Dietz Verlag, 1985.

McAdams, James A. *East Germany and Detente. Building Authority after the Wall.* Cambridge: Cambridge University Press, 1985.

Mühlberg, Dietrich. *Woher wir wissen, was Kultur ist.* Berlin: VEB Deutscher Verlag der Wissenschaften, 1983.

Mushaben, Joyce Marie. "Swords to Plowshares: The Church, the State and the East German Peace Movement." *Studies in Comparative Communism* 17, no. 2 (1984): 123–35.

Musil, Jiří. *Urbanization in Socialist Countries*. New York: M.E. Sharpe, 1980.

Nickel, Hildegard M. "Geschlechtersozialisation in der Familie und als Funktion gesellschaftlicher Arbeitsteilung—Ein erziehungssoziologischer Erklärungsansatz für die Herausbildung weiblicher und männlicher sozialer Identität." Diss. (B), Berlin: Humboldt University, 1986.

Niederländer, Loni. *Arbeiten und Wohnen in der Stadt*. Berlin: Dietz Verlag, 1984.

Röder, Karl-Heinz, ed. *Politische Theorie und sozialer Fortschritt*. Berlin: Staatsverlag der DDR, 1986.

Rueschemeyer, Marilyn. *Professional Work and Marriage: An East-West Comparison*. London: Macmillan & Co.; New York: St. Martin's Press, 1981.

—————. "Integrating Work and Personal Life. An Analysis of Three Professional Work Collectives in the German Democratic Republic." *GDR-Monitor*, no. 8 (1982–83).

—————. "New Family Forms in a State Socialist Society: the German Democratic Republic." *Journal of Family Issues*. Forthcoming.

Rueschemeyer, Marilyn and Scharf, Bradley. "Labor Unions in the German Democratic Republic." In *Trade Unions in Communist States*, ed. Alex Pravda and Blair Ruble. London and Boston: Allen and Unwin, 1985.

Runge, Irene. *Ganz in Familie*. Berlin: Dietz Verlag, 1985.

Scharf, C. Bradley. *Politics and Change in East Germany*. Colorado: Westview Press, 1984.

Schellenberger, Gerhard. *Technische Neuerungen—sozialer Fortschritt*. Berlin: Dietz Verlag, 1980.

Sodaro, Michael J. "Limits to Dissent in the GDR: Fragmentation, Cooptation, and Repression." In *Dissent in Eastern Europe*, ed. Jane Leftwich Curry, 82–116. New York: Praeger, 1983.

Soziale Triebkräfte ökonomischen Wachstums. Materialien des 4. Kongresses der marxistisch-leninistischen Soziologie. Berlin: Dietz Verlag, 1986.

Staemmler, Gerlind. "East Germany." In *Housing in Europe*, ed. Martin Wynn. London: Croom Helm; New York: St. Martin's Press, 1984.

Staritz, Dieter. *Geschichte der DDR 1949–1985*. Frankfurt/M.: Suhrkamp, 1985.

Statistisches Jahrbuch der DDR. Berlin: Staatsverlag der DDR, annually.

Staufenbiel, Fred et al. *Soziologische Untersuchung von Wohngebieten der Stadt Rostock*. Weimar: Hochschule für Architektur und Bauwesen, 1983.

von Beyme, Klaus and Zimmermann, Hartmut, eds. *Policymaking in the German Democratic Republic*. New York: St. Martin's Press, 1984.

Voss, Peter, ed. *Die Freizeit der Jugend*. Berlin: Dietz Verlag, 1981.

Wallace, Ian, ed. *The GDR under Honecker 1971–1981*. GDR-Monitor Special Series, no. 1. Dundee, 1981.

Whetten, Lawrence. *Germany East and West. Conflicts, Collaboration and Confrontation*. New York: New York University Press, 1980.

Winkler, Gunnar. *Lexikon der Sozialpolitik*. Berlin: Akademie Verlag, 1987.

Wynn, Martin, ed. *Housing in Europe*. New York: St. Martin's Press, 1984.

Zimmermann, Hartmut. "Power Distribution and Opportunities for Participation: Aspects of the Socio-political System of the GDR." In *Policymaking in the German Democratic Republic*, ed. Klaus v. Beyme and Hartmut Zimmermann, 1–108. New York: St. Martin's Press, 1984.

Zimmermann, Hartmut; Ulrich, Horst; and Fehlauer, Michael, eds. *DDR Handbuch*. Köln: Verlag Wissenschaft und Politik, 1985.

Zur Sozialpolitik in der antifaschistisch-demokratischen Umwälzung 1945–1949, Dokumente und Materialien. Berlin: Dietz Verlag, 1984.

About the Editors

MARILYN SCHATTNER RUESCHEMEYER, educated at the University of Toronto and at Brandeis University, where she received her doctorate, is Associate Professor of Sociology at the Rhode Island School of Design and Adjunct Associate Professor of Sociology at Brown University. In 1979 and 1982, she was a senior associate member of St. Antony's College, Oxford. Rueschemeyer chairs the GDR Study Group at Harvard's Center for European Studies and Russian Research Center where she is a Fellow. She is the author of *Professional Work and Marriage: an East-West Comparison* and co-author (with Igor Golomshtok and Janet Kennedy) of *Soviet Emigre Artists: Life and Work in the USSR and the United States*.

CHRISTIANE LEMKE is a German Academic Exchange Service Visiting Associate Professor in Political Science at the University of North Carolina, Chapel Hill. She received her doctorate at the Freie Universität, Berlin. From 1978 to 1987, she was a researcher at the Zentralinstitut für sozialwissenschaftliche Forschung and Lecturer in the Political Science Department at the Freie Universität, Berlin. She is the author of *Personlichkeit und Gesellschaft, Zur theorie der Personlichkeit in der DDR*, and ''Politische Sozialisation in der DDR,'' manuscript submitted as Habilitation thesis, Freie Universität, Berlin. Lemke is also co-editor of *Studies in GDR Culture and Society*, Volumes 5, 6, and 7.

About the Other Contributors

LOTHAR BISKY is Rektor of the Hochscule für Film und Fernsehen der DDR, Potsdam-Babelsberg.

JOAN DEBARDELEBEN is Associate Professor of Political Science at McGill University, Montreal, Canada.

MICHAEL DENNIS is Senior Lecturer in Contemporary History, The School of Humanities & Cultural Studies, at Wolverhampton Polytechnic, Great Britain.

IRENE DÖLLING is Professor in the section Ästhetik und Kunstwissenschaften, Humboldt Universität, Berlin (DDR).

GERT-JOACHIM GLAESSNER is Professor of Political Science at the Zentralinstitut für sozialwissenschaftliche Forschung, Freie Universität Berlin (BRD).

ROBERT F. GOECKEL is Associate Professor of Political Science at the State University of New York in Geneseo.

VOLKER GRANSOW, a political scientist and sociologist, is a German Academic Exchange Service Visiting Professor in the German Department at the University of California, Berkeley.

HELMUT HANKE is Professor of Sociology at the Hochschule für Film and Fernsehen der DDR, Potsdam-Babelsberg.

HILDEGARD M. NICKEL is an Instructor of Sociology at the Humboldt Universität, Berlin (DDR).

C. BRADLEY SCHARF is Professor of Political Science at Seattle University, Washington.